D1349921

COUNTRY LIVING

a seasonal guide to

# soft furnishings

ideas & inspiration
projects & patterns

Gabi Tubbs

with photographs by Pia Tryde

techniques & projects written by Lucinda Ganderton

illustrations by Alison Barratt

**Quadrille**

First published in 1997 by

Quadrille Publishing Limited

Alhambra House, 27–31 Charing Cross Road, London WC2H 0LS

Published in association with the National Magazine Company Limited

Country Living is a trademark of the National Magazine Company Limited



Creative Director • Mary Evans

Editorial Director • Jane O'Shea

Art Director • Françoise Dietrich

Editors • Alexa Stace and Maggi McCormick

Design Co-ordinator • Sara Jane Glynn

Design Assistant • Nathalie Hennequin

Editorial Assistant • Katherine Seely

Production Manager • Candida Lane

Picture Researcher • Helen Fickling

Additional text • Lucy Naylor



British Library Cataloguing-in-Publication Data

A catalogue record for this book is available from the British Library.

ISBN 1 899988 41 6

Printed and bound by Mohndruck Graphische Betriebe GmbH, Germany

# contents

# a natural palette

*I have had a passion for fabrics since I was about five or six. My earliest memories are of my mother's wedding dress being unpicked, dyed pale blue and made into a party dress for me by a seamstress known to us as Tante Annie. Tante Annie came to our house about once a month to do mending or alterations, and she always made clothes for me, often out of dresses that my mother no longer wore. I remember driving her mad, as I would never stand still for long enough!*

*The most exciting times for me were just before the local carnival, known in Munich (where I come from) as* Fasching, *or when I was invited to someone's dressing-up party. I always had the most wonderfully fantastical clothes which I would choose out of a pattern book, adding unexpected touches for my own amusement. I was in turn dressed as a powder puff, an inkwell, a strawberry, a geisha girl, flamenco dancer or whatever else my fancy let me be. The hats too were always eyecatching and quirky, the fabrics and trimmings a mixture of old and new.*

*It is scarcely surprising, with this background, that I eventually became a fashion editor, and then a decorating editor, since my love for working with wonderful antique fabrics and contemporary designs has never left me.*

*When the idea for this book was first broached, I was aware of how many good decorating books there were already. None of them, however, seemed to tackle the making and designing of soft furnishings in equal measure, which I feel we have achieved with this book.*

*To give the book another twist, I have divided it into the four seasons, to create an ambience naturally associated with certain times of the year. Fabrics for each section are defined by colour, weight, and texture; the colour schemes and designs by association of certain moods influenced by temperature and weather.*

*These themes are there to help you decide what kind of mood is right for you and your house and to show how you can have a 'change of clothes' for every season, without having to change the furniture. In spring, for example, an armchair can be dressed in a pretty frock; in winter, it switches to sophistication with a silk dress. Colour, texture and fabric can be used to make each basic piece of furniture look quite different.*

*In spring, for example, we cannot wait to open doors and windows to let the light and warmth come flooding in. This is when enthusiasm for decorating is in plentiful supply. Carpets of spring flowers – bluebells, tulips, primroses – and trees laden with blossom all inspire a multitude of ideas. Fresh greens and radiant pink ginghams are used with ticking stripes and floral prints. Pink and yellow toiles de Jouy sit happily with checks. A truly carefree ways of creating decorating schemes.*

*In summer, decorating themes are on the whole clean and unfussy. The feel is cool rather than cosy, and the house should be clean and invigorating. Bring the outdoors into your home with the colours of sea and sand, lush meadows, ripe juicy fruit and bright splashy flowers. Allow the sun to find its way through white linen blinds and flimsy voile drapes.*

*In the autumn, the countryside is alive with purple hills, tawny trees and ripening harvests in a splendid array of colours. Fabrics are reminiscent of turning leaves, golden pumpkins, red berries and glowing heather and bracken. Soft traditional tweeds and flannels jostle with bright tartans – fabrics which are not just confined to the country, but can look equally good in a town house, in relaxed mode or tailored.*

*By the time we reach winter, when the weather is often cold and miserable, there is a need for energizing colours and touches of magic in the home to keep up our spirits. Use an abundance of opulent fabrics and rich colour: decorate with velvets, brocades and damasks; introduce exotic shades and fabrics inspired by the Far East, like sheer muslins, silks and chiffons. For a more refined look, swathe, furniture, walls and windows in silvery greys and pearly whites.*

*This book is designed to rejuvenate and transform your home, as well as to inspire. The designs have been carefully worked out, and are clearly illustrated with straightforward instructions – there are even a few special designs for each season to encourage you to be more adventurous. I hope you enjoy these ideas as much as I enjoyed creating them!*

# *spring* awakening

*There is no better way to spend an early spring morning than to watch tentative rays of sunshine filter through newly unfurled leaves. Wander on to see sunny daffodils dancing on grassy slopes, carpets of bluebells rippling beneath trees and radiant tulips, pansies and primroses, in blushing pinks, brilliant reds and royal purples, lifting their heads up to the sky. It is all so familiar – a canopy of blossom showers its delicious scent, white tides of snowdrops seem to melt the frosted earth – yet every spring it is as if the earth is opening its eyes for the first time.*

# natural inspiration

*Optimism breathes from every blade of grass in spring. After being curled up against the cold for months on end, you want to throw open all the doors and windows. Traditionally, spring is a time to clean the slate and start afresh, so enthusiasm for decorating is in plentiful supply. Inspiration is just as abundant, and is everywhere you look. Year after year, spring awakens new textures, patterns and colours. Hence the pictures that will greet you on the following pages. Rooms are newly painted in pale shades. Fresh green and white ginghams recall young leaves bursting from buds; sprigs of purest pink and warmest red sing out from toiles de Jouy and taffetas; clusters of daisies and cowslips on dappled lawns and young petals in waking borders smile from floral prints, checks and chintzes, voiles and linens. The secret is to pilfer nature's bright ideas in great blossoming armfuls.*

# striking companions

*to mix & match*

It is a truth universally acknowledged that harmony in interior design means uniform codes of co-ordination. Discard this theory at once! So long as you ensure that one or two colours run through your palette to create a definite look, there are no other rules to follow, and that includes rules about which colours can or cannot be seen together. The most interesting and attractive rooms are the result of trial and error. Take pink and yellow, for example, and put them side by side. They make striking companions, especially with the added depth of rich purples against natural and white backgrounds. In fact, all colours are mutually compatible until proven otherwise – by holding them up against a wall, or over a sofa. Similarly, when choosing patterns, stay away from repeating a single design throughout a room. Try mixing ticking stripes with checks and florals of varying sizes. The effect is liberating.

## **crisp & soft**
## *textures for contrast*

Just as juxtapositions of pattern and colour bring a room to life, so a variety of textures and weights of fabric add interest to the look. The most surprising combinations of fabrics can bring out the best in each other when placed side by side in a room. Fine floating voiles are ethereal next to stately toiles. Glazed cotton is flattered by soft, warmer, smooth cotton. The glorious earthiness of a slubby linen is emphasized by a lining of delicate lightweight cotton, and the same lining gives depth to a fine linen. You can even team crisp, regal taffeta and folds of glossy chintz with homely, strong matt ticking. Pick up samples of all the fabrics that catch your eye and build up a collection. Gather your swatches together and try holding different weights and textures of fabric in your hands. If they feel right together, they are likely to look so, too.

# light affair

## *checks & toiles*
## **in a garden room**

A garden room, bathed in natural light, is the perfect setting in which to enjoy spring mornings. It is a room for writing letters, sprawling on a sofa with a book, or arranging vases of the first flowers of the year. Airiness and comfort are all. Windows are framed with simple swedish swags, and either roman blinds or unlined toile curtains, neatly tied back to make way for the spring sunshine. An antique sofa bed is piled with pillows, bolsters and cushions, blatantly encouraging sloth. The collection of fabrics throughout the room creates the atmosphere of a spring garden party. Bold woven linen checks on an armchair are reminiscent of cloths laid out for picnics, finely-printed toiles recall the sweep of eighteenth-century skirts across a lawn, and a chair dressed in a flirtatious floral print is partnered by a matching lampshade.

The room is uncluttered, and the walls, too, are left mostly naked. Gardens are understated affairs in spring; airy rooms should reflect that subtlety. A couple of natural wreaths break the blue expanse of one wall and a simple gilt mirror reflects the light on another. On the floor, pale earthy tiles are ideal, not least because of their practicality, while a well-chosen rug in warm colours comforts chilly feet on cool mornings.

THE LARGE CUSHIONS OF AN OLD CHAIR ARE RE-DRESSED IN A STURDY LINEN CHECK, WITH STRONG TIES TO HOLD THEM IN PLACE.

**See pages 164–5 for gathered-corner cover.**

right

AN UNEXPECTED COLOUR COMBINATION – SPRING GREENS FOR THE UNLINED PASTORAL TOILE CURTAINS, SOFT ROMAN BLINDS AND SIMPLE SWAGS, AND GENTLE MAUVES FOR THE SOFA BED AGAINST THE PALE BLUE OF A FRESHLY PAINTED WALL.

**See pages 149 for unlined curtain, 146 for soft roman blind and 153 for swags.**

opposite

AN ANTIQUE SWEDISH SOFA BED IS DRESSED WITH A PAINTERLY TOILE SHEET AND SCATTERED WITH MATCHING CUSHIONS AND PILLOWS IN CRUSHED BERRY COLOURS. THE TAFFETA GINGHAM BOLSTERS ARE TIED LIKE CRACKERS.

**See pages 158–60 for cushions and 161–3 for bolsters.**

# *light & space*
## in sun-dappled rooms

Pattern is a magical phenomenon. You can use it to make a room seem larger or smaller, brighter or darker. In a garden room, where the emphasis is on light and space, it is best to choose delicate, small-scale designs rather than overpowering bold patterns. The smaller the pattern, the further away it seems to the eye, so an artistic 'distance' is achieved and therefore a sense of space. And where there is space, there is light. Of course, if you have the enviable problem of a room that is so large you feel slightly lost in it – perhaps it has very high ceilings, for example – then richer colours and busier patterns will wrap the room around you and make it seem cosier. If space and light are a priority, more than one pattern in a room begs for a solid plain background. For an airy garden room, walls should be pale and interesting behind more extrovert fabrics – soft matt pastels work well.

The texture of your fabric is just as important to the eye. Glossy chintz, for example, can brighten up a room immeasurably as it reflects the light, though a room over-dressed in shiny fabric is not conducive to relaxation. At the other end of the scale are matt fabrics such as homely, rough linens. These soak up the light and have a calming, cosy effect, but too much can be frumpy. If you have found one fabric that you like, take as large a sample of it as possible and use its texture as well as its pattern and colour as a reference when you look for other fabrics. Although the colours in a room do not have to co-ordinate, a sense of unity is achieved if, say, the fabric of a lampshade matches the skirt of a covered chair, or the sprig on a floral print curtain is the same colour as the check on a cushion or bolster. Even a curtain tie-back that echoes the shade of a sofa is a unifying accessory. A little discreet co-ordination goes a long way, but too much is claustrophobic. The secret, as ever, is balance.

This fitted seat cushion and bolster in a traditional Scandinavian blue check was chosen to echo the painted wooden bench and the blue emulsioned walls.

**See pages 165 for fitted box cushion and 161–3 for bolsters.**

This simple lampshade has a deep fabric border and a handkerchief skirt.

**See page 154 for lampshades.**

A flirty summer frock in smooth Provençal cotton transforms a plain chair.

**See pages 168–9 for two-piece chair cover.**

Lightly padded and quilted placemats have matching napkins made out of fine floral cotton.

**See page 185 for table linen.**

Shiny chintz and crunchy taffeta for a Sunday-best dining-chair skirt and top.

**See pages 168–9 for two-piece chair cover.**

## *soft prints*
## **for a garden setting**

Thanks to an ever-balmier climate, garden parties are becoming a real possibility. Instead of plastic, wipeable chairs and tables that can be quickly ferried indoors when the weather turns nasty, we can bring furniture outside for the occasion and make a 'room' out of a corner of the garden. With the warmer weather come comfortable, covered chairs and a table laid with a cloth.

Take afternoon tea, for example. Such a civilized institution needs an elegant setting to be enjoyed to the full. Served outside, it can be raised to an art form. Jam and cream become the inspiration for a colour scheme of chintzy floral prints, while cucumber sandwiches influence the choice of thinly-striped green and white taffeta for chairs. Chair coverings are tied with bows like old-fashioned dresses and aprons, and a secret love of frills and flounces can be indulged without constraint. Follow the colours of the flowers and the blossom, but add earthy colours and textures to balance the sweetness. Vary the designs and fabrics of the chair covers, especially if the dining chairs come in different shapes and sizes.

The rougher influence of a fabric such as slubby linen makes a good rustic tablecloth and plain cream and white china looks smooth and calm above the busy patterns. Even indoors, an arrangement such as this, at one end of a large sitting-room for example, will create the fresh atmosphere of a late spring garden and the perfect setting for any meal. If you are lucky enough to have a conservatory or garden room, why not turn it into a dining-room with these frilled chairs and invitingly laid table.

ON THE FIRST BALMY DAY OF SPRING THE DINING TABLE AND CHAIRS ARE WHISKED OUTSIDE. THE TABLE WEARS A SLUBBY LINEN TABLECLOTH WITH A SMALLER OVERCLOTH IN FLOWER-SPRIGGED COTTON AND QUILTED TABLEMATS TO MATCH. THE SKIRTED CHAIRS ARE DRESSED IN SUNDAY-BEST CHINTZ AND TAFFETA.

**See pages 184–5 for table linen.**

An iron day bed is framed by two windows dressed with swedish blinds and prettily ruched pelmets gathered on to narrow curtain poles. The valance which conceals the legs of the bed is in fact a short curtain with a gathered heading.

**See pages 145–6 for swedish blind, 153 for ruffled pelmet and 151 for gathered heading.**

**For picture bow see page 144.**

# sugar sweet

## *pastoral overtones* **in a country day-room**

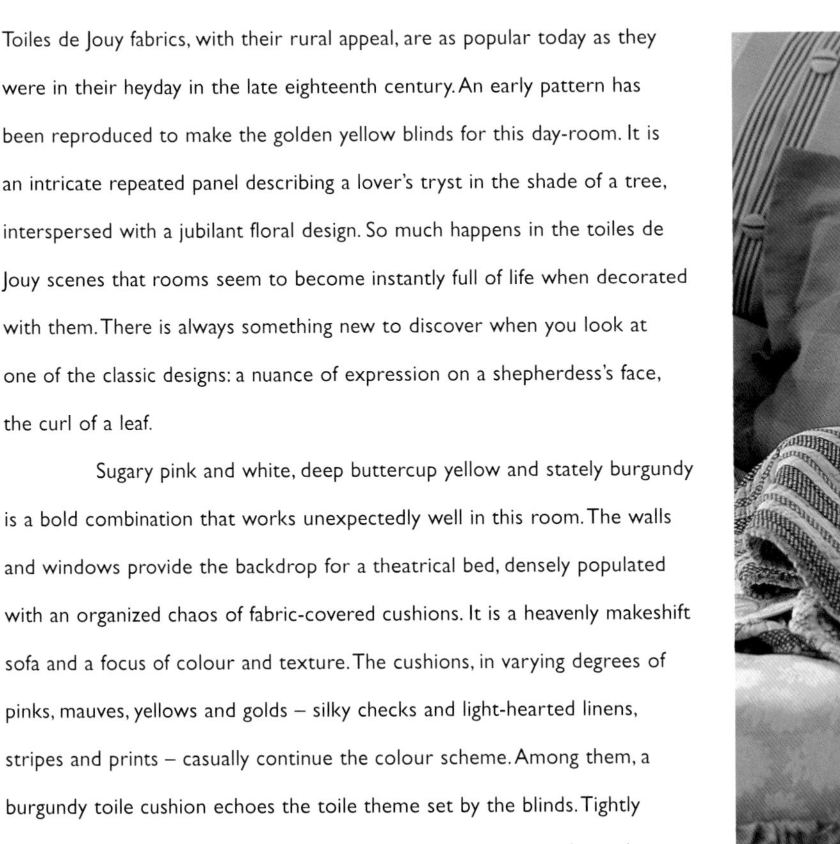

Toiles de Jouy fabrics, with their rural appeal, are as popular today as they were in their heyday in the late eighteenth century. An early pattern has been reproduced to make the golden yellow blinds for this day-room. It is an intricate repeated panel describing a lover's tryst in the shade of a tree, interspersed with a jubilant floral design. So much happens in the toiles de Jouy scenes that rooms seem to become instantly full of life when decorated with them. There is always something new to discover when you look at one of the classic designs: a nuance of expression on a shepherdess's face, the curl of a leaf.

Sugary pink and white, deep buttercup yellow and stately burgundy is a bold combination that works unexpectedly well in this room. The walls and windows provide the backdrop for a theatrical bed, densely populated with an organized chaos of fabric-covered cushions. It is a heavenly makeshift sofa and a focus of colour and texture. The cushions, in varying degrees of pinks, mauves, yellows and golds – silky checks and light-hearted linens, stripes and prints – casually continue the colour scheme. Among them, a burgundy toile cushion echoes the toile theme set by the blinds. Tightly ruched pelmets in a taffeta check are simply threaded on to a slim pole, whereas the deep valance, in yet another fine cotton toile, is gathered on to curtain header tape. The exquisite demoiselle looking out of the gilded frame is a fabric copy of an eighteenth-century print. With so much richness of pattern, a plain natural floor is called for.

THE DAY BED IS PILED HIGH WITH SCATTER CUSHIONS, PILLOWS AND BOLSTERS IN SUGARY PINKS, YELLOWS AND MAUVES.

**See pages 155–63 for pillows, cushions and bolsters.**

A SILKY TAFFETA FABRIC IS GATHERED INTO A SKIRT AND THEN SLIPPED OVER A MATCHING LAMPSHADE.

**See page 154 for gathered lampshade.**

# *made to measure* **a cover for a storage unit**

An amusing and extremely useful touch for any room is a tented wardrobe or shelf unit. Here we have used an architectural toile named *Les vues de Paris* for the dress, and a less defined toile of similar colouring for the top and shelves. The scalloped shelf lining is fixed to the wooden shelves with velcro. The whole tent slips easily over the unit and can be taken off quickly for dry-cleaning or careful washing. A colour-matched cord is threaded through a buttonhole in the side seams and ties back the front curtains on either side. Both the top and shelf panels are lined for neatness. A quirky touch is the wired top knot. The height of the roof can be altered to suit the proportions of your room by changing the length of the wooden struts.

*fig 1*

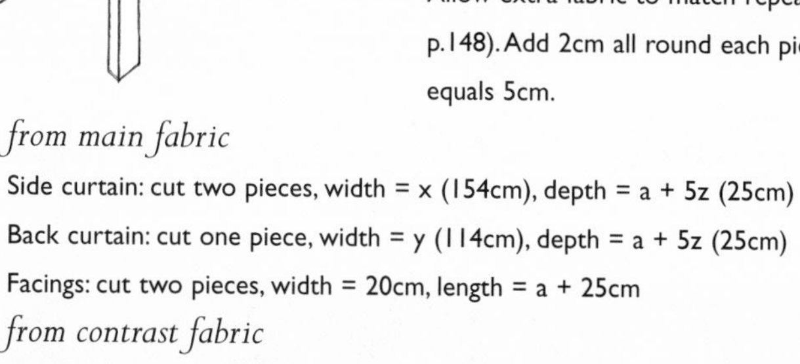


*materials*

Main fabric (x = 154cm wide), contrast fabric, lining fabric, wooden shelf unit (approx 2m high, 1m wide, 50cm deep), 4 lengths of 5 x 20mm battening (70cm long) for struts, masking tape, drill, strong twine, 4 screws, fusible bonding web 15 x 45cm, 1m millinery wire, 5m cord for tie-backs, drawing pins, craft knife, velcro (50cm per shelf), craft glue

*measuring & cutting out (figs 1 & 2)*

Allow extra fabric to match repeats (see p.148). Add 2cm all round each piece. NB: z equals 5cm.

*from main fabric*

Side curtain: cut two pieces, width = x (154cm), depth = a + 5z (25cm)

Back curtain: cut one piece, width = y (114cm), depth = a + 5z (25cm)

Facings: cut two pieces, width = 20cm, length = a + 25cm

*from contrast fabric*

Main roof: cut two pieces, sides of triangle = d, width = b, border height = 4z (20cm)

Side roof: cut two pieces, sides of triangle = d, width = c, border height = 4z (20cm). Notch the sides of each roof piece, 5cm below the point

Shelf cover: cut one piece for each shelf, width = b, depth = c + 2z (10cm)

Shelf facing: cut one piece for each shelf, width = b, depth = 2z (10cm)

Top knot: cut one piece, 30 x 85cm

*from lining fabric*

Roof facings: cut two pieces, width = 4z (20cm), length = b

Side roof facings: cut two pieces, width = 4z (20cm), length = c

*making the roof framework*

**1** Assemble the unit as instructed. Drill a 5mm hole 12mm from one end of each length of battening. Drill a 2mm hole 2.5cm in from the other end. Thread the twine through the large holes. Knot securely, but loosely enough for the struts to move freely. Tape the frame in position on the top of the unit and mark the points where the struts meet the uprights. Drill into the uprights at the correct angle, then screw the frame in place *(fig 3)*.

*making the curtain*

**2** Zigzag one long edge of each facing. With right sides together, pin and stitch the unstitched edges to the outside edges of the side curtains. Press the seam towards the facing. If you are using a non-reversible fabric, put the curtain together so that the right side of the back piece faces forwards. Pin and stitch the right side of each side piece to the wrong side of the back, matching the raw edges. Turn up a 12cm hem along the lower edge.

**3** With a drawing pin, secure the centre back of the curtain to the centre back of the top shelf and the top corners to the centre front. Make three small pleats

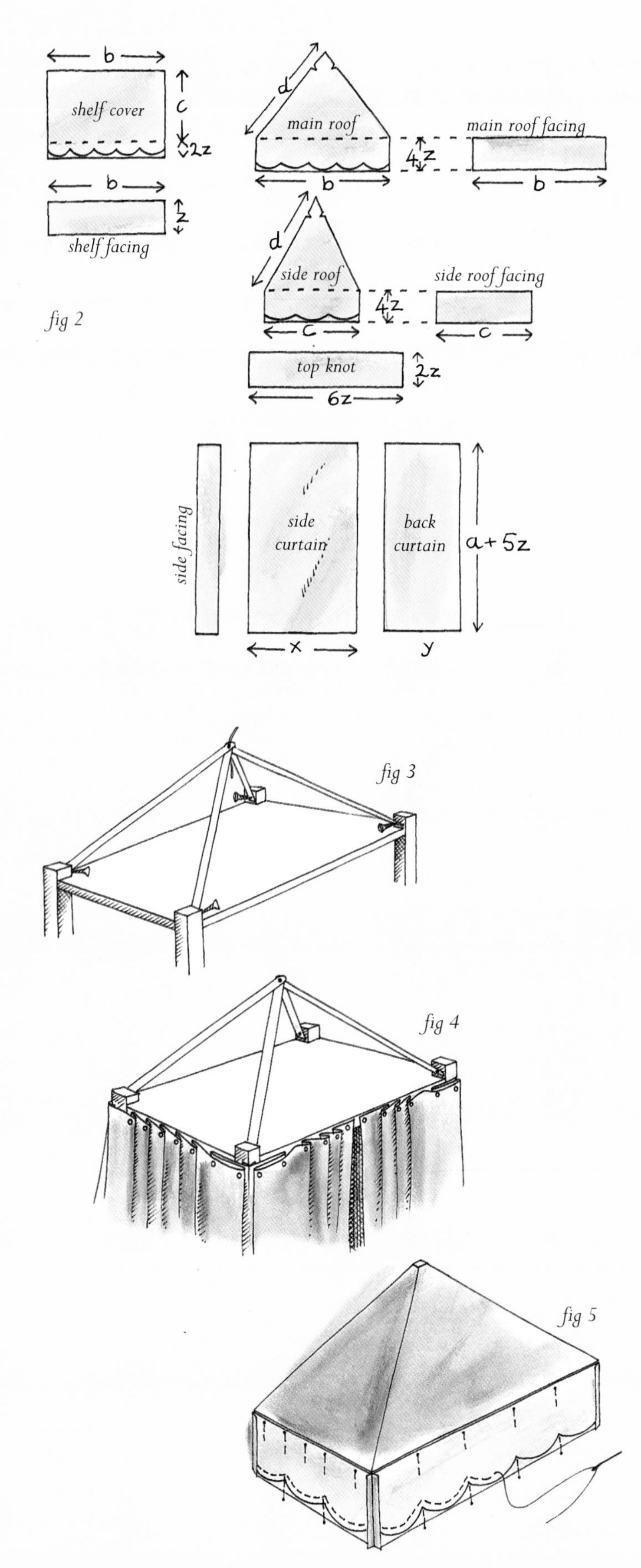


*fig 2*

*fig 3*

*fig 4*

*fig 5*

either side of the opening and fix to the shelf with drawing pins. Fold and pin a 15cm inverted box pleat at each front corner. Pin the side seams to the back corners and then fold and pin the remaining loose fabric in small pleats *(fig 4)*.

*making the roof*

**4** Right sides together, pin one side roof to each side of one main roof piece along short and diagonal edges. Stitch from notch to 2cm from lower edge, leaving a 2cm allowance. Join second main roof piece to the two free sides. Press seams open.

**5** Pin one side roof facing to each end of one main roof facing, then pin the remaining main piece to the loose ends. Stitch 2cm from the edges, and press the seams flat. Neaten one edge. Mark three shallow scallops along the other edge of the side facings and five along the main facings, following the method on p. 156.

**6** Pin the facing to the bottom edge of the roof with right sides together, matching the corners. Tack together close to the scallops *(fig 5)* and stitch along the line. Trim and clip the curves and points (see p.139). Turn right side out and press. Pin the free edge of the facing to the roof fabric.

*making the top knot*

**7** Join the short ends with right sides facing and press the seam open. Fold in half lengthways with wrong sides together. Press and open out again. Lay the bonding web on the wrong side of one half of the loop and press *(fig 6)*. Peel off the backing paper and fold again along the crease. Twist the ends of the millinery wire together to form a ring the same size as the fabric loop. Place the wire inside the fold and pin it in place. Press the fabric to join the two sides together. Using a zipper foot, stitch along the fold, close to the wire.

**8** Carefully bend the loop into a series of pleats, and pin them together at the lower edge *(fig 7)*. Slip the top knot into the hole at the top of the roof and adjust the pleats so that it fits tightly. Remove and slip stitch each pleat in place 3cm from the lower edge. Pin back on to the roof and stitch firmly in place.

**9** Drop the roof over its frame so that the scallops hang over the top edge of the curtain. Match the corners, then pin the roof to the curtain through the facing, adjusting the pleats to fit. Top stitch all round twice.

**10** Hang a tie-back cord around the front upright next to the centre shelf. Mark the point where it will come through on the inside of the box pleat and remove the tent. Cut a 6cm square of fabric and press under 5mm along each edge. Draw a long oval on the wrong side, large enough for the cord to pass through easily. Pin the patch to the mark with right sides together and stitch around the mark. Clip into the opening *(fig 8)* and turn the patch to the wrong side. Press, pin in place and top stitch the edges to secure. Do the same with the other side.

*making the shelf covers*

**11** Draw five scallops as on the roof facing and make up. Neaten the remaining sides. Cut short strips of velcro and separate. Sew four pieces to the wrong side of each back edge at intervals. Stick the other pieces to the shelves to correspond.

**12** Fix all covers in place, then put the tent back on the frame. Loop the tie-backs around the uprights, thread through the openings and knot the ends loosely.

*fig 6*

*fig 7*

*fig 8*

# *room for change*

## *imagination realized* **in a simple bedroom**

Dreams can be triggered by one sentence in a book; or by a picture that catches the imagination. Inspiration for interior design works on the same principle. It begins with something small but captivating and grows to fill the whole room. And nowhere are you more free to indulge the imagination than in a bedroom.

Take a curtain tie-back, for instance. It is a tiny feature in a room, and one that is normally a finishing touch rather than a beginning, but it can quickly set off a train of thought. Looking at an old gilded tie-back, we are transported to the faded charm of a crumbling French manoir at the turn of the century, where hints of former opulence mingle with simpler country style. From this one small object, you could build up a scheme for the whole room.

Consider the shape and size of the space you have before you begin. In most cases, sleep must be the foremost concern, so dress the bed and build up a scheme for the rest of the room around it. In a little bedroom, it is best to echo the patterns and colours of the bed elsewhere, so that you avoid contrasts that could make it an over-dominant presence, seeming to fill the room completely.

This does not mean that you must limit yourself to only one pattern, if any, when working with a smaller space. As long as a link is achieved with repeated colours, several designs can work harmoniously together without seeming crowded. In this room, the green of a nostalgic toile is picked up by a contemporary gingham. And the deep red edges of petals on a floral print cotton match a pink and cream checked glazed cotton. Pictorial toiles are teamed with childish prints and modern checks; gloriously decadent sheer fabrics with homespun linens and smooth floral cotton.

above

The faded charm of an antique gilded wooden tie-back complements whimsical toile curtains.

A fabric screen provides privacy when needed. Here a fabric panel has been gathered at top and bottom with curtain header tape and attached to this wooden frame screen with matching ties.

**See pages 151 for gathered heading and 144 for ties.**

A plump duvet slips neatly into a cover of grey toile and green gingham.

**See page 182 for tie-on duvet cover.**

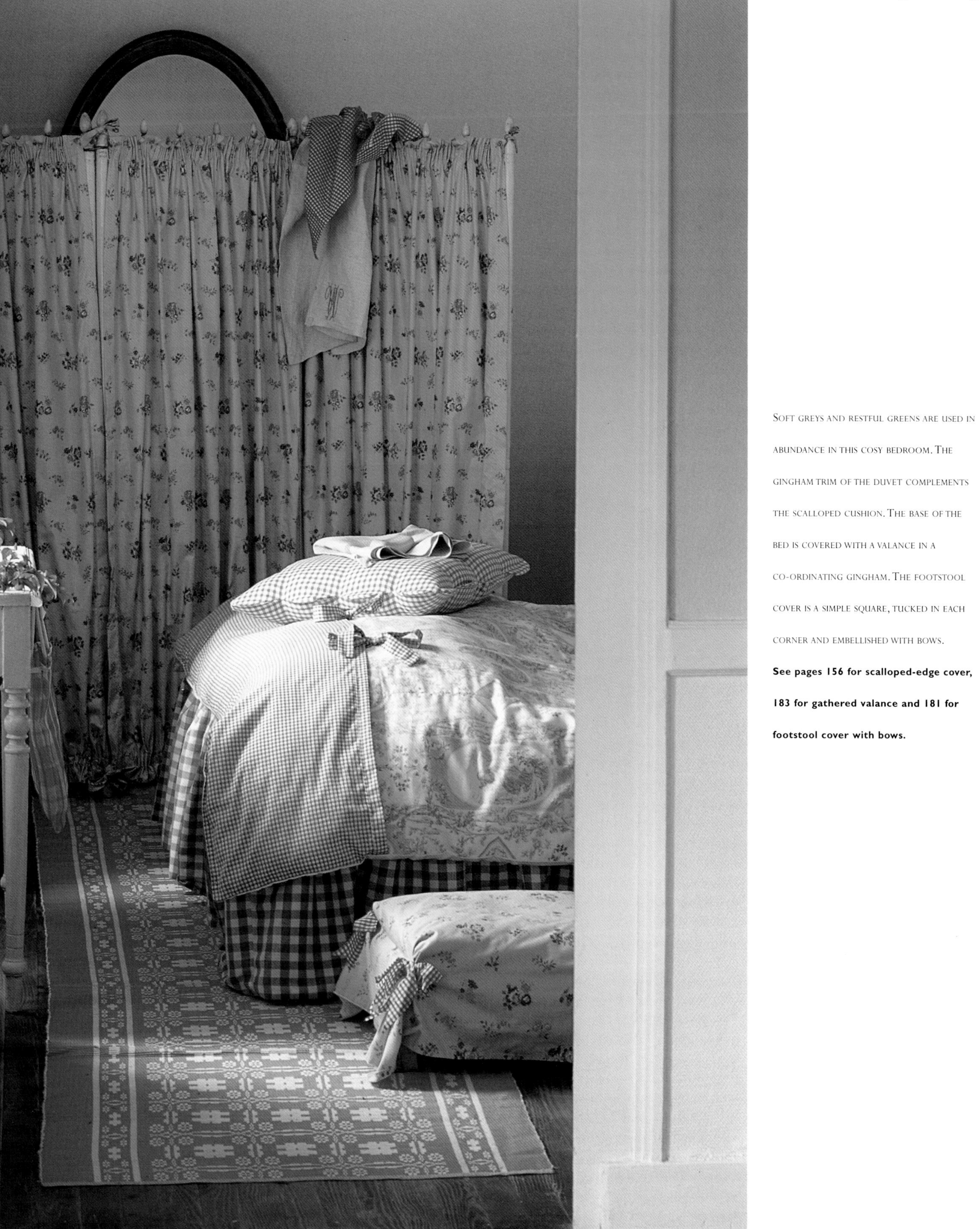

Soft greys and restful greens are used in abundance in this cosy bedroom. The gingham trim of the duvet complements the scalloped cushion. The base of the bed is covered with a valance in a co-ordinating gingham. The footstool cover is a simple square, tucked in each corner and embellished with bows.

**See pages 156 for scalloped-edge cover, 183 for gathered valance and 181 for footstool cover with bows.**

An unusual effect is created by framing an unlined roman blind, made out of a fine green and grey cotton print, with translucent voile curtains which also have a delicate design. **See pages 146 for soft roman blind and 149 for unlined curtains.**

This layette basket is lined very much like the Moses baskets **(see pages 128–9)** with additional pockets to hold the baby's toiletries.

## *spring greens & budding pinks*
### **for detail & finish**

Be generous with fabric in a bedroom. The billowing duvet undulates like restful waves with intermittent bows, while the cushion covers are finished with scalloped, ruched and gathered edges. Using inexpensive country checks and stripes means that you can be more generous with other fabrics and accessories. The combination of the simple with the splendid is always effective. Here we used a simple and inexpensive ticking fabric to cover a chair. A little luxury is the frilled piping and bows made out of expensive silky taffeta – a leftover from a pair of curtains. The footstool's generous bows are made out of the same fabric. A background of gentle curves has been introduced with the addition of gathered fabric on a covered screen. A rug underlines the pinks and reds of floral and checked fabrics in the room for both an aesthetically and physically soothing presence.

Paint natural base colours on the walls and add accessories such as fabric-filled wicker baskets and wooden picture-frames to give an earthy, solid framework to the network of colours and pattern.

Simulate the bright French sunshine with a light-catching, floaty voile tucked behind the gilded tie-backs. Hang up a more substantial blind with ruffled edges, to formalize the effect neatly. Heap broderie anglaise and gingham pillows and cushions with frilled edges on to painted country furniture.

PICKING UP THE GREY FROM THE TIE-ON DUVET COVER, THE HANDSOME TICKING STRIPE FOR THE ARMCHAIR IS PRETTIFIED WITH PINK TAFFETA BOWS.

# *passion for red*

## *bold sophistication* **in a master bedroom**

Red is always a glorious colour. We are encouraged to wear red clothes to feel confident, to cheer ourselves up, to radiate warmth. It is astonishing, therefore, that a predominance of red is a rarity in 'room-dressing'. There is no doubt that it is a bold statement. But it is one worth making. Screw up your courage, be brave and enjoy red's rewards.

Think of a late spring garden, full of poppies and peonies, rhododendrons and camellias. Carry those rich pinks and reds around in your head to choose fabrics that will recreate that freshness. Try monochrome toiles de Jouy – there are masses of delicious designs to choose from that are the perfect excuse for indulging a passion for red. On previous pages, pretty toiles have blended in with contemporary checks, florals and stripes, a cushion here, a curtain there. But like all brilliant designs, the characteristic toile patterns deserve to be given centre stage in the master bedroom. Mix contemporary interpretations with reproductions of original designs, but use varying shades of one colour on a neutral background throughout the room to show off the toiles to greatest effect. Use a range of weights and textures to add visual interest.

Lavish toiles on the bed, sofas, chairs, curtains, cushions, wall hangings and dressing-table – anything that can be covered. Your philosophy should be more is more! Keep the floor and ceiling in neutral colours to offset the richness of the red.

opposite

A view from the bedroom into the en-suite bathroom, also decorated in fine toiles. The circular table is covered with a trimmed circular cloth with a smaller square overcloth.

**See page 184 for tablecloths.**

right

Covering the bed is a reversible quilt – the pictures on the toile pattern have been outlined with machine stitching. The pillowcases and the lined bed curtains are in the same red tone but with different pictorial designs. The head of the antique bed is panelled in a complementary fabric. The bedside tablecloth is made like a circular placemat with cord piping and a frilled edge.

**See pages 38–9 for outline quilted bedspread and drapes, 155–7 for pillowcases.**

# *coronet* for a luxurious bedroom

Children love secret dens, and as adults are merely grown-up children, why not create a regal enclave for yourself, complete with canopy and coronet to make a kind of private room within a room? Antique French bows and swags in brass embellish the velvet-covered coronet.

The double-sided quilt has a finer, less heavy toile design on the underside which looks pretty turned over against the busier outside toile. The outline stitching emphasizes the pictorial images of the fabric.

## *materials*

### *for the curtains & tie-backs*

Main fabric, contrasting fabric, fringed braid (length = 150cm, + 2a + 6 widths), chalk pencil or fading pen, 50 curtain hooks, 550cm covered narrow piping cord, 2 small brass rings, 2 cup hooks

### *for the coronet*

Semi-circle of 2.5cm chipboard (48cm in diameter), contrast fabric, PVA adhesive, bradawl, 50 eye screws, 2 angle brackets with screws, 150 x 10cm mounting board, 65 x 150cm velvet, 160cm x 1cm-wide velvet-covered piping cord, upholstery tacks

## *measuring & cutting out* *(figs 1 & 2)*

The coronet is fixed to the wall above the centre of the bed; the height will depend on the proportions of your room. Decide where it should go before calculating the fabric amounts. Allow extra fabric to match repeats (see p.148). NB: z equals width of fabric: this can vary between 120 and 154cm.

Back curtain: cut one piece from main and one piece from contrast fabric, width = 3 widths of fabric, length = a + 4cm

Side curtains: cut two pieces from main and two pieces from contrast fabric, width = 1.5 widths of fabric, length = a + 4cm

Tie-backs: cut two pieces from main and two pieces from contrast fabric, width (x) = 15cm, length = 150cm

Coronet lining: cut a 60cm semi-circle from contrast fabric

Pelmet cover: cut from velvet, width (x) = 15cm, length (y) = 155cm

## *making the coronet*

**1** Cover the chipboard with contrast fabric, pulling it tightly over the edges and gluing with PVA. Make a row of small holes, 4cm apart, 1cm in from the outside edge, with a bradawl, leaving a 10cm gap at the centre front. Fix an eye screw into each hole, twisting it until secure, so that the eye lies parallel to the edge. Fix the two angle brackets to the top of the board, each 30cm in from the edge.

**2** Cover the mounting board with velvet, and hand stitch or glue the covered piping along the long top edge, neatening the ends. Bend the lower edge gently around the curved edge of the chipboard and fix with tacks *(fig 3)*. Glue on the fringed braid to cover the tacks. Add any further decoration at this stage, then screw the board in place on the wall.

## *making up the curtains & tie-backs*

**1** Cut the selvedges from the curtain fabric. Join widths together as on p.143, then join back and side curtains and make one large curtain by the bagging method (see p.143). Stitch the fringed braid to the right side along the seamed edges. Press under 2cm along both sides of the top edge and top stitch together.

**2** Hand stitch a series of pencil pleats along the top of the curtain, to draw up

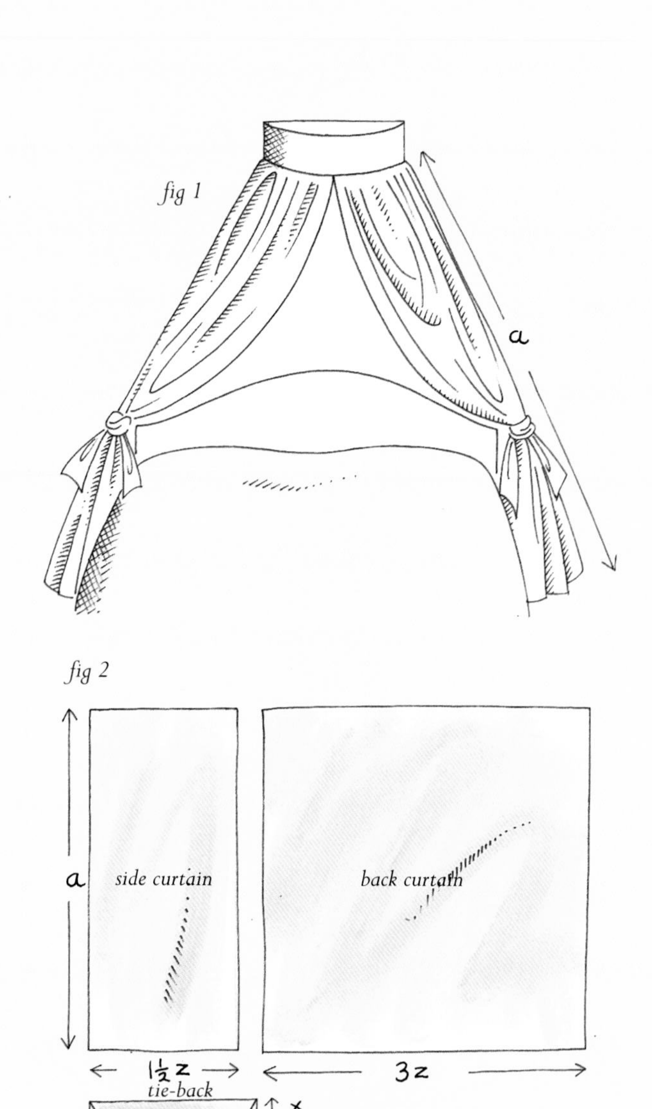

*fig 1*
*fig 2*
*fig 3*
*fig 4*

the width up to 200cm. Mark two lines, 1cm and 5cm from the top on the wrong side. Thread two strong needles with double lengths of buttonhole thread and secure one at the beginning of each line, 4cm in from the edge. Sew 2cm running stitches along both lines, drawing up the fabric at intervals and fastening off tightly before starting a new length *(fig 4)*. Continue to within 4cm of the end. Sew the curtain hooks so that they are concealed inside the folds with just the tips showing, at 4cm intervals.

**3** Pin the two pieces of each tie-back together at the ends, then cut the corners at an angle. Pin and stitch a round of piping to the right side of each contrast fabric piece, then with right sides together, pin each main fabric piece in place. Sew each tie-back together, just inside the previous stitch line, leaving a 5cm gap in the centre of one long edge. Clip the corners and turn right side out. Press and slip stitch the gap closed. Sew a brass ring to the centre on the main fabric side.

**4** Hang up the curtain, starting at the centre front and slotting one hook through each screw eye. Fix a cup hook on each side of the bed at the height where the tie-backs will hang. Mark the seams between the back and side curtains at this height. Take down the curtains and unpick the seam on both sides of the curtain for 8cm on each side of the mark. Slip stitch the front to the back along the previous stitch line to form a slot. Hang the tie-backs on the wall and re-hang the curtains. Pass one end of each tie-back through the slots and tie loosely.

## outline quilted bedspread

### *materials*

Main fabric, contrast fabric, plain fabric, polyester wadding, walking foot for sewing machine, quilter's safety pins, quillting clips

### *measuring and cutting out (fig 1)*

Front: cut one piece from main fabric, width = a, length = 2b, + 3cm all round
Backing: cut one piece from contrast fabric, as front
Wadding: cut one piece, as front, joining widths with a loose herringbone stitch
Binding: cut one 8cm strip from plain fabric, length = 2a + 2b + 40cm

### *making up*

**1** Lay the wadding flat and place the front piece on top, right side up. Join together with tacking or quilter's safety pins. Take time to do this, smoothing the fabric as you go. Work from the centre out to the four corners, then to the middle of each side. Continue making parallel lines 25cm apart, to cover the whole surface *(fig 2)*. When finished, roll up the sides and hold in place with quilting clips, leaving a 40cm area on which to work *(fig 3)*.

**2** Decide in advance which areas to quilt. Using a medium straight stitch, sew slowly and steadily along the outlines. When complete, re-roll the sides to expose the next section. Work from the centre out to each side in turn.

**3** Finish off the loose threads on the wrong side. Trim and square off the edges. Pin the backing, right side out, to the front. Stitch together, 1cm from the edge, then bind (see p.140).

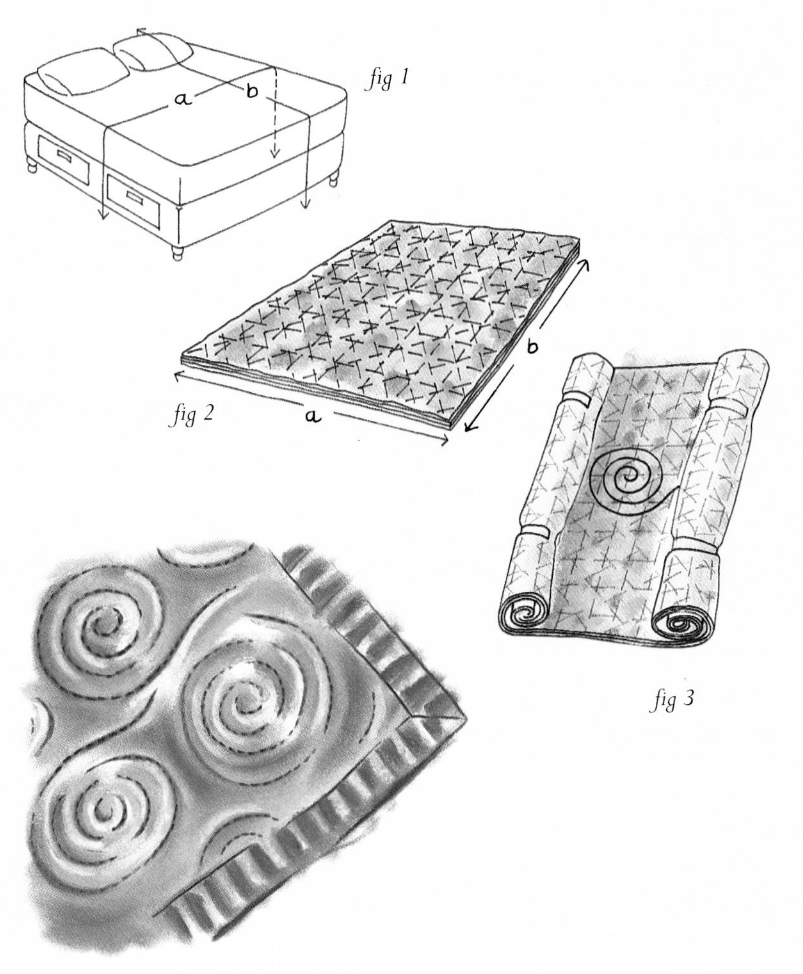

right

French painted furniture, decorative accessories and delicate china from the seventeenth and eighteenth centuries enhance fabric designs from the same period. A sumptuous print curtain sets the scene.

**See page 149 for loose-lined curtains.**

Scatter cushions in toiles and checks, trimmed generously with fringing, bobbles, ties and rope, are piled high on a stool.

**See pages 158–60 for cushions and 166 for footstool squab.**

# *fabric opulence*
## **for a boudoir**

There is no doubt that opulent swathes of fabric draped lavishly around windows are an extremely civilized addition to a bedroom. This is where a secret yearning to have been born in the age of rustling, full-length gowns will out. Treat a bedroom window to a rich fabric hanging in deep folds. Or try weighty red and white leafy toiles lined with dark cream cotton.

By no means should you confine a love of material excess to curtains. There are limitless possibilities for fabric extravaganzas. Play with favourite toiles around the room. Colour schemes can be repeated in an en-suite bathroom or dressing-room to create continuity and a sense of space. Choose red and white toile for both the bed hanging and the bathroom curtains, for instance. Or echo the pattern of the bedspread with a wallpaper to line the shelves of the dressing-room cupboard. Choose linen and towels in pure white, or with contrasting red borders or embroidery to relieve the eye of too much pattern. Of course, those of you who prefer to be wrapped up completely in pattern can opt for toile bedlinen in a monotone print. Choose red and white rugs for both bedroom and bathroom. Accessories such as eighteenth-century china, gilt picture frames and mirrors, candlesticks and old portraits on the walls, are in the spirit of the busy toile designs.

The inside of a painted cupboard is full of surprises, with shelves trimmed and lined with scalloped toiles.

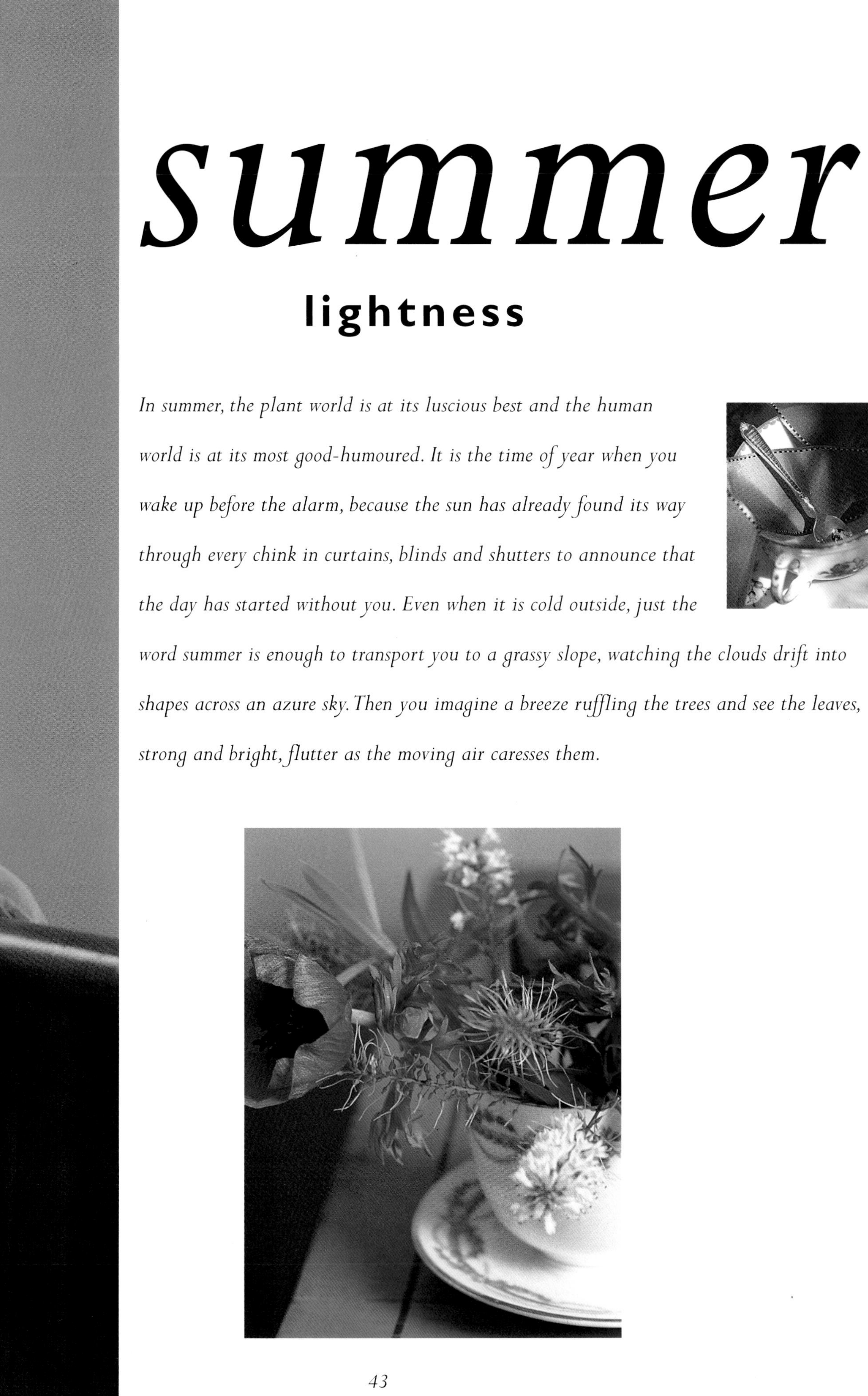

# *summer*

## lightness

*In summer, the plant world is at its luscious best and the human world is at its most good-humoured. It is the time of year when you wake up before the alarm, because the sun has already found its way through every chink in curtains, blinds and shutters to announce that the day has started without you. Even when it is cold outside, just the word summer is enough to transport you to a grassy slope, watching the clouds drift into shapes across an azure sky. Then you imagine a breeze ruffling the trees and see the leaves, strong and bright, flutter as the moving air caresses them.*

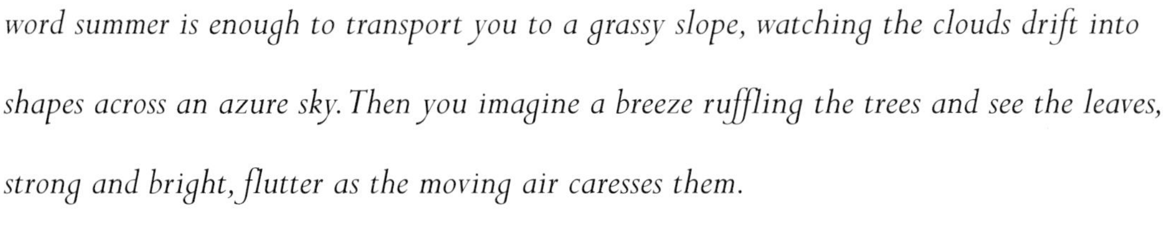

# natural inspiration

*People have tried to bottle and sell the scent of clean washing that has gently dried on a line between two trees in a summer garden. But the truth is that nothing can rival the real McCoy. There are other ways and means of bringing a sense of the outdoors into your house, however. Decorate rooms with fabrics that reflect the elements of your favourite summer days. Let white sand, clear sea and bright sun influence your choice – expanses of blue mixed with white and natural. The colours of lush meadows, ripe juicy fruit, burgeoning flowers and healthy foliage should also play their part. Think of the warmth of summer scenes painted by Rousseau and Dufy. Remember the sort of afternoon that was made for croquet greens and cricket whites. And don't be afraid to change a heavily-clothed winter room into one that looks and feels like a light summer dress.*

# plain & bright

## *for summer effects*

In the heat of summer, the inside of your house should look and feel clean, sharp and invigorating to make it a refreshing retreat from the midday sun. There should be no murky shades left lurking: let pure, plain hues and bright, splashy, blowsy flowers take over. Choose white and natural fabrics, cool indigo blues, fresh blue and white, tangy lime and rich, exotic flowery prints to bring summer inside. The checks are large, the patterns bold and joyful, reflecting gardens in their full glory. Decorating schemes are, on the whole, clean and unfussy. A more urban, architectural, plain look is beginning to take over from the sprigs and buds, rustic toiles and ginghams of a spring-like atmosphere, and the effect is cool rather than cosy. But don't totally discount the idea of a smattering of antiquated, flowery cottons, because these will always have a place in design.

## **airy & crisp**
*textures for contrast*

Let the natural world of summer also inspire the textures and weights of your fabric choices. Imagine trailing a hand in the wake of a sailing boat and find silky, fluid, fine washed cottons to remind you of that feeling. And don't stop there – make a frothing waterfall of floaty sheers and voiles that fall to the floor – these fabrics will let the sun shine through, making the most of bright days. Slubby natural linen and fine smooth linen on sofas, curtains and cushions recall the holiday feeling of sand underfoot. Crisp broderie anglaise is as cool and fresh as white crests of waves for soft pillows and cushions. And choose slender, airy feathered duvets, quilts and pillows, not only because they are light but also because they are reminiscent of summer scenes of lightly billowing sails or fresh washing blowing in a faint breeze.

If a cottage garden were made of fabrics, they would be pink and white faded cottons and sheer voiles. In the right setting an antique curtain makes an ideal table cover.

**See pages 158–60 for cushions, 166 for frilled cushion for basket chair and 167 for tie-on squab.**

# under a greenwood tree

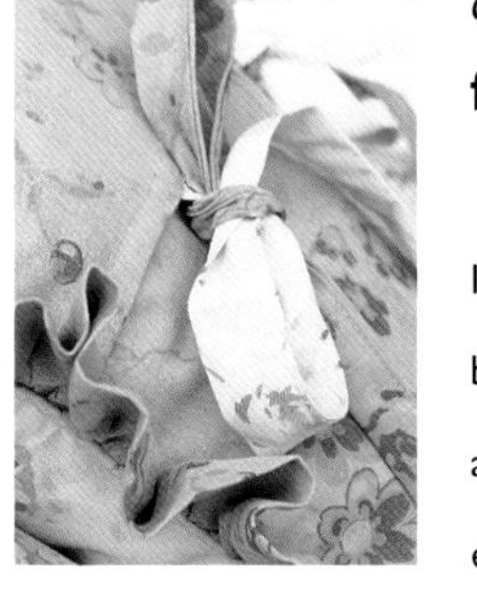

## *abundant flowers*
## **for a lazy afternoon**

It is very satisfying to see a rhododendron or a rose-bush repay your hard graft with a blaze of colour. This is the kind of display that might tempt you to abandon the house altogether in the summer and set up camp in the garden. And why not? But you could equally recreate that freshness of colour in a decorating scheme for inside. Try a rich green solid background for walls and painted furniture and bring it to life with deep pink flowers, shown off against smooth white cotton. Alternatively, clad your walls with painted boards in pale washed shades, and put up decorative shelves to house terracotta pots of flowers such as geraniums and pansies. Use the colours of your garden for inspiration when planning a conservatory, and it will become an attractive transitional area between outside and in. Look at the trees or flower borders and choose fabrics to match. Or imagine your dream garden, and choose the colours and textures that best conjure up its characteristics. You will then have the perfect setting for idyllic summer lounging, whether spent indoors or out. And when the blooms in the garden have long since faded, the flower-scattered fabrics will be a delightful reminder of sunny days and balmy nights.

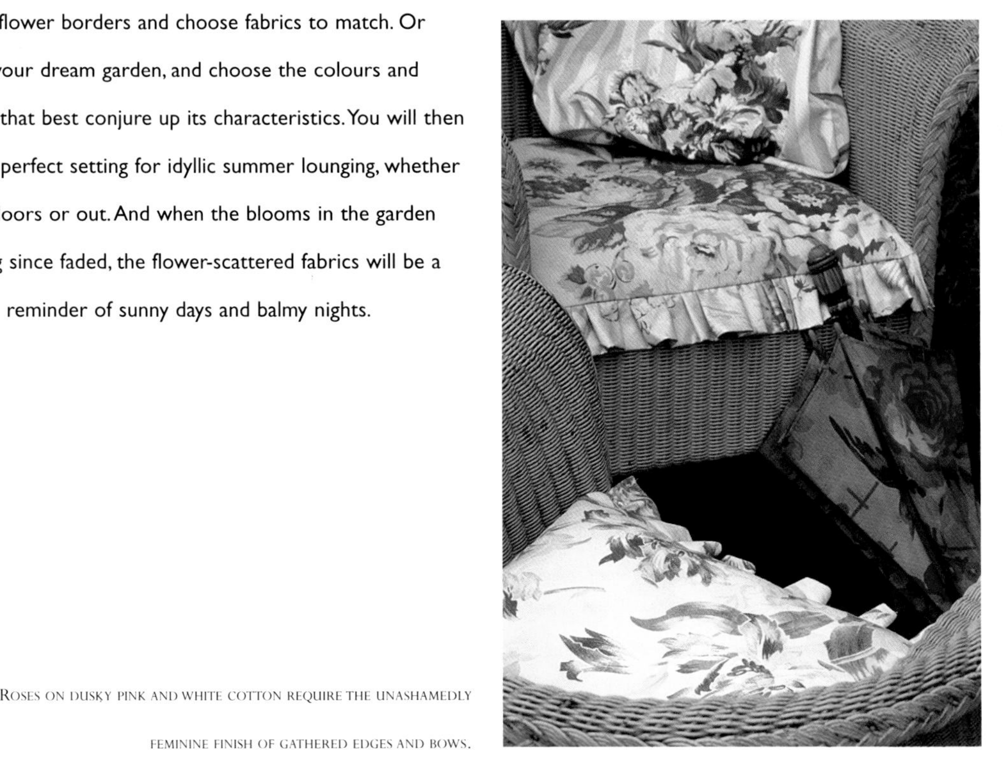

Roses on dusky pink and white cotton require the unashamedly feminine finish of gathered edges and bows.

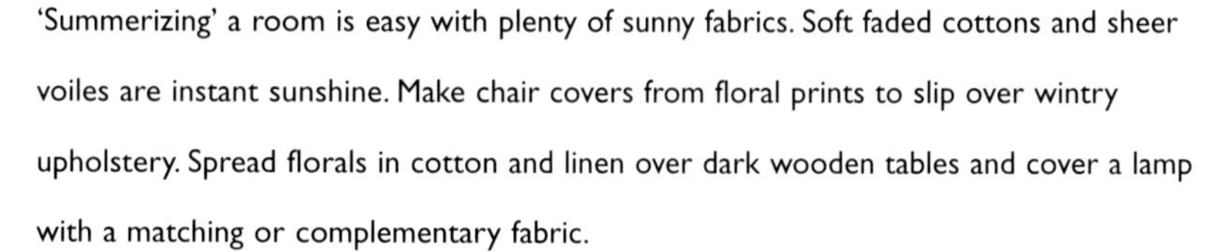

# *scattered posies*
## for furniture al fresco

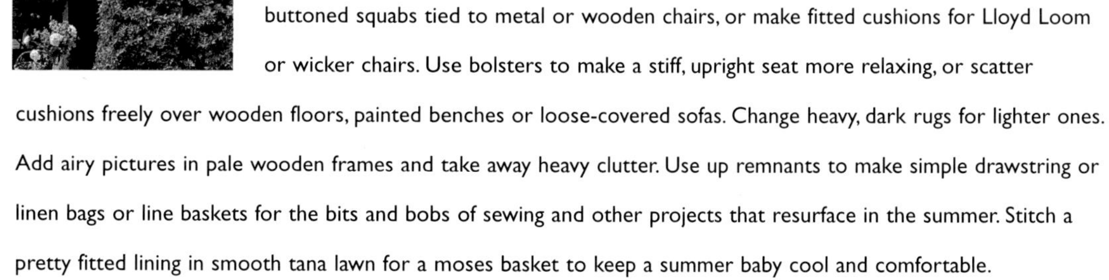

'Summerizing' a room is easy with plenty of sunny fabrics. Soft faded cottons and sheer voiles are instant sunshine. Make chair covers from floral prints to slip over wintry upholstery. Spread florals in cotton and linen over dark wooden tables and cover a lamp with a matching or complementary fabric.

Cushions are an excellent way of bringing brightness into a room. Try mattress-buttoned squabs tied to metal or wooden chairs, or make fitted cushions for Lloyd Loom or wicker chairs. Use bolsters to make a stiff, upright seat more relaxing, or scatter cushions freely over wooden floors, painted benches or loose-covered sofas. Change heavy, dark rugs for lighter ones. Add airy pictures in pale wooden frames and take away heavy clutter. Use up remnants to make simple drawstring or linen bags or line baskets for the bits and bobs of sewing and other projects that resurface in the summer. Stitch a pretty fitted lining in smooth tana lawn for a moses basket to keep a summer baby cool and comfortable.

For a dining-room, make the most of a pretty dinner service by choosing fresh linens that echo its pattern, or pick up one or two colours, and make a set of napkins and placemats from them. And don't fold them away into drawers when not in use: pile them on a sideboard as an accessory.

Here we have chosen faded pink florals on an ecru background, roses and cherries on dusky pink and grey, a whole rose garden against sky blue, and the collected riot of colour creates the atmosphere of a typical summer's day. Don't be restrained in your choice of florals – the blowsier the better. Big blooms are part of the full glory of summer. The fabrics can be as varied as you like and a mixture of interesting piping and scalloped edges will frame the different designs. And don't forget to bring inside posies of the flowers that have inspired your scheme. A small pot of roses and some rich greenery is enough to make the connection.

right & opposite

A frilly lampshade and a matching drawstring bag pick out the pinks in a scalloped-edged loose cover for a chair. The cover is secured at the back of the chair with fabric bows.

**See pages 178–80 for tie-backed chair cover and 154 for frilled lampshade.**

left

A basket of cherries inspires the fabric for luscious summer pillows, cushions and antique soft quilts, with pretty pink flounces and plain piped edges.

**See pages 158–160 for cushions.**

below

Sky blue and roses for a drawstring bag and a moses basket. Bright yellow gingham trimming makes a sunny contrast.

**See pages 128–9 for moses baskets.**

# *fabric folly* for a summer canopy & stools

A summer house to sit and dream in is a luxury that funds do not always allow. Next time you are planning your ideal garden, complete with a gothic gazebo in the wildest spot, think about constructing a canopy instead – equally blissful but much easier to realize. All you need is a fabric roof, scalloped in the style of its medieval ancestors, and sides that can be hitched up or unfurled depending on the angle of the sun. Choose fabric that picks out the colours of a nearby border or hedge and re-cover garden stools in fabrics that complement rather than match. Putting the framework together is a family effort, as three people are needed to assemble the parts. Do this before sewing the cover, so that you can check for a perfect fit.

*materials*

*for the frame*

2 x 3cm poles (30cm long) for the vertical roof struts, 3 x 3cm poles (2.5m long) for the long horizontal roof struts, 2 x 3cm poles (1.5m long) for the short horizontal roof struts, 4 x 4.5cm poles (2m long) for the uprights, roll of heavy-duty adhesive tape, 4 x 3-way corner connectors (A20, size 7), 2 x T-connectors (A4, size 7), 2 x right-angle connectors (A6, size 7), Allen key, 4 long nails, 4 x 2.5m lengths of twine, 4 tent pegs, chisel, drill

*for the canopy*

Main fabric, contrast fabric, thin card, chalk pencil or fading pen

*for the stools*

Small folding stool, main fabric, 2cm upholstery tacks and hammer

*fig 1*

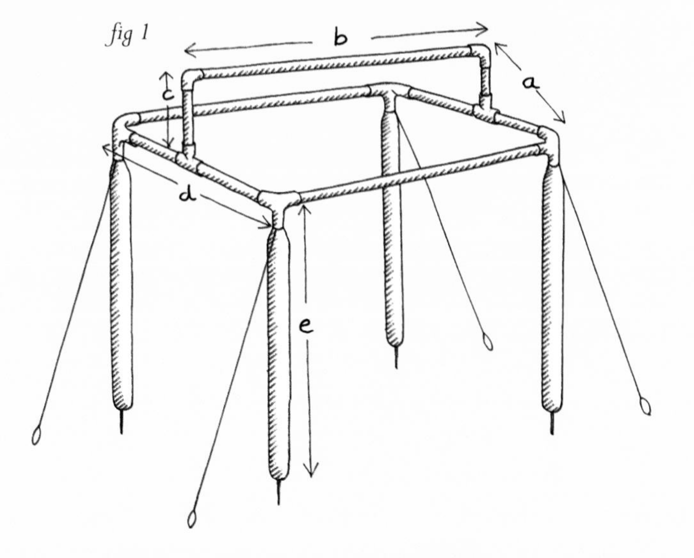


*making the frame*

**1** Chisel down one end of each upright to make it fit into the 3-way corner connector. Drill a hole in the other end and hammer in a nail to make a spike.

**2** Wrap two layers of tape around both ends of each roof pole. Thread the T-connectors on to the short horizontal struts. Position them centrally, with the empty connection facing upwards, and tighten the nuts with the Allen key. Push the taped ends of the short and two of the long horizontal struts into the 3-way connectors to make a rectangular frame and tighten.

**3** Push one end of each vertical strut into an empty T-connector. Put the right-angle connector on the other end and tighten. Put each end of the remaining long roof pole into the free ends of the right-angle connectors and tighten.

**4** Lay the roof frame out on the grass where the canopy will stand. Mark each corner with a tent peg and use these as a guide to plant the uprights firmly in the lawn. Tie a loop in both ends of each piece of twine to make guy ropes. Loop one over the top of each upright so that the loop rests on the flange. Lift the roof and place the empty sockets of the 3-way corner connectors over the top of the uprights and tighten *(fig 1)*. Stretch out the strings and peg down.

*fig 2*

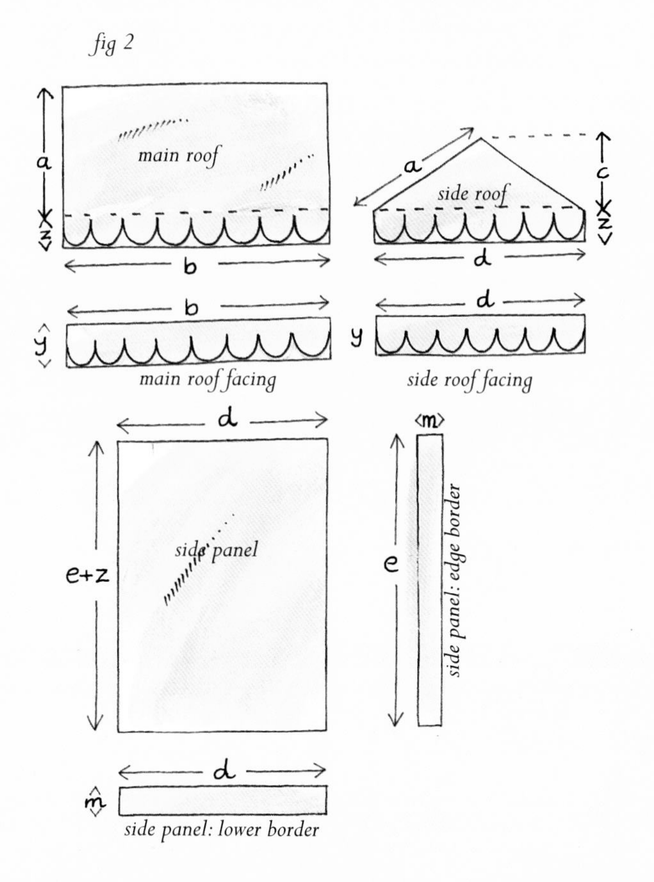


*making the canopy*

*measuring & cutting out (figs 1 & 2)*

Add 2cm all round each piece except the ties. The shaded areas represent fabric that will be cut away. NB: z equals 20cm in the cutting instructions below.

*from main fabric*

Main roof: cut two pieces, width = b, depth = a + z (20cm)

Side roof: cut two pieces, width = d, depth = c + z (20cm)

Side panels: cut two pieces, width = d, depth = e + z (20cm)

*from contrast fabric*

Main roof facing: cut two pieces, width = y (22cm), length = b

Side roof facing: cut two pieces, width = y (22cm), length ≐ d

Side panel edge border: cut four pieces, width = m (14cm), length = e

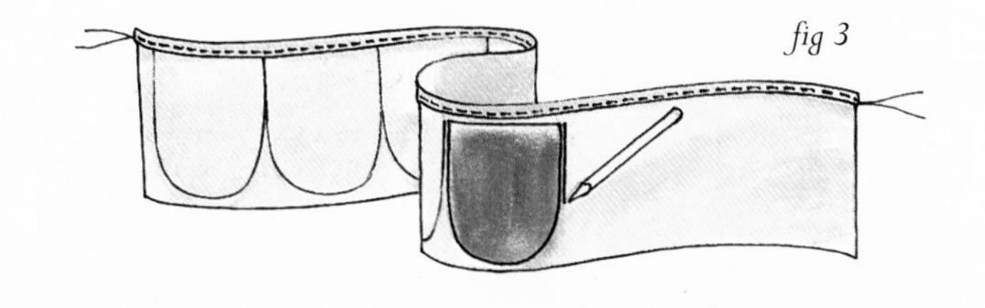

*fig 3*

Side panel lower border: cut two pieces, width = m (14cm), length = d

Ties: cut ten strips, 6 x 30cm

Panel ties: cut four strips, 14 x 200cm

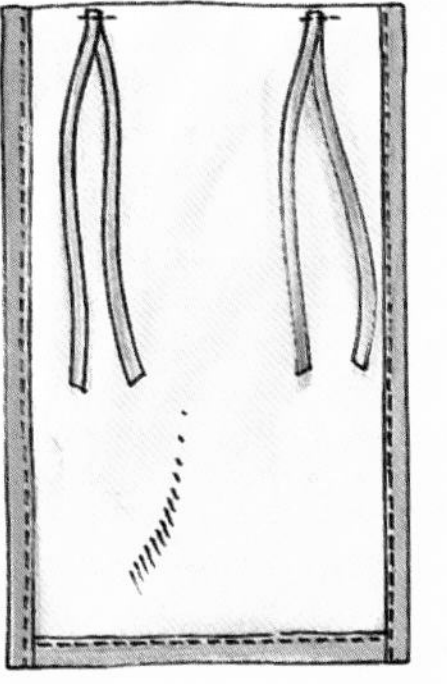
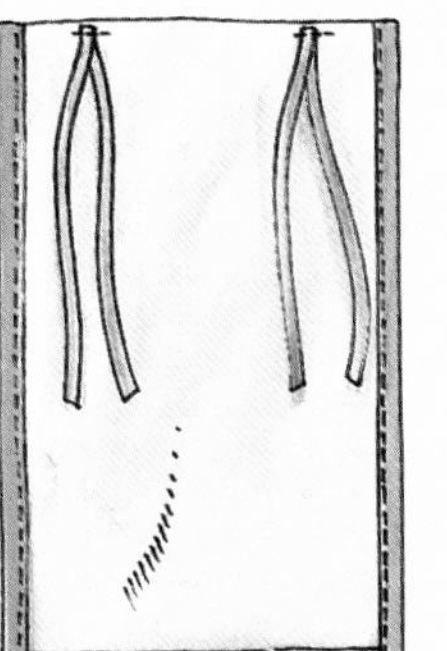
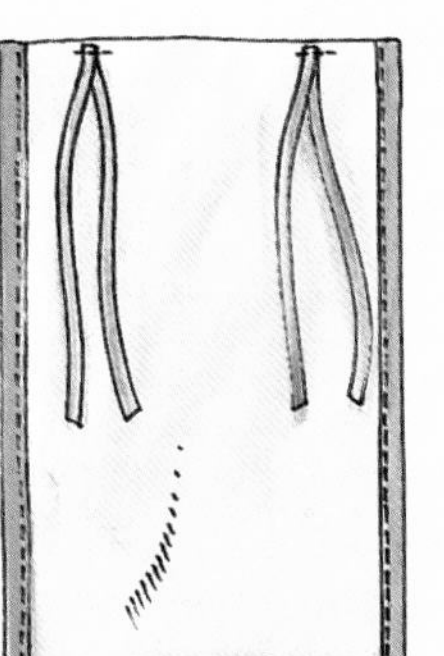

fig 4

fig 5

## making up

**1** Make a template for the scallops by subtracting 4cm from length d and dividing by six. Cut a piece of card this width by 18cm. Draw a deep scallop shape and cut out. Make a 1cm double hem along the top edge of one side roof facing. Starting 2cm in from the side and matching the top to the hem fold, draw around the template seven times or to make the desired number of scallops *(fig 3)*.

**2** With right sides together, pin the facing strip to the lower edge of the side roof. Tack close to the scallop line, then stitch. Trim and clip the curves and points (see p.139). Turn right side out and press. Stitch the hemmed edge of the facing to the main fabric. Do the same with the other side roof, and make an edging of eight scallops along the lower edge of the main roof pieces in the same way.

**3** With right sides together, pin and stitch the two main roof pieces together along the top edge, leaving a 2cm seam allowance. Pin and stitch the side roof pieces to each end. Make the ties as on p.144. Fold them in half and sew one securely to each corner, one to the centre lower edge of each side roof, and two, evenly spaced, to the lower edge of each main roof piece *(fig 4)*.

**4** Press under 1cm along the long edges of each panel border, and press in half lengthways. Pin and stitch one short strip over the lower edge of each side panel. Press under 1cm at the lower end of each long border. Pin and stitch in place down the sides, so that the folded edge lies along the hem line.

**5** Make the panel ties as on p.144. Fold in half and pin to the top of the side panels, 40cm in from each edge *(fig 5)*. Pin the upper edge of each panel in position against the hemmed scalloped roof edge, with the right side facing outwards and stitch in place, catching in the ties. Tie the canopy on to the frame.

## making the stools

### measuring & cutting out

Seat: remove the existing cover. Use it as a guide to cut a rectangle the same length by twice the width, plus 3cm

Frill: cut two pieces 10cm strips, length = twice the width of the seat

### making up

**1** Fold the seat piece in half widthways with right sides facing. Pin, and stitch 1.5cm from the long edges. Press the seam flat and turn right side out. Press so that the seam lies along the centre back.

**2** Make a narrow double hem along the sides and one long edge of each frill piece. Gather the raw edge to fit the width of the seat (see p.142). Mark where the seat folds over the frame. With right sides facing, pin and stitch the frills along these lines, with the neatened edges facing into the centre *(fig 6)*. Fix the cover to the underside of the wooden frame with tacks.

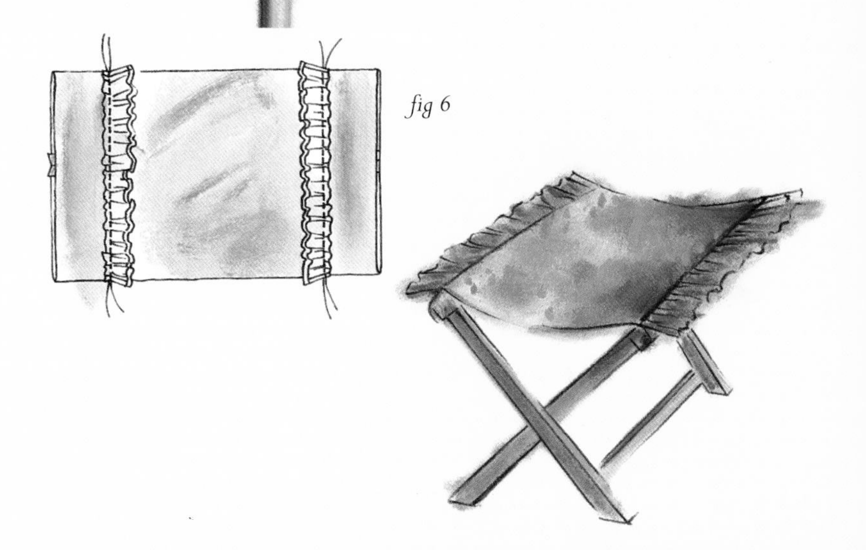

fig 6

A plain canopy balances the chintzy sweetness of this table dressing. A bow for a tablecloth requires fabric that is substantial enough to stay in place.

**See pages 184–5 for fitted buffet tablecloth and 144 for bows.**

## *table manners*
# **frocks for furniture**

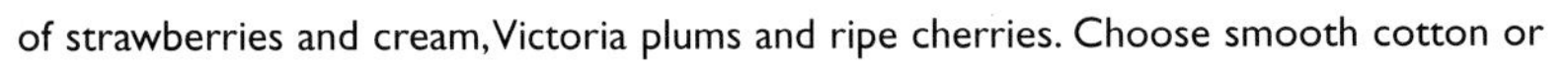

The Victorian obsession with covering chairs and tables with floor-sweeping fabric stemmed from a general feeling among polite society that chair and table legs were unseemly. Just as limbs were swathed in long skirts, so furniture was kept under wraps. A side-effect of this attention to morals was that chairs, trestle tables, dressing-tables and side tables were made into colourful features with imaginative fabric creations.

Revive these niceties with a trestle table in floral cotton. Find colours that remind you of strawberries and cream, Victoria plums and ripe cherries. Choose smooth cotton or shiny chintz that is heavy enough to sweep in folds to the floor. Lift the tablecloth at each corner to reveal a daring, pure-white 'petticoat' undercloth in linen or broderie anglaise and attach four generous bustle-like bows. The effect is perfect for a traditional wedding reception or garden party. Beg, borrow or trawl old curiosity shops for a miscellany of Victorian glassware and china for the day, too. A plain blue and white awning or canopy makes an attractive sun-shade for the festive feast – an unfussy contemporary shape balances the old-fashioned look of the table underneath.

You could translate this idea for a bedroom, too. Make a layered valance for a bed with floral and pure white cottons, and bows. Construct a cool white linen canopy – either over the whole bed to make a fourposter, or over the headboard in a coronet with drapes. Indulge in a spot of table-dressing here, too. Pick out simple ginghams and sweet floral prints to mix and match. Make a cotton skirt for a dressing-table and top it with a frilled cover in a contrasting patterned cotton – use piping from the first fabric to connect the two designs. Make accessories such as lampshades or picture frames that echo one of the fabrics. A dressing-table stool could be covered in the same way, but reverse the order of the fabrics to make the table and stool more intriguing as a pair.

Plain checked cotton contrasts with pretty smooth cotton florals for a bedroom. The summery spectrum of warm pinks is given a sunny yellow background. Accessories and fresh flowers echo the scheme. Adapt the instructions given for the tartan sequence **(see pages 104–5)**, for this lighter version.

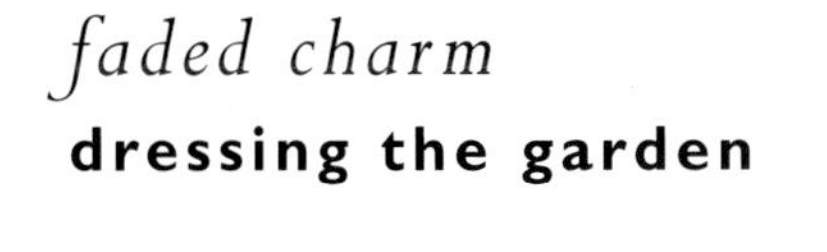

# *faded charm*
## dressing the garden

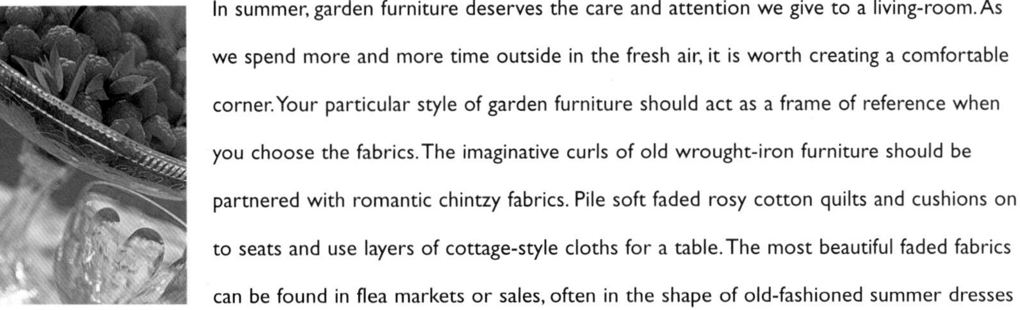

In summer, garden furniture deserves the care and attention we give to a living-room. As we spend more and more time outside in the fresh air, it is worth creating a comfortable corner. Your particular style of garden furniture should act as a frame of reference when you choose the fabrics. The imaginative curls of old wrought-iron furniture should be partnered with romantic chintzy fabrics. Pile soft faded rosy cotton quilts and cushions on to seats and use layers of cottage-style cloths for a table. The most beautiful faded fabrics can be found in flea markets or sales, often in the shape of old-fashioned summer dresses or an old curtain. When unpicking your finds, make sure to launder the pieces before making them up into new furnishings. Where changes in colour occur, usually in seam allowances or hems, either cut around them, or make them part of the faded charm. More contemporary natural or painted wooden benches and tables can be teamed with plain linens – either in bright or neutral colours or simple, sharp geometric designs. Of course, the cushions and cloths can also be taken inside to bring freshness and light into a dining area.

**opposite**

Wrought-iron garden furniture, a straw hat and a vase of chintzy roses set off a train of imaginative thought for dressing up garden furniture.

A pretty basket can be lined with left-over fabric.

Squab cushions are loosely tied to garden chairs for quick release should a balmy day turn stormy.

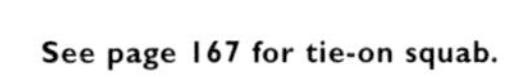

**See page 167 for tie-on squab.**

An old screen is easily cheered up with a patterned fabric cover.

**See page 143 for fabric-covered panels.**

# *blue indigo*

## *bright ideas* **with cool colour**

It might be unbearably hot on the beach, but as long as you are transfixed by the swell of blue in front of you, and the occasional white breaker, you will feel refreshed. For a refreshing summer decorating scheme, take an array of blues and indigos, whites and naturals in linen, cotton, sheer voile and denim to form an escape from the heat of the day. Clear blues have an unrivalled freshness which brings every room to life. You cannot fail, mixing intense and washed shades of the same colour spectrum. Add a splash of warm yellow in a vase of fresh flowers, a picture or a lampshade for a light-creating contrast.

Turn a bedroom into a cool airy retreat with sheer watery drapes and a miscellany of indigo and blue cottons and denims for cushions and a softly pleated valance. Mix pure white and blue for a simple duvet cover and a mound of smooth cotton pillows. A sandy-coloured floor and plain wooden furniture and accessories provide warm contrasts. Make sure the windows are not obscured with heavy curtains – blue is a light-absorbing colour, so let in plenty of sunshine to brighten the room during the day.

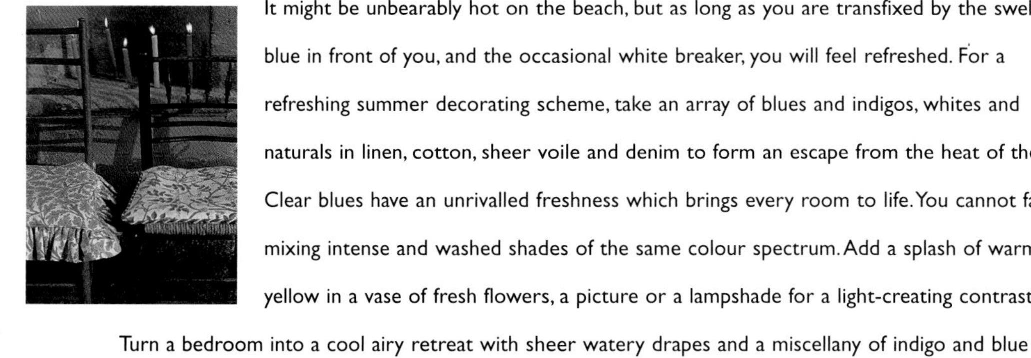

A ROW OF CHAIRS DRESSED FOR AN EVENING PERFORMANCE IN COMPLEMENTARY BLUE AND WHITE PRINTS.

**See page 167 for tie-on squabs.**

A PEACEFUL SUMMER BEDROOM IS AWASH WITH BLUE. TRANSPARENT BED CURTAINS OF VARYING WEIGHTS AND DESIGNS ARE COMPLEMENTED BY AN INDIGO COVER AND CRISP, FRESH BLUE AND WHITE BEDLINEN, FOR COOL SLUMBER ON A HOT SUMMER'S NIGHT. THE CURTAINS ARE ATTACHED TO THE BEDFRAME BY BUTTONED LOOPS.

**See pages 149 for unlined curtains, 150 for buttoned loops and 155–7 for pillowcases.**

A WINDOW-SEAT AND CURTAINS ARE PARTNERS IN FABRIC. THE PLAIN PIPED CUSHIONS CONTINUE THE COOL COLOUR SCHEME WHILE RELIEVING THE UNIFORMITY. ROMAN BLINDS IN WHITE PURE LINEN ARE LINED IN WHITE AND MERELY DIFFUSE THE INCOMING LIGHT.

**See pages 165 for fitted box cushion, 160 for piped cushion edging, 147 for lined roman blind and 149 for loose-lined curtains.**

# *light reflections*
## **in cool settings**

If the eyes are the windows of our souls, it follows that windows should aptly reflect the spirit of a house. Windows are especially important in summer, as they are our first point of contact with the sunny outdoors when we wake up in the morning. Sleepy eyes look through them even before they focus on anything else, to register the colour of the sky and the wind in the trees.

Capitalize on a pleasant view or morning sun with a window-seat padded with plenty of cushions. A Saturday morning breakfast of warm croissants and fruit undeniably tastes best when enjoyed with sunlight and/or greenery behind you. Alternatively, place a table by a well-dressed open window for a dinner party, to make the most of the evening air.

For summer days, plain roman blinds in slubby linen or unlined voiles look fresh and natural. Add simple navy and white cotton curtains to offset the brightest sunshine. If you choose fabric for your window seat to match your curtains, then add cushions in contrasting patterns and a mixture of different blues to break the uniformity. Pure, unfussy, lightweight fabrics and simple designs work well by a window and will not detract too much from an attractive windowframe, or a stunning view. White or cream blinds are supremely effective during the day – for bearing the brunt of the strong sun without casting the room into gloom and, of course, for showing the dancing silhouette of a tree or a rose-bush outside. Be sure to line them if you like a neat crisp finish, and if you cannot sleep unless the bedroom is dark, you can have separate blackout blinds made.

**above**

FITTED OVER A SHEER VOILE PANEL IS A NEATLY TAILORED ROMAN BLIND, LINED IN WHITE COTTON FOR CRISPNESS.

**above right**

A BASKETFUL OF BLUE AND WHITE CUSHIONS, BROUGHT IN FROM THE GARDEN AT THE END OF THE DAY.

A GARDEN CHAIR WITH A SMOCK-LIKE COVER HAS POCKETS ON EACH SIDE – FOR BOOKS AND READING GLASSES, OR SECATEURS AND GARDENING GLOVES. BLUE AND WHITE WIDE AND NARROW STRIPES ARE COOL AND FRESH, AND A COUPLE OF SUNFLOWERS BREAK THE ICE.

**See pages 172–3 for tailored cover.**

# *limelight*

## *a burst of citrus* **for a town house**

An easy way of shedding limelight is to use the colour of the fruit in a decorating scheme for a room. The colour lime gives out a thoroughly modern glow, full of vitality, conjuring up an invigorating sense of the freshness of summer inside a house. It is a stimulating colour that works best in the living areas of a house rather than the bedrooms, which should be decorated in more restful shades.

Start with a contemporary chair upholstered in lime and build your scheme around it. Continue the lime theme throughout the room but don't match all the shades exactly. Graduate from warm lemony lime on the walls to sharp acid lime for the furniture, and a mixture of more muted greens and sherbet limes for the curtains. As always, accessories will bring the scheme together masterfully. A dining-room or kitchen, for instance, will benefit from a display of creamy ceramics with traces of lime and a collection of lime napkins, and keep a stash of the real thing in a fruit bowl with some apples, pears and lemons.

With one section of the colour spectrum so dominant in a room, a range of contrasting textures and weights of fabrics is important. Mix delicate muslin with slubby natural linen in different weights, smooth cotton with shiny glazed cotton, and see the room take shape. A smooth, leafy cotton curtain, neatly drawn back in the daytime, is a solid background for a concentration of different greens. But a flimsy voile under-curtain with a mixture of crisp opaque and delicate translucent squares plays with the sunlight in the room and is more ethereal. Its natural and lime squares are alternately prominent, depending on the angle of the sun. The checks of this curtain echo the multi-panelled window behind – always look at the patterns that already exist in the framework of the room before you start decorating. Even the curve of a cornice or a knot in a floorboard will throw up an idea for a fabric. Pale wooden floors have a calming effect on citrus, soaking up some of its impact. Rush matting, natural rough linen in a loose chair cover or a tablecloth, a pale wooden table or chair will all have the same effect. Remember, too much of any one colour soon dates.

left, from the top

A curly wrought-iron tie-back is neater and more modern than a fabric one for this room.

Neutral rough linens for a loose chair cover and cushions are a passive addition to an otherwise colour-dominated room. Cherrywood and gentle cream cotton and ceramics balance the acidity of smartly contemporary lime-green chairs.

**See pages 173–4 for basket chair cover and 184 for rectangular tablecloth.**

A lime-coloured scheme for walls, furniture and curtains brings a modern interpretation of a zestful summer day to a town house. The outer curtain has a gathered heading and the unlined inner curtain is attached to the pole with tape ties on a straight heading.

**See pages 151 for gathered heading and 150 for tape ties on straight heading.**

# *zigzag finish* **for a table cover**

Follow in the footsteps of the court jester, and make a head-turning feature out of an uninteresting table. Dress it in linen and, with another shade of finer linen, make a zigzag-edged cover for the top. Line the top layer so that it holds its shape: the lining will also ensure that the zigzags are well defined and do not fray. Lime green and natural linen make an eye-catching contrast. Little beads, tassels or even bells sewn on to the tips are excellent courtly accessories. This would work equally well in a patchwork of primary colours or wide blue and white stripes. You could also vary the design by swapping zigzags for a scalloped edge.

### *materials*

Main fabric, contrast fabric, cotton lining fabric, 20 x 1cm glass beads, thin card and pencil

### *measuring & cutting out*

#### *tablecloth*

Top: cut one circle from main fabric, diameter = diameter of table top, plus 5cm

Skirt: cut one rectangle from main fabric, length = circumference plus 24cm, width = distance from table top to floor + 3cm

NB: To make a fuller fitted circular tablecloth in a finer fabric, the length of the skirt must equal twice the circumference of the table.

#### *cover*

Top: cut one circle from contrast fabric, diameter = diameter of table top, plus 7cm

Edging: cut one rectangle from contrast fabric and one from lining, length = length of slirt, plus 3cm, width = 25cm

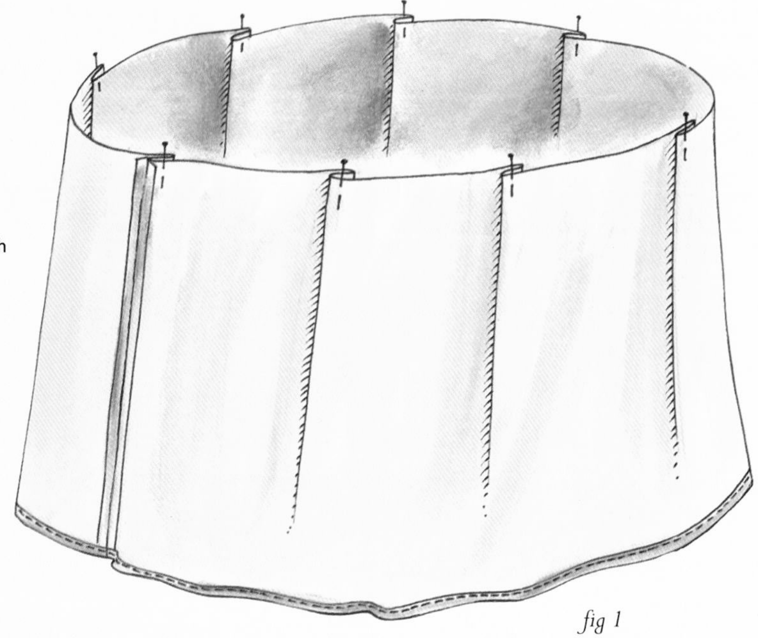

*fig 1*

### *making up the tablecloth*

**1** With right sides facing, join the two short edges of the skirt, leaving a seam allowance of 1.5cm. Turn up and stitch a 2cm double hem along the lower edge. Fold in half from the seam, then into quarters and eighths. Mark each fold point with a pin. Starting at the seam, make a 1.5cm pleat at each fold and pin in place *(fig 1)*.

**2** Fold the circular top into half, then quarters, then eighths. Mark these folds with pins at the outside edge and then, with right sides facing, pin the skirt around the edge of the top, matching the pleats to the pins. Adjust the fullness of the pleats as necessary. Check the fit on the table itself, then sew together, leaving a 1cm seam allowance.

*fig 2*

### *making up the cover*

**3** To work out how large each point should be, subtract 3cm from the length of the edging strip. Divide the remaining amount by 20 and cut out a rectangular cardboard template which is this distance (x) wide and y (23cm) long. Draw a horizontal line z (10cm) from the top and another which divides the rectangle in half lengthways. Draw a triangle in the lower half *(fig 2)* between these lines.

**4** Starting 1.5cm in from one short edge, and lining up the top with the upper edge of the fabric, draw around the template on to the wrong side of the lining fabric 20 times to form a zigzag line. Leave 1.5cm at the other end *(fig 3)*.

**5** Sew into a loop with right sides together, with a 1.5 cm seam allowance, and press flat. Join the main fabric into a loop with right sides facing, 2cm from the ends. Press the seam flat.

*fig 3*

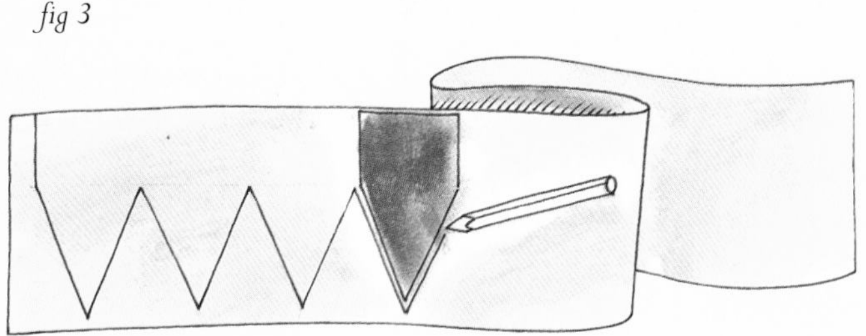

**6** With right sides facing, pin the lining loop around the outside of the main fabric loop along the top and bottom edges. Tack close to the zigzag line *(fig 4)*, then stitch along it. Trim the surplus fabric, clip the corners (see p.139) and turn right side out. Pin and stitch the two sides of the top edges together.

**7** Pin and stitch the edging around the outside of the top with right sides together, leaving a 1cm seam allowance. Stitch a glass bead securely to each point.

*fig 4*

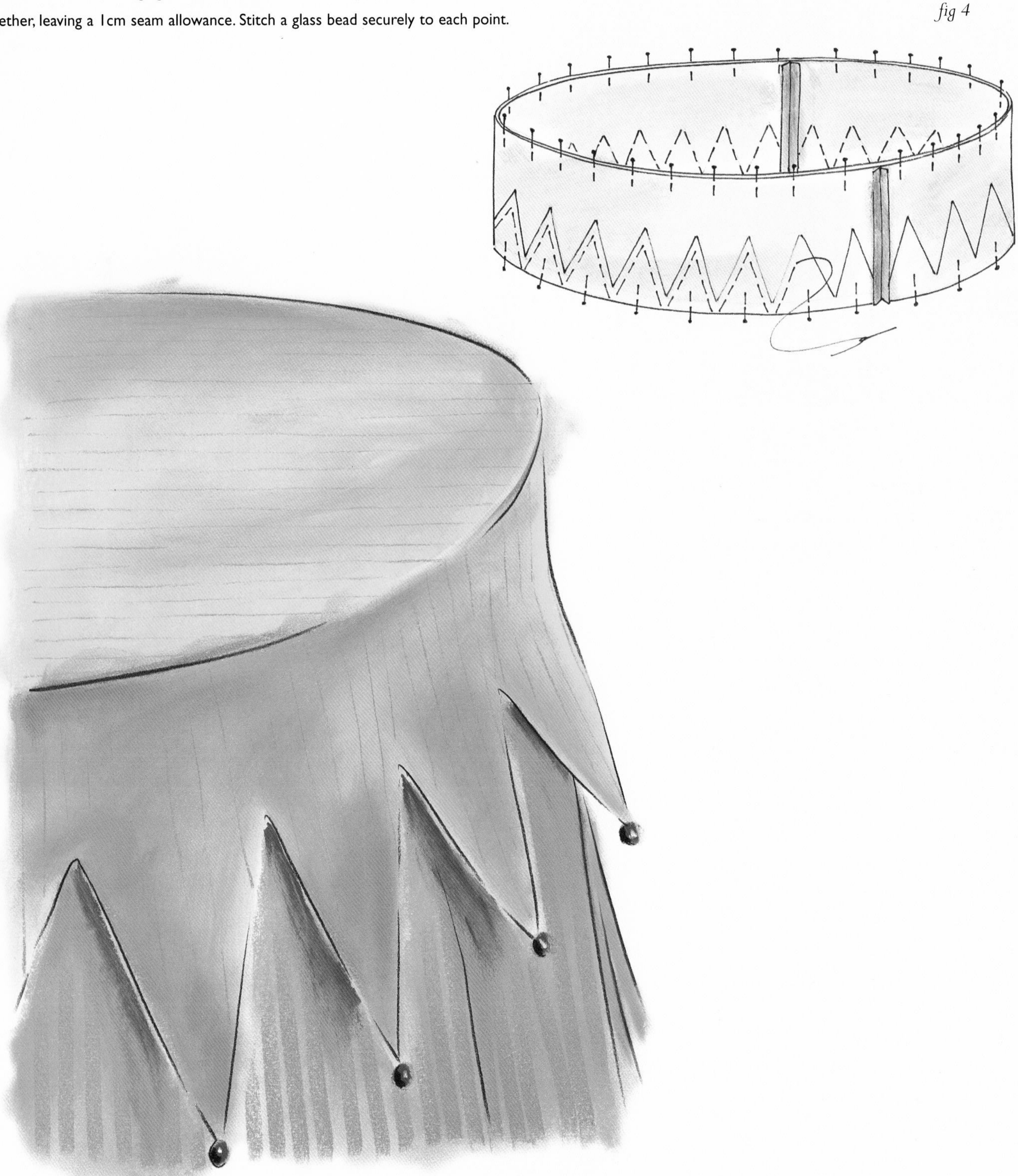

# *white havens*

## *peace and tranquillity* **for simple guest rooms**

White is a symbol of peace, so it stands to reason that it is conducive to sleep. Swathe your bedroom in white cotton and linen and the odds are you will wake up each morning feeling completely refreshed.

Depending on which part of the world you live in, it is safe to say that blue and lime whites enhance a scheme in a sunny climate and gentler porcelain and cream shades look prettier in northern climes. Decorating history has it that the French used to favour fabric for the walls of their houses while the English preferred to battle with paper and glue, or paint. As several coats of paint are needed to achieve really solid white walls, you could join the French school of thought with white cotton wall hangings instead. This can be achieved by stapling fabric panels to battens fixed to the wall, or by simply stretching a wire from one wall to another and threading the hemmed fabric panels over the wire. Or you can tie the fabric at short intervals to a Shaker pegboard fitted to the walls at picture-rail level with fabric tape, ribbons or elastic bands. Fabric-covered screens can be used too, to soften the corners of a room. Continue the French influence with square pillows and bolsters. A few hints of colour in a stain for the floor add a sense of warmth – a rug, painted furniture or pictures would do the same.

ROMANCE BY CANDLELIGHT – A FOUR-POSTER BRASS BED IS DRESSED IN FINERY OF CRISP COTTON, DELICATE LACE AND TRANSLUCENT ORGANZA.

**below**

A PRETTY ORGANZA CURTAIN SCREENS OFF A ROLL TOP BATH IN AN ENSUITE BATHROOM.

COOL COTTON AND LINEN PILLOWCASES ARE CRISPLY STARCHED TO LOOK THEIR BEST.

# *permutations of white* **for simple luxury**

A white sofa has the same comforting aura of luxury as a huge, thick white towel in a country house hotel. It is the kind of luxury that you enjoy away from home, but rarely think of including in your own domestic arrangements. People shy away from white in their houses for two reasons. One is that they fear it will be too difficult to keep clean, though in fact, a pre-shrunk loose cover can be washed and dried quite easily, and is unlikely to attract the layers of dust that darker colours do. The second qualm is that white is considered too bold a statement for smaller houses. The accepted wisdom is that an expanse of white will dominate the room and make it seem crowded.

But in fact the opposite is true: a white sofa will introduce a sense of light, air and space, opening up the room by bringing in a feeling of freshness and just a touch of abandon. Continue the holiday humour with other shades throughout the room. Deep blue mixed with white in natural fabric cushion covers, patterned wallpaper and accessories is a nod to dappled summer skies and seas; textured creams and natural hues for curtains and paintwork are a reminder of sandy beaches. A bed covered in freshly laundered linen is one of the most delicious and inviting sights. Here, a trousseau containing embroidered and lace-trimmed Victorian and French linen is made into a big patchwork cover. Placing and sewing the pieces on to a large cotton sheet will save the more fragile edges from tearing, and will also make laundering and ironing less of a delicate operation.

**left, above**

Cushions, covers and linen in every permutation of blue and white are piled on to a lit bateau.

**left**

A forgotten bottom drawer of embroidered linen and lace remnants, napkins and runners is made into a magnificent bedspread.

A COMFORTABLE SOFA NEED NOT LOOK BATTERED. MAKE A LOOSE COVER OUT OF WHITE TEXTURED FABRIC THAT IS GUARANTEED NOT TO SHRINK IN THE WASH.

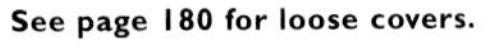

**See page 180 for loose covers.**

# *chequered history* for country bedrooms

Three ingredients in the recipe for an old-fashioned bucolic bedroom – be it in deepest Provence or the wilds of Manhattan – are unpolished wooden floors, bold checked fabrics and old French or Italian bed-tables and chairs of polished wood. These basic elements – plus a couple of mirrors to give the illusion of extra space, and perhaps a cupboard – are all that is needed for a summer bedroom. Move heavy wardrobes and clutter elsewhere, if possible, to leave space for light and air. It is a good idea to keep the layout of a bedroom fluid, so that you can change the position of the bed should the mood take you, or to escape the heat of the morning sun.

A high-ceilinged space in a town house, with cool wooden floors and large bright windows, is perfect for a children's summer bedroom. But this is only the framework. The art of making a shared room for children is a delicate one. The solution is to create individuality within the communal space. For instance, old iron beds in different designs (allow them to choose their own if possible) and variations on the same theme of pillows and duvets (red, white and black checks) give each child his or her own special space, but still lend the room a cohesive, overall decorating scheme. Plain wooden floors and windows without curtains not only add to the brightness of the room, they rid the area of the usual dust-traps. Practical considerations in children's rooms include washable rugs on the floors and ornaments kept to a minimum. But do allow enough personal clutter for each room-mate to stake out their territory.

A SWEETHEART-SHAPED SCREEN, LIGHTLY PADDED, IS COVERED IN EMBROIDERED LINEN ON ONE SIDE, PLAIN ON THE OTHER.

**See page 143 for fabric-covered panels.**

left, above

A BURST OF ORANGE CHECKS AROUND THE SUN-SOAKED WINDOW LIGHTS UP THIS SIMPLE BEDROOM. WHITE WALLS SET THE COOL, CALM TONE OF THE REST OF THE SPACE. THE CURTAINS HAVE A FALL-BACK FRILL HEADING.

**See page 152 for fall-back frill.**

left

READING A SECRET BEDTIME STORY TAKES PRECCEDENCE OVER SLEEP.

A children's town house bedroom becomes a rustic dormitory with red, black and white checks of varying sizes for duvets and pillowcases.

**See pages 155–7 for pillowcases and 182 for duvet cover.**

# *autumn*

## warmth

*Despite what the calendar says, autumn is undoubtedly the natural beginning of the year, the time when everyone settles back down to work or other more serious pursuits after the distractions of summer. There is still light in the early evenings but a chill steals in on the air, and the cool blue skies make the pace of life seem newly quickened. The countryside is very much alive with ripening harvests, everywhere there is a mellow feel of burgeoning nature. Though some days are filled with mistiness, like a prolonged dawn, the light is often gently golden. And though the leaves may be dying and falling, they do so with such splendour that this is their finest hour.*

# natural inspiration

*Autumn keeps some glowing embers of the burning summer sun to make the rain-dampened mosses and hedgerows shine. The light enriches purple hillsides and tawny trees, and makes the grass greener and the earth a deeper brown.*

*On crisp days, when the sky is a perfect blue and the air is clean and still, the countryside seems at its most stately and mature. But on misty mornings, the world is in limbo and the colours are sleepy and muted. Yet all the time, whatever the weather, the countryside swells with ripe fruit: fat plums languish on the ground, rosy apples weigh down branches and berries jostle in the bushes. There is bountiful inspiration for the designer in all of the layers of colour, pattern and texture. Take home an armful of this decorative bounty, fill up a dish, jug or basket and use the glorious colours to build up a decorating scheme.*

# classic & contemporary

## *for new variations*

The colours and patterns of the autumnal tweeds and tartans in this chapter take their lead from nature. They are the fabric equivalent of turning leaves, silver-white seed heads, golden pumpkins, blood-red berries, green and purple heathers and bracken, hydrangea flower-heads, garlic and artichokes. Dyers, textile designers and weavers have always enjoyed tapping into this season's landscape to fire their imaginations, so the choice of fabric is a rich one. You will see old-fashioned houndstooth check tweed, for example, transformed with luminous green and pink. And contemporary tartans that play with the ancient framework using new combinations of red, blue, mauve, yellow and green. All the rich contrasts and gentle muted patterns in the autumn landscape have been copied and developed to suit a range of different houses. Year after year the fashion world sends classic tweeds and tartans with a contemporary twist along the catwalk. Interiors, too, can enjoy infinite variations and combinations.

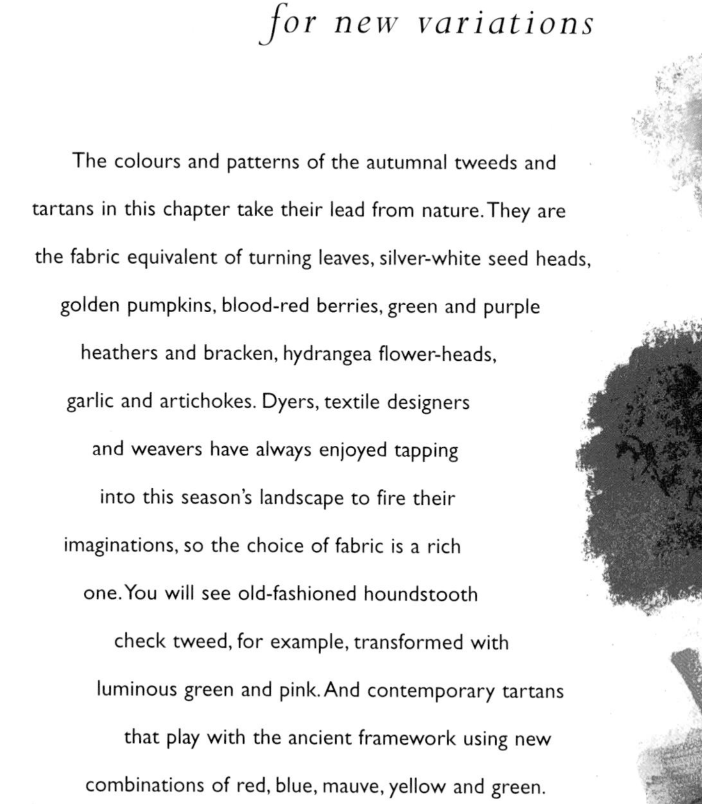

## **rough with the smooth** *textures for contrast*

An autumn theme begs for heavier, rougher, earthier fabrics. When nights draw in like a blanket, soft furnishings should add to the cosy, fireside atmosphere that is the bonus of colder weather. But instead of an entirely rustic look, mix in smoother, glossier yarns too, for a more urban feel.

The authenic-looking acrylic pile fabrics that imitate wild animals are exciting and innovative next to traditional tweeds or tartans. Knitted fabrics like Arans or Fair Isles also combine brilliantly with less textured autumn fabrics. In a large room you could easily mix a variety of textures; in a more confined space, you need to limit yourself to one or two – say tartan or flannel with Aran or suede.

# character study

## *contemporary pattern*
## **for an old-fashioned room**

Tartan is about the most famous pattern there is, and comes complete with layers of history and the strong personality of its country of origin. A fabric with such character can never be subsumed into the overall look of a room, but is an interesting feature in its own right. With such a traditional basis to work with you can afford to be as daring as you like in the colours of tartan that you decide on. There are now endless variations on the originals to choose from, and the beauty of tartan is that, unlike the clans themselves, it never clashes.

This old-fashioned sitting-room with dark woodwork and furniture is given a traditional muted tartan flooring reminiscent of hillsides carpeted with bracken and heather. The painted background on the walls is the pale blue of an island sea. But the whole look is immediately updated with a bright blue and red tartan chair. None of the traditional character of the room is lost with this contemporary splash of vibrancy, but the gloom of dark autumn nights bounces off the chair. The same effect can be achieved with a cheerful tartan throw over the back of a plain old sofa, or a tartan cover for a dressing-table or side table.

left

A traditional sitting-room, originally fairly gloomy, is updated with new upholstery. The armchair is the same comfortable old friend it was before, but its new cover immediately makes dark nights more cheerful.

**See pages 178–80 for loose covers for armchairs and 160 for piped cushion.**

right

A bare dressing-room is easily warmed with the addition of a cosy tartan covering for a table. The top and the sides of the cover are made separately, and stitched together so that the skirt can fall in generous folds. The instructions for the zigzag finish table cover **(see pages 70–1)** can be adapted for the top cover.

# *cosy nights* **under a lined duvet**

This bed is a tribute to tartan, checks and late lie-ins. Comfort is what counts here, and the all-enveloping curtains, plump pillows and dense duvet add to the snugness of the sleeping den. The curtains keep out the light and also any draughts, their soothing shades of blue a natural background to the plum and berry colours on the bed. They are made by the bagging method (see p.143) and held on to the frame with buttoned loops. The tartan duvet cover is protected by a fresh white linen sheet with hand-stitched buttonholes, which marry up with large mother-of-pearl buttons at the top and bottom of the woollen cover. This bed works well whether it is in a small room of its own, or simply curtained off in a living-room.

*materials*

Main fabric for duvet cover, linen or cotton sheeting, red embroidery thread, 18 2cm buttons

*measuring & cutting out (see fig 1)*

Join widths as necessary, with a flat fell seam (see p.139)

*duvet*

Cut two: width = a + 16cm, depth = b + 20cm

*sheet*

Cut one: width = a + 120cm, length = b + 120cm

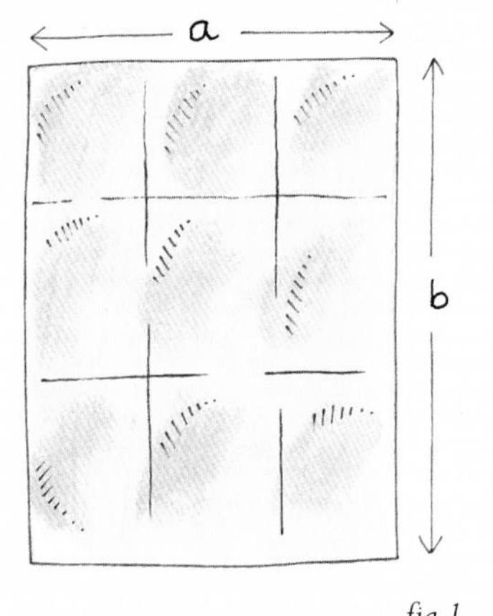


*fig 1*

*making up*

**1** Pin the front and back together with right sides facing, and stitch around the two long and one short edge, leaving a 1.5cm allowance. Trim the seam and stitch with a zigzag to neaten.

**2** Press under 1cm around the open end, then turn under a further 6cm. Stitch down close to the fold and press. Make six evenly spaced buttonholes along the front, 2cm from the edge, by hand or machine. Sew six buttons to the inside of the back edge in the corresponding positions to close.

**3** Sew a further six buttons to the top and six to the bottom of the front, 50cm from the edge.

**4** Make a 3cm double hem round all four edges of the sheet, mitring the corners (see p.140) if desired. Make six buttonholes by hand or machine along the double border at each short end to match the buttons on the duvet. Put the duvet inside the cover, then button the two ends of the sheet in place.

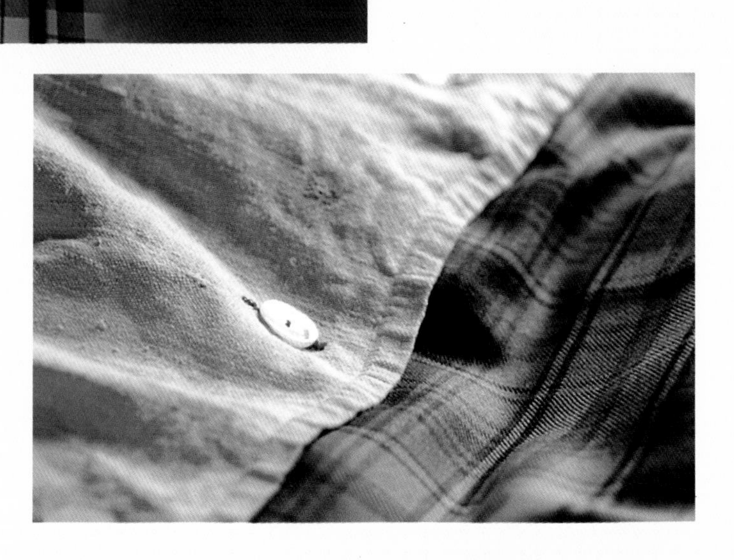

# *tartan for all*

## *formal & informal*
**from castle to cottage**

Historically associated with grand gothic mansions and shooting lodges, tartan needs neither imposing spaces nor formality to look magnificent. It works equally well in a compact cottage or smart town house. Tartans in every combination of blues, pinks, yellows, greens, lilacs and reds fill a home with colour, light and comfort. Keep a medley of extra tartan blankets piled on a shelf for bedtime. Use less predictable designs than a predominance of Black Watch and Royal Stewart, and try instead tartans in duck-egg blue, Bordeaux-red, olive and grey. Why not take your lead from the colours of favourite possessions, such as a warm dressing-gown, and use them as a starting-point for choosing fabrics?

In the bedroom, the mattress is tucked up with fresh blue and white checked cotton sheets. Its valance picks up on the theme with a tartan interpretation of blue checks, warmed by lines and squares of cream – and sewn into the corners of the valance, interrupting the gentle blues, are flashes of the traditional Royal Stewart. These crimson corners could be echoed in the rest of the room with a similar tartan throw over a bedside chair, a dressing-table cover or a pelmet over a blue and white checked cotton blind at the window. Just a red cushion or blanket over the bed is enough to give the effect some substance. Walls painted the colour of a pale blue autumn sky or the smokiest white mist, natural wooden floors and stone window-ledges will offset the richness of the red.

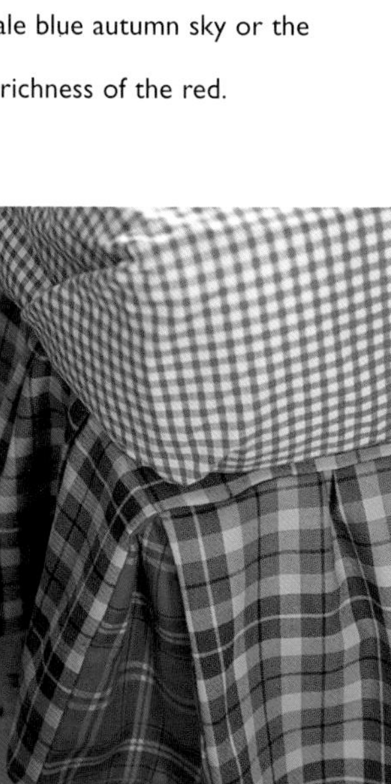

Flashes of Royal Stewart tartan set into the corners of this valance set off the blue and white checks of the bed linen.

**See page 183 for box-pleated valance.**

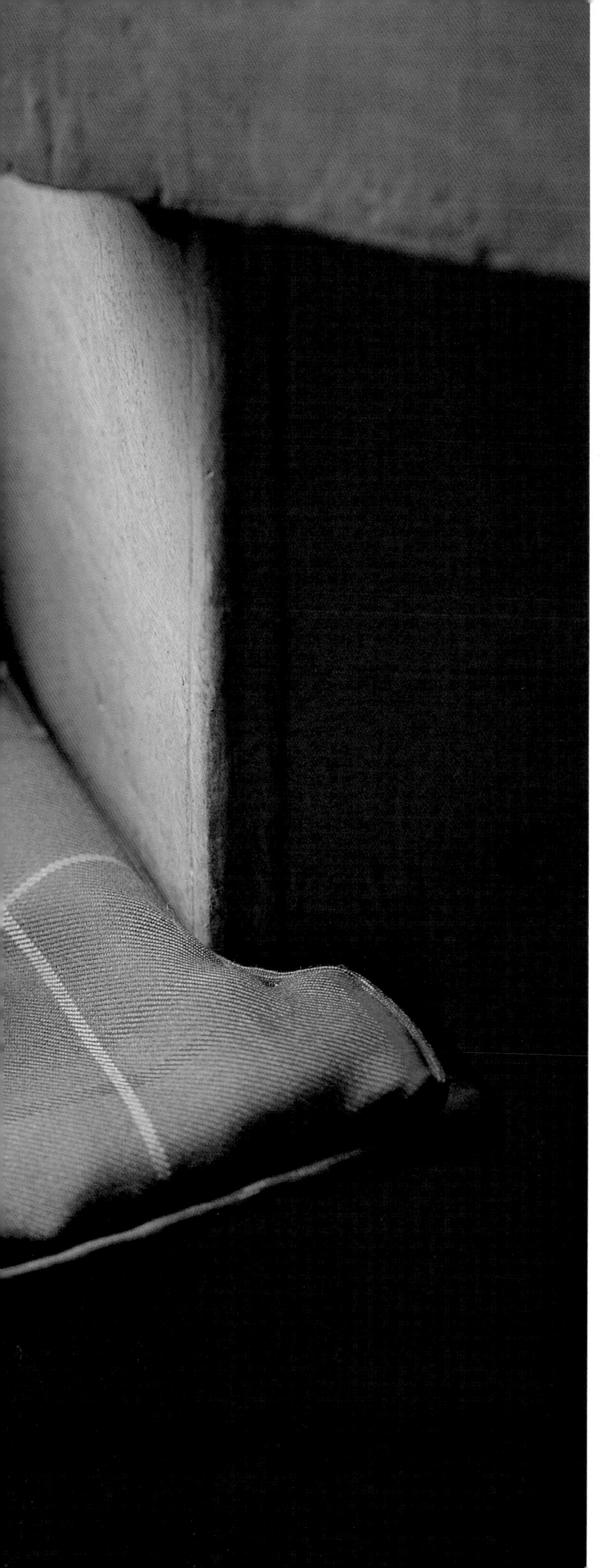

left

A piped tartan window-seat is a neat, urbane use of rustic fabric.

**See page 165 for fitted box cushion.**

below

Footstools are comfortable as well as practical. Here wool tartan remnants are used for a generous cover made in a similar way to the tartan sequence **(see pages 104–5)**.

Thick tartan blankets are *de rigueur* for moorland picnics. Not only do they adapt well to the outdoors life, they are just right as extra layers of warmth when the mists draw in.

# *oasis in the heather*
## for a picnic

A tartan blanket spread out in the midst of an expanse of heather or under a chestnut tree provides an oasis on an autumnal ramble. It is the perfect setting for a picnic of thick soup and nutty bread, with the picnickers swaddled in layers of wool and furry throws, enjoying the pure air and a heightened appetite. Tartan blankets, fringed, tassled or plain, make a perfect base for an early-morning mushrooming expedition or an afternoon blackberry hunt. This is why the use of tartan inside a house can be so effective in creating a country atmosphere: it conjures up these scenes from a hearty, outdoors life.

These blankets lead a double life as picnic rugs, and sofa or bed throws. They are crafted from weighty wool tartans, some with hand-plaited fringing. Not only are they beautiful, they are also incredibly warm and comforting. Try backing a flannel throw or blanket with soft fun fur to wrap up a sleepy child after lunch. Take a folding director's chair with a tartan cover, so that you can admire the view in comfort. A more ambitious, but still simple, project is a frock covering for a chair. Heather-coloured tartan helps to adapt a black canvas, urban-style director's chair for the country. Don't go for a toned-down version of heather: look closely at the vibrant colour of the real thing – take a bunch with you to the fabric shop if you like –and choose a modern tartan, check or tweed that does justice to that true purple hue, mingled with mossy or bracken-green checks.

A PLAIN FOLDING DIRECTOR'S CHAIR PAYS TRIBUTE TO THE VIBRANT COLOUR OF HEATHER WITH ITS NEW FROCK COVER. THE FABRIC HAS BEEN CAREFULLY CUT SO THAT THE LINES OF THE TARTAN LIE SYMMETRICALLY ACROSS THE CHAIR. THE KICK PLEATS AT EACH CORNER GIVE THE SLIP COVER A GENEROUS FEEL.

**See pages 174–5 for director's chair cover.**

# *dressing for warmth*
## wool tartans & snug fur

The creative use of tartan remnants and ribbons can be very effective accessorizing a room, making it cosy and inviting. It can be introduced in many different and quite simple ways: try making placemats, serviettes, a curtain tie-back, a trimming for a lampshade, a lining for a log basket or a hamper. Deep royal purple mixed with dark forest green is a particularly rich combination in tartan. Here it is used for picnic cutlery rolls, tied with another length of fabric or a tartan ribbon. When not being used for picnics, these rolls have another life as attractive placemats.

A FLANNEL THROW IS BACKED WITH SOFT FUN FUR.

**See page 182 for throws.**

One of the most exciting new textures is the almost realistic animal fur imitation fabric. There is no shortage of choice: the patterned or plain designs vary in thickness of pile and smoothness of texture. They are so beautifully soft to the touch that they make the most wonderfully comfy covers and throws. Backed with flannel, tartan or tweed, they are as chic in a smart apartment or town house as they are down to earth in a hunting lodge or country house.

opposite

A CUTLERY ROLL IN DEEP PURPLE AND FOREST GREEN TARTAN CAN BE USED FOR A PICNIC, BUT IS SMART ENOUGH FOR A DINNER-PARTY PLACEMAT, TOO. MATCH IT WITH BONE-HANDLED CUTLERY MIXED WITH SILVER.

**See page 185 for cutlery roll.**

# *modern eccentrics*

## *trendy tweed suits* **in a town setting**

Describing a person as tweedy means that they are slightly quaint and old-fashioned, and probably bookish. Tweed soft furnishings can give the same characteristics to a room. But just as this perception of tweed has been turned on its head by fashion designers in their autumn collections, so interior designers can transform its fusty charm into artistic urban sophistication. Mixed with modern, colourful, tweed variations and an array of other, more vibrant, fabrics, old-fashioned herringbone and houndstooth weaves take on a whole new life. Two of the most important considerations are tailoring – the suit must sit well on the shape of the sofa or chair – and attention to detail in buttons, piping and fringing.

Traditional herringbone tweed is used for curtains, and its colours are picked up in a more eccentric modern weave used for an armchair. The chair's tailored cover is made from high-quality Scottish tweed in bold checks of mustard and blue. The traditional sofa is swathed in a donkey-grey velvet cover, updated with contemporary throws and cushions in more exotic colours. Tweed cushions are fringed and neatly buttoned. The curtains are fringed too, and gathered on to a header tape. Coconut shell buttons are stitched on to the fold of each pleat – an attractive, discreet detail. The curtains are left unlined to let the light filter through the weave. If you want a cosier feel, and more protection from light and draughts, line them with a mellow tartan of a similar colour.

above & detail right

Curtains are made of herringbone tweed suiting material; the frayed edges make excellent fringing when gathered on to a header tape. The armchair picks up on the flecks of colour in the curtains in a more flamboyant tweed design.

**See pages 151 for buttoned pleat curtain heading and 178–80 for loose covers for armchairs.**

above

Bright tweed and tartan throws and cushions are used to update a cosy sofa and brighten the room.

**See pages 182 for throws and 158–60 for cushions.**

left

These cushions are made like pyjama cases, and then fringed and buttoned to match the curtains.

# *red, white & blue*
## for a child's room

The same golden cream paint can be used on the walls throughout a house, and the effect is a mellow autumnal glow. Tartans and tweed themes are then repeated and developed in each room, and in the hallways and landing. Themes from the main bedroom's colour scheme and its fabric off-cuts can be used for a child's bedroom. For babies who began life sleeping in the main room with their parents, a continuation of pattern and colour will help develop a sense of security, while toddlers will be proud to have the parental colour scheme in their own room. It also has the advantage of being easy, and less expensive.

The baby's cot has decorative surrounds in a blue plaid. The sheet is a blue and white cotton check and the cover is a warm blue and cream tartan. A fresh linen sheet is tied to the coverlet to protect it. The splash of rich red in the tartan pelmets echoes the red seen in the chair covers. These pelmets are decorated with multicoloured pompoms; they top plain linen blinds with running stitch embroidery. Red tartan window-seats double as beds for teddies and dolls. Children's rooms should not be over-sweet. Decorate them so that they can be adapted to more sophisticated tastes as their occupants grow up, or so that they can be easily returned to the status of guest room when the need arises.

**top**

Detail of the chair cover tied with bows at the back.

**above**

A zigzag-edged pelmet with pompoms fringes the window, which is covered with an embroidered linen blind at night.

**See pages 152 for pelmets and 146 for soft roman blind.**

**left**

An old wooden kitchen chair is transformed for a bedroom with a simple red tartan frock cover tied with bows at the back.

**See pages 172–3 for tailored cover and 165 for fitted box cushion.**

**opposite & detail left**

This cot has an embroidered white cotton over-sheet tied back to protect the coverlet and make a softer, more decorative edge. Running stitch embroidery and a simple zigzag pattern recur to add finishing touches in the room.

A mahogany hall chair is dressed in a red tartan frilled skirt to brighten the landing. Traditional tartan works better than floral prints or modern stripes on sturdy dark wood or gothic furniture.

**See page 169 for box-pleated seat cover.**

A bedroom chair is given a shapely new cover in close-woven wool tartan. Strong colours will fade in time, but age becomes tartan.

**See pages 176–7 for bedroom chair cover.**

# *chair lifts*
## re-covering in red tartan

There are many recognized shades of red in the colour spectrum: scarlet, crimson, cherry . . . But there should also be one called maple-leaf red, best seen reflected in the lakes of New England in the fall. It is a mature, glowing red intermingled with golden yellow, brown and touches of green.

Maple-leaf red plaid is used here for a bedroom chair. The cover fits tightly and gives the chair a neat, urban look – though the frilled skirt is a nod to country style. Make up a mock cover first, using an old sheet, then use that as a template for the real thing. Loose covers are especially practical for lighter colours and fine fabrics as they can be removed and cleaned easily. If the look of an upholstered chair or sofa appeals, but you prefer the facility of removing a cover for cleaning, make sure that the cover fits snugly with little room for movement. This can be achieved by making the cover like a tailored suit. Darts and velcro or zip fastenings are essential.

The scope for re-covering tired furniture with tartan and tweed is limitless. Wrap the seat of an old chaise in new tartan and pile it with cushions to match. Cheer up a sombre hall chair by tying on a squab cushion with a full skirt. Always add skirts or frills to the cover last of all – experiment with length and shape until the right proportions are achieved. As a rule, keep the skirt short if the legs are beautiful, cover them if they are unsightly.

Tartan should not be confined to the country, as it can be equally smart in less rustic surroundings. Just think how exquisitely smart a bridegroom looks when wearing a kilt and beautifully tailored wool jacket. Imagine an elegant tartan dinner jacket with satin lapels. Apply these combinations to your city dwelling for curtains and chair covers, cushions and tablecloths – the result can be quite stunning.

below

THE SEAT CUSHION OF THIS PAINTED CHAISE WAS RE-COVERED IN TARTAN WITH CORD-EDGED CUSHIONS TO MATCH. ALWAYS MINGLE DIFFERENT COLOURS AND PATTERNS OF CUSHIONS ON A SOFA TO MAKE THE EFFECT MORE INTERESTING.

**See pages 165 for fitted box cushion, 141 for decorative cord edgings and 162–3 for gathered-end bolsters.**

# *tartan sequence* **on a dressing-table & stool**

An old-fashioned dressing-table and matching stool furnishes a bathroom or dressing-room that opens on to the bedroom, and serves as a continuation of a colour scheme. In this case, the fabric of the chair covering in the bedroom is echoed in the covers for table and stool. This link is all it takes to make the two rooms into a suite. Alternatively, you could pick up the colours in a bedroom rug to decorate your en-suite furniture. In the case of a dressing-room or bathroom, covers should be loose so that they can be easily removed and cleaned.

## *materials*

Main fabric, contrast fabric, piping cord (length = a + 2c + 15cm)

## *measuring & cutting out (figs 1 & 2)*

Make a paper template to fit the top of both table and stool, following the method shown on p.166. For a dressing-table that has a fixed mirror, cut the frill and skirt in two pieces and leave two gaps to fit around the struts. Lengths 'a' and 'c' refer to the template pieces, which allow an extra 1cm all round the actual size of the furniture, so that the fit is not too tight.

## *table*

Top: cut one as template from contrast fabric, plus 2.5cm all round

Frill: cut one from contrast fabric, width = z (22cm), length = 1.5a

Skirt: cut one from main fabric, width = b + 5cm, length = 2a

## *making up the table cover*

**1** Cut a length of piping cord, measuring a + 5cm, and cover it with a strip of the main fabric. Pin the covered cord to the right side of the top. Clip the curves and join the edges (see p.141). Stitch in place with a zipper foot.

**2** Pin the frill into a loop with right sides together, and stitch 1.5cm from the short edges. Press the seam flat. Zigzag one long edge of the frill, then turn up and stitch a 2cm single hem. With right sides together and matching the raw edges, pin around the edge of the top, making 1cm pleats at 5cm intervals *(fig 3)*. (Divide the circumference by eight, then follow the technique for attaching a frill to a rectangle on p.142 to make sure that the fullness is distributed evenly.) Adjust the pleats as necessary, so they look even. Stitch in place 1cm from the edge, using a zipper foot.

**3** Zigzag the short edges of the skirt and turn under a 2cm single hem, then do the same along the lower edge. With right sides facing, pin the two unhemmed corners to the centre front of the top. Pin the right side of the skirt around the edge to the wrong side of the frill, making 3cm pleats approximately every 7cm. Put the cover over the table to check the fit, then stitch through all the layers, close to the piping. Press.

*fig 1*

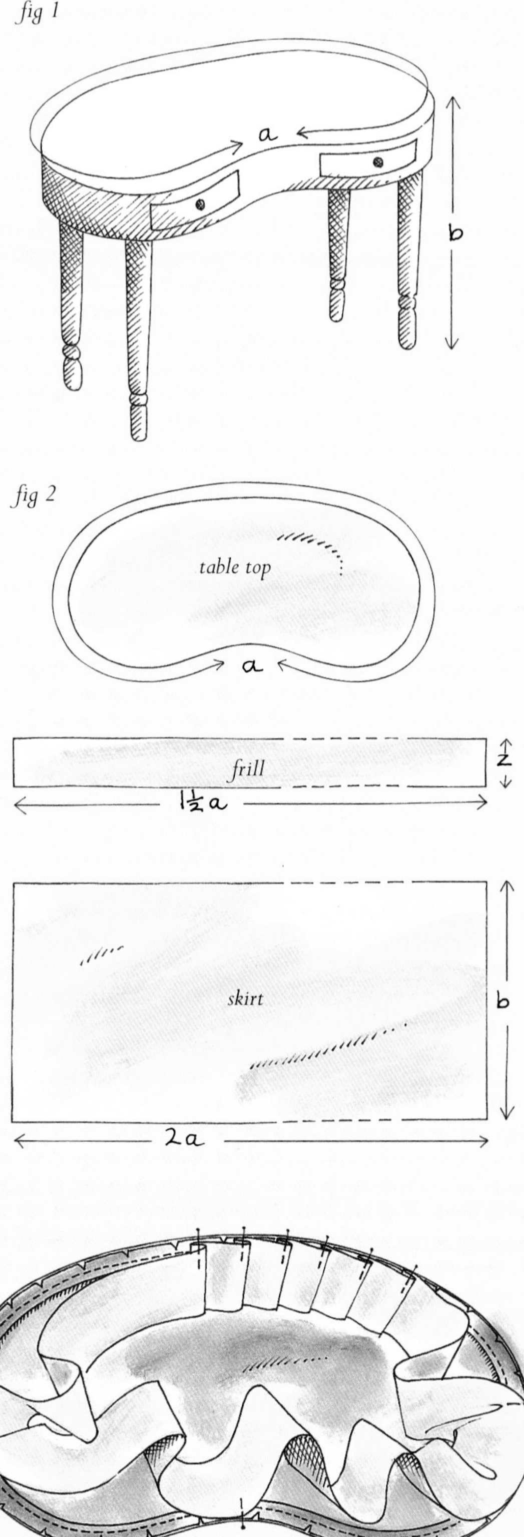


*fig 3*

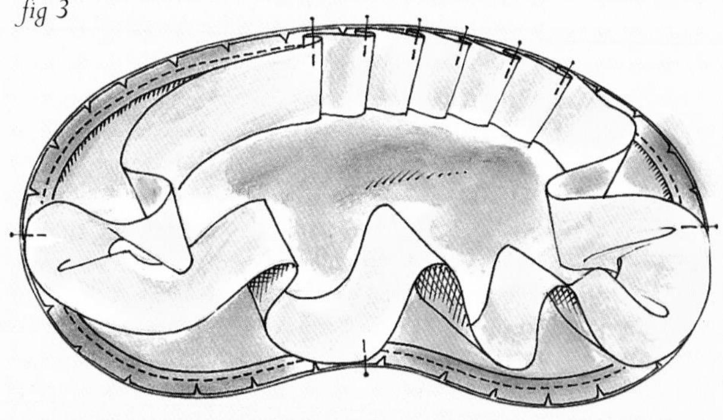

*stool (fig 4)*

Top: cut one piece as template from main fabric, plus 1.5cm all round

Collar: cut one piece from main fabric, width = d + 3cm, length = c + 3cm

Frill: cut one piece from main fabric, width (y) = 20cm, length = 1.5c + 3cm

Skirt: cut one piece from contrast fabric, width = e + 4cm, length = 2c + 5cm

## *making up the stool cover*

**1** Cover the remaining piping cord with contrast fabric and cut in two. Sew one length to the right side of the stool top, joining the ends neatly. Pin the two short ends of the collar with right sides facing and stitch, 1.5cm from the edge. Press the seam open, then sew the second length of piping to the right side of the lower edge. Pin the top edge to the stool top and check the fit before stitching *(fig 5)*.

**2** Sew the frill and skirt into loops along their short edges. Turn up 2cm double hems at the lower edges. Pin the frill to the collar along the piping with right sides together, distributing the fullness evenly. Make a series of 2cm pleats, 8cm apart. Pin the skirt to the frill, as in step 3 opposite, making a 2.5cm pleat every 5cm. Stitch through all the layers, and press.

*fig 4*

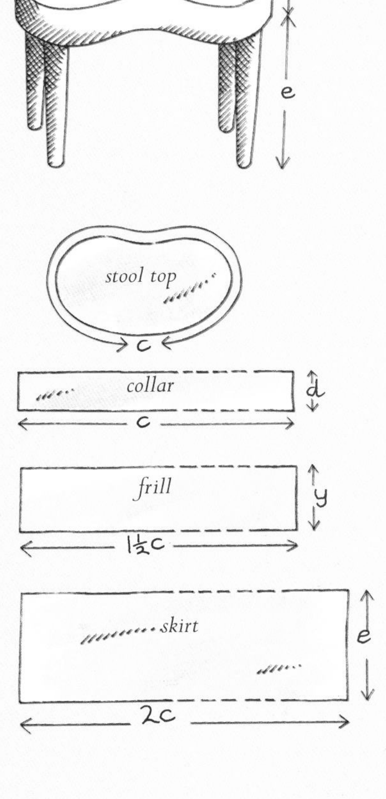


*fig 5*

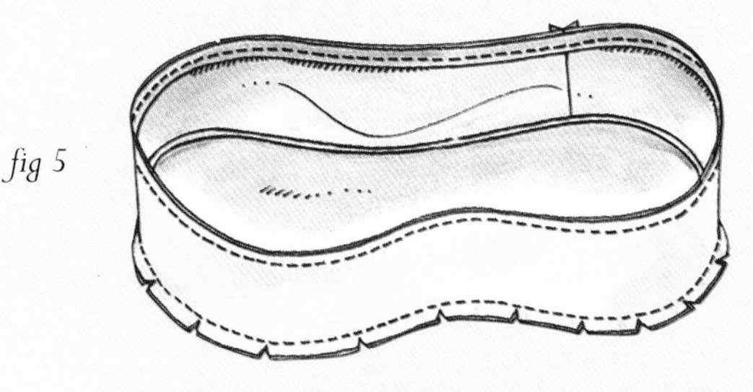

# winter
## glow

*We talk about the dead of winter, when the life of the countryside is mostly buried, the landscape is blank and the view out of the window is bleak. However, the view in through the windows, from the outside, is never warmer nor more inviting than now. Log fires, thick blankets, tinsel, fairy lights, mulled spices, mince pies and presents – all the festive accessories more than compensate for cold weather. It is worth a walk through an exhilaratingly biting wind to visit friends and family and enjoy the sociability which makes winter probably the warmest season of all.*

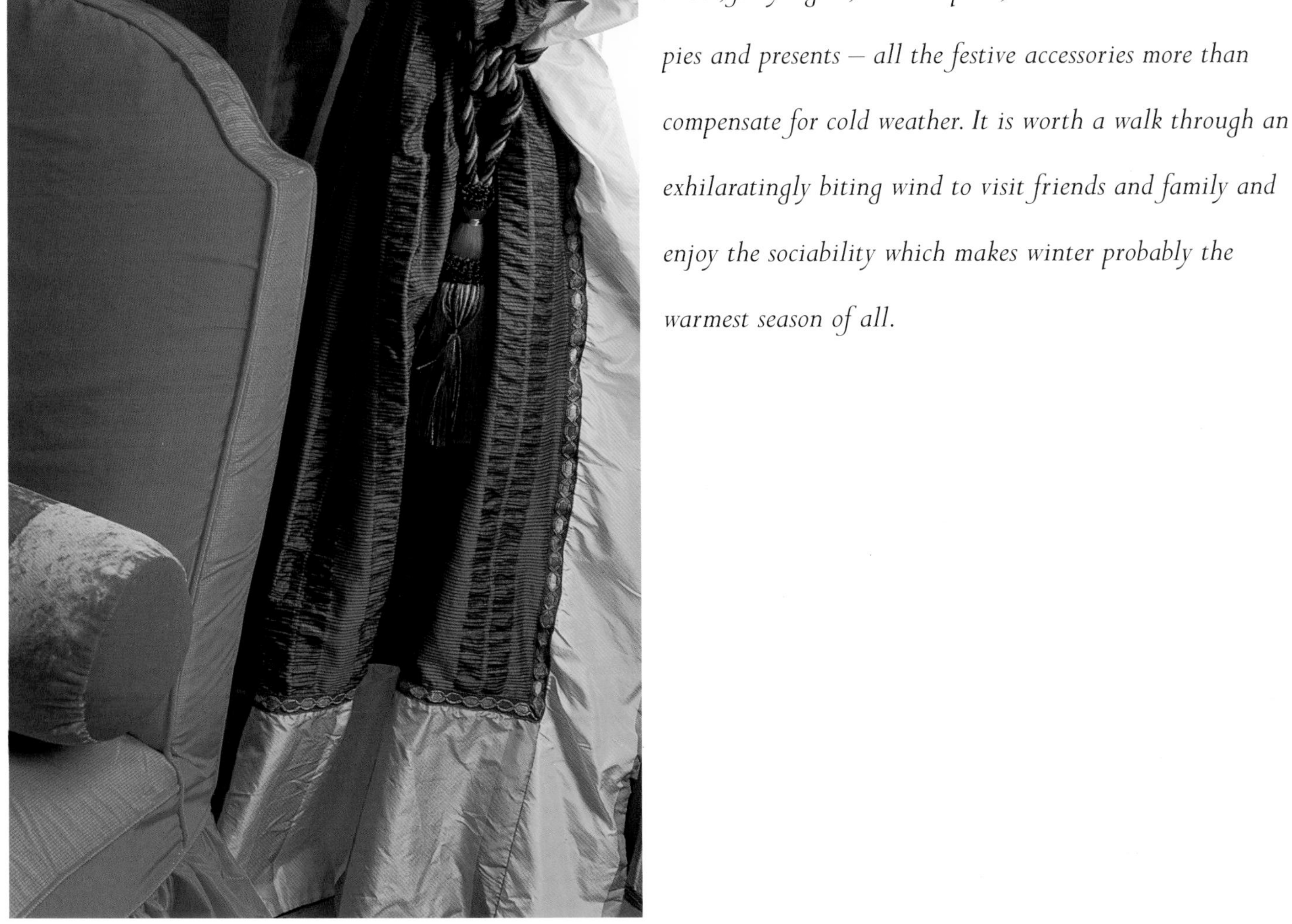

# natural inspiration

*Far from feeling miserable in the cold weather, we can create our own winter wonderland where it is vital to eat, drink and be merry, wrap up in luxuriously thick layers, sing together around the piano or solo in a richly scented bath, roast chestnuts on the fire and make vats of hot fudge sauce for the chocolate cake – all in the name of keeping up spirits. To create an atmosphere of good cheer, houses should also be allowed to enjoy excess – in an abundance of opulent fabrics and rich colours.*

# rich & sophisticated

*for dramatic effects*

Much of the inspiration for the fabric in this chapter comes from the street markets of Asia, giving an exotic, spiced warmth to the proceedings. There is no delicate Saxon subtlety here: the ideas are based on glorious gaudiness and startling displays – in stark contrast to the grey skies, sleeping trees and frozen ground outside. Colours are rich and festive, and should be put together with the same gay abandon with which you might decorate a Christmas tree. We have used gold and scarlet, silver, bronze and caramel creams, and mingled them with greens, blues, shocking pinks and royal purples. Patterns – stripes, paisleys and embroidered florals – are intricate and dramatic by turns; they are all sumptuously detailed and a feast for the eye. The theatrical flamboyance of Renaissance fashions also plays its part here – you will see a revival of that era's luxury, which of course benefited hugely from foreign imports.

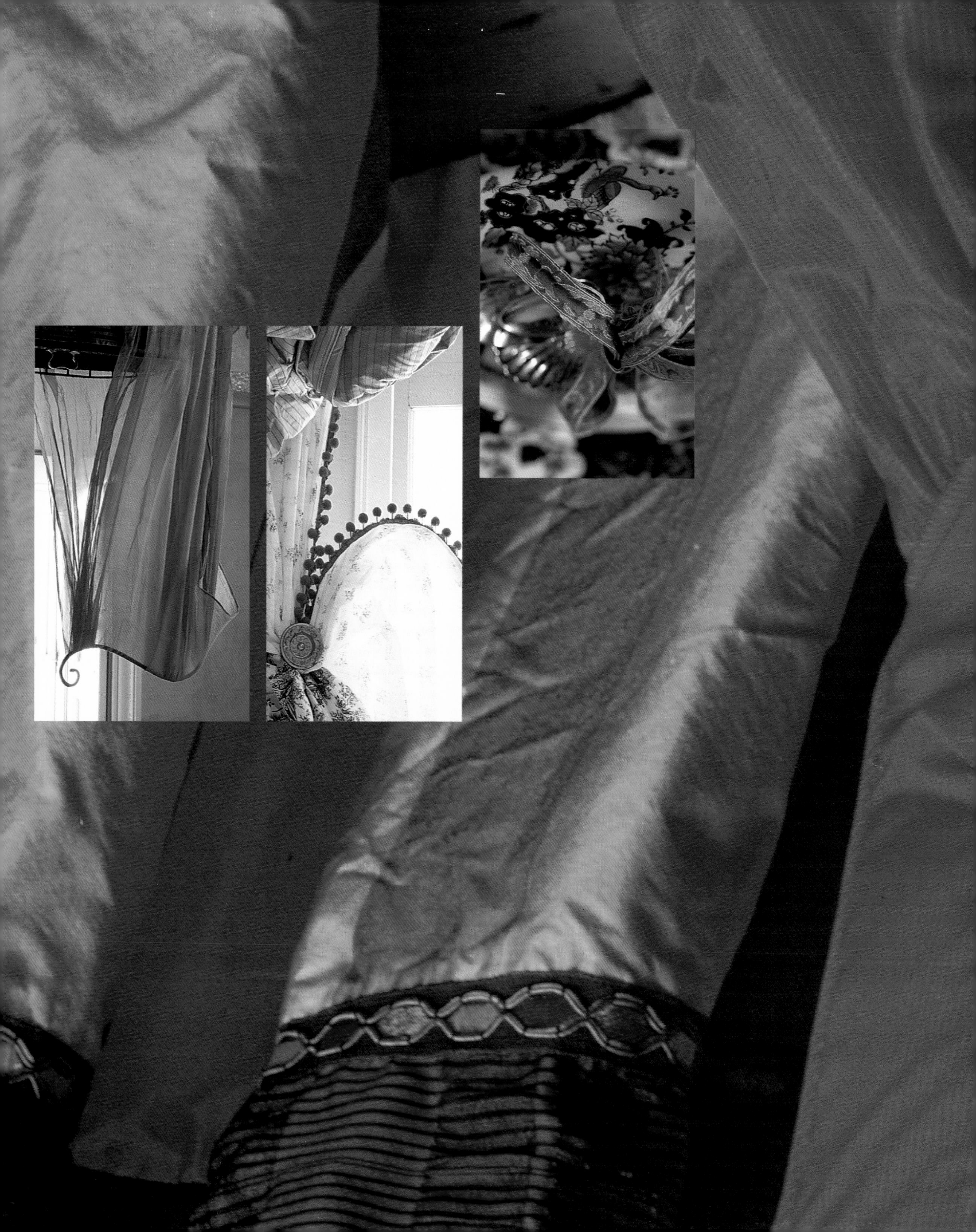

# soft & luxurious
## *textures for contrast*

In this chapter you will see how easy it is to create a sense of luxury with the right textures and weights of fabrics – soft, flowing velvets, textured brocades, stiff taffetas and dress silks. For a winter theme, the feel of materials, their sheen, their depth, the three-dimensional map of their embroidered designs, is probably most important of all. And jùst as Christmas presents under the tree are so much more enticing when wrapped with a flourish of ribbons and other finishing touches, so these fabrics benefit from a large helping of trimmings such as tassels, braided edging and piping. Once you have chosen your fabrics, the other point to remember is that you need plenty of them. Curtains that drape to the floor in great folds look more luxurious, and indeed warmer, than neat little window-coverings. So be generous.

# *winter wonderland*

## *shimmery & sophisticated*
### dresses for furniture

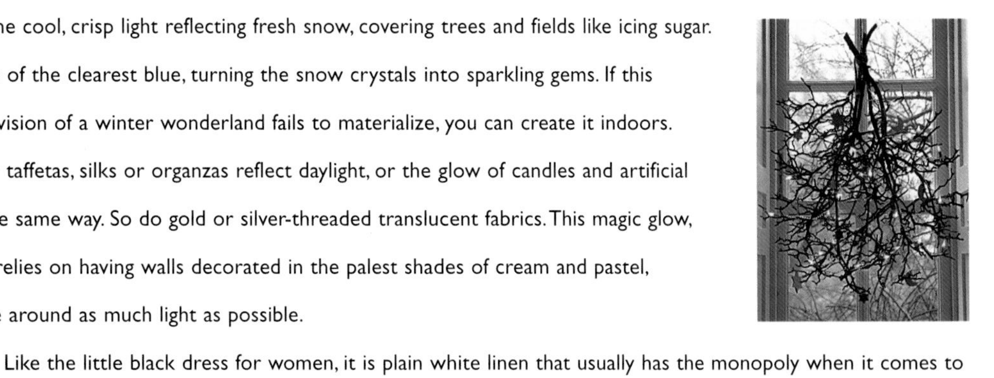

Just imagine cool, crisp light reflecting fresh snow, covering trees and fields like icing sugar. The sky is of the clearest blue, turning the snow crystals into sparkling gems. If this romantic vision of a winter wonderland fails to materialize, you can create it indoors. Shimmery taffetas, silks or organzas reflect daylight, or the glow of candles and artificial light, in the same way. So do gold or silver-threaded translucent fabrics. This magic glow, however, relies on having walls decorated in the palest shades of cream and pastel, to bounce around as much light as possible.

Like the little black dress for women, it is plain white linen that usually has the monopoly when it comes to tablecloths. But for special occasions it is worth playing with surprising fabrics in different textures and colours for more of a party atmosphere: such as the festive silvery silk for this table covering. The table top has a cover which is shaped to a flattering point like a drop-waisted skirt, and the rest of the silk hangs in rustling folds. It is over-long, trailing on the polished floor, to give a sense of the ballgown that inspired its design, and indeed provided the material for its construction! Recycling is always a satisfying way to find raw materials. Search out crystal or cut-glass champagne glasses and silver or wrought-iron candelabras from second-hand or junk shops to place on top.

right

A SILVERY SILK TABLE COVERING WITH AN OVERLAY MADE OUT OF STIFF ORGANDIE EDGED WITH TINY GREY PEARLS MAKES A DRAMATIC SCENE-SETTER FOR A CHRISTMAS PARTY. THE GATHERED CIRCULAR TABLECLOTH IS A FULLER VERSION OF THE ZIGZAG FINISH TABLE COVER **(see pages 68–9)**.

An antique iron cot handed down through generations is decorated with layers of dreamy oriental fabrics – lilac and hibiscus pink chiffon and richly woven brocades. The curtains in the baby's room (see opposite, also) are layers of orange muslin and yellow embroidered chiffon which bathe the room in calm light.

**See page 149 for unlined curtains.**

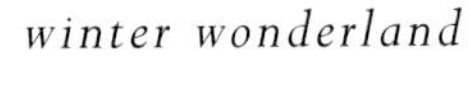

## *sleeping beauty*
## **from cot to four-poster**

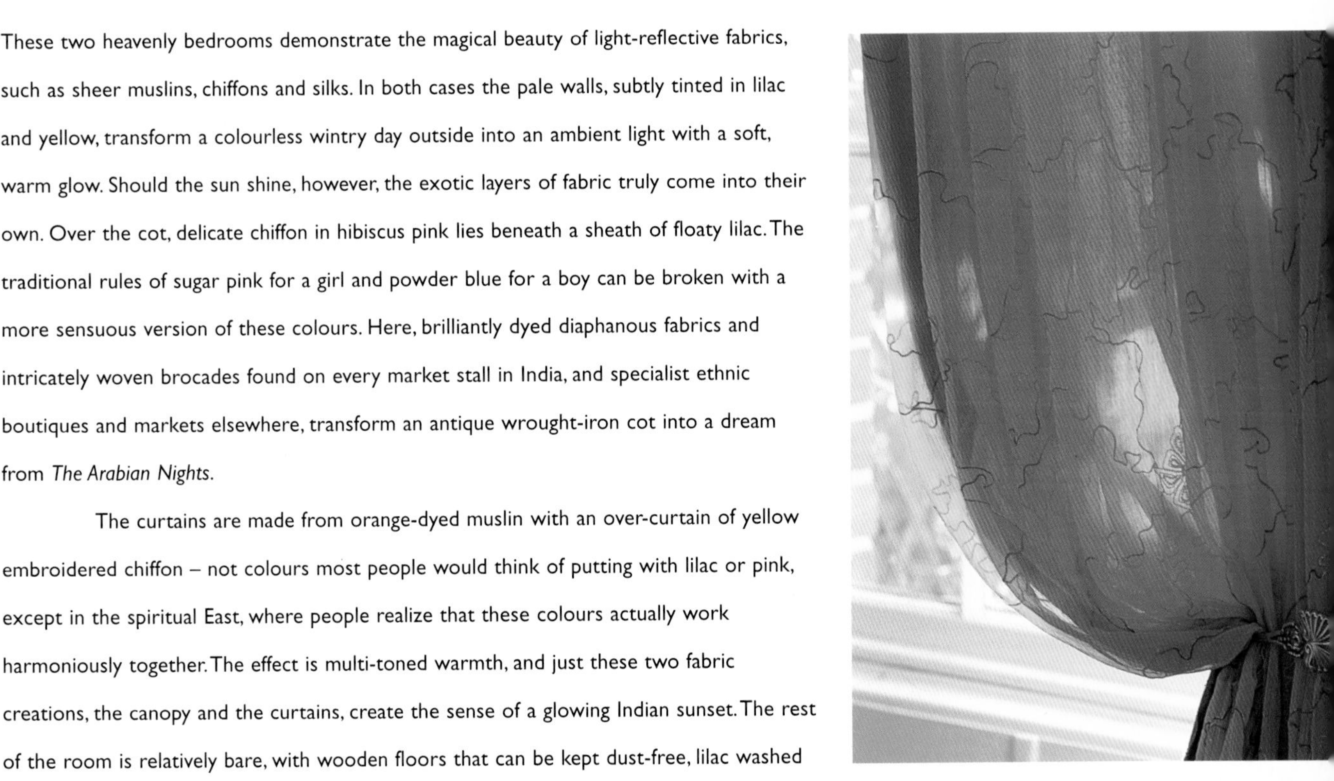

These two heavenly bedrooms demonstrate the magical beauty of light-reflective fabrics, such as sheer muslins, chiffons and silks. In both cases the pale walls, subtly tinted in lilac and yellow, transform a colourless wintry day outside into an ambient light with a soft, warm glow. Should the sun shine, however, the exotic layers of fabric truly come into their own. Over the cot, delicate chiffon in hibiscus pink lies beneath a sheath of floaty lilac. The traditional rules of sugar pink for a girl and powder blue for a boy can be broken with a more sensuous version of these colours. Here, brilliantly dyed diaphanous fabrics and intricately woven brocades found on every market stall in India, and specialist ethnic boutiques and markets elsewhere, transform an antique wrought-iron cot into a dream from *The Arabian Nights*.

The curtains are made from orange-dyed muslin with an over-curtain of yellow embroidered chiffon – not colours most people would think of putting with lilac or pink, except in the spiritual East, where people realize that these colours actually work harmoniously together. The effect is multi-toned warmth, and just these two fabric creations, the canopy and the curtains, create the sense of a glowing Indian sunset. The rest of the room is relatively bare, with wooden floors that can be kept dust-free, lilac washed walls and a simple gilded curtain tie-back.

The painted four-poster bed, reminiscent of magic journeys, is draped with diaphanous and gold-threaded silks. In this room, the yellow walls are a reminder of constant sunshine and the colourful kelims, scattered on bare boards, of native weavers.

right

The winter sun streams through tall windows, enhancing the heavenly silks and chiffons draped across the eastern four-poster bed, imported from sunnier climes.

A dayroom in French Empire style is decorated in pale greys, lilac, blues and white. The fabrics are new and old damasks and brocades.

**See pages 170–1 for flounced cover skirt and 158–60 for cushions.**

## *crisp & even*
## **serenity in wintry rooms**

Looking over fields of snow in the early morning is one of the most peaceful pleasures in nature. Not least because all sounds are absorbed into that blanket, leaving a hushed world above.

Instead of counteracting the winter landscape with warm exotic fabrics, one room of a house could reflect some of this bare beauty of winter, using a mixture of silver, white and grey fabrics. The effect is serene. In the dayroom, these wintry colours are tempered with pale blues and lilac. The cooler sitting-room details of which are shown below, has upright chairs in grey silk frocks, shiny ballgowns trimmed with gold brocade. The double-ended day bed is covered in white ribbed fabric with grey piping: a soft ivory velvet or moiré silk would work equally well. An impressive gilt-framed crackle-glazed mirror adds to the frosty scene, but there are few other ornaments or decorations. The walls are pure white, the ceiling is sky grey and the floor is stained palest silvery grey.

A hint of colour in a table warms the effect without loosing the icy theme. The curtains, in fine cotton, are a warmer contrast to the glossy silks on the seats.

If you cannot live with too many neutral colours, a hint of colour in a painting or a larger splash in a rug will break the spell. The table by the window, painted in cool blue, sweetens the room a little as do the countrified grey and white curtains with zigzag edges. A marble-topped table or a stone-hearth fireplace would also be fitting additions, though they would be more austere than painted wood, and would serve to underline the ethereal atmosphere of a wintry room.

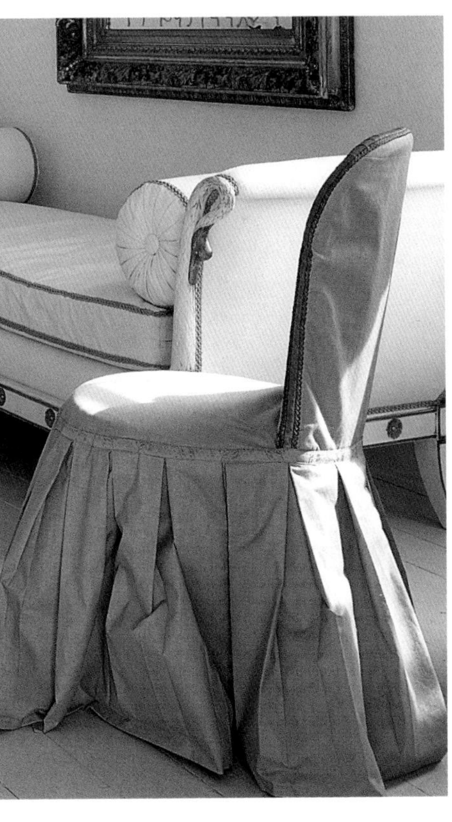

right

A snowy landscape is translated into grey silk fabric for the chairs and chaise longue.

**See page 171 for pleated chair cover and 161 for bolsters.**

# *piping & buttons* for a luxurious quilt

Silk is a fabric that we usually confine to dressmaking, but it can also be used for house-dressing. It may be delicate, but it is also extremely warm, and so is ideal for winter. The choices of silk substitutes and treated washable silks available are just as practical and inexpensive as linen and cotton, so it is no longer an option only for the élite. Silk has the affinity to deep, rich colours and bold designs that cotton has to pretty faded floral prints. The bed is luxurious in red and ochre silk with Indian-influenced bold stripes.

## *materials*

Main fabric for the top, contrast fabric for the back, length of covered piping = 2a + 2b, plus 5cm, chalk pencil, strong thread, 12 x 3cm self-cover buttons

## *measuring & cutting out* *(see fig 1)*

Cut top and back alike: width (a) = width of duvet, length (b) = length of duvet, plus 1.5cm all round

Cut 12 circles from each fabric using the template supplied with the buttons.

## *making up*

**1** Mark three points on the right side along each long edge of both pieces; two 40cm from the corners and the third halfway between them. Pin the piping facing inwards around the right side of the edge of the back. Curve it gently at the corners and join the ends (see p.141). Stitch, using a zipper foot *(fig 1)*.

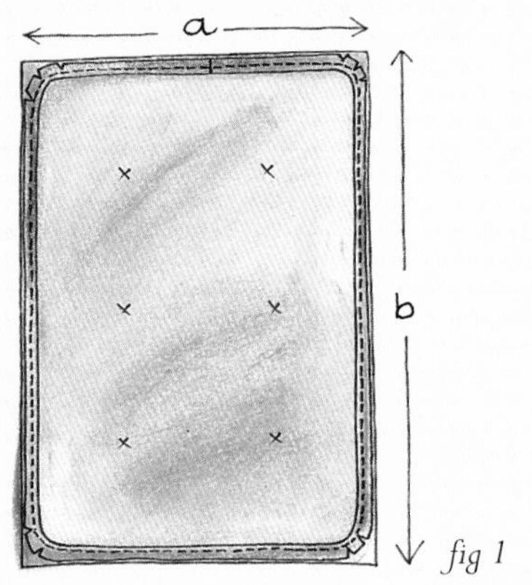


*fig 1*

**2** With right sides facing, pin the top to the back. Sew together just inside the previous stitch line, close to the cord. Leave a 1m opening along one short edge. Fold back and press the unstitched seam allowance on the front. Clip the corners, turn right side out and press. Insert the duvet and slip stitch the opening.

**3** Make up the buttons according to the instructions and thread a long needle with a double length of strong sewing cotton. Thread the needle through the shank of the first button and tie it on securely, 10cm from the knot. Push the needle through the duvet at the first mark and out the other side at the corresponding point. Thread it through the shank of the second button and take it back to the right side *(fig 2)*. Stitch through the duvet again once or twice, then knot the thread tightly and clip the ends. Repeat for the other buttons.

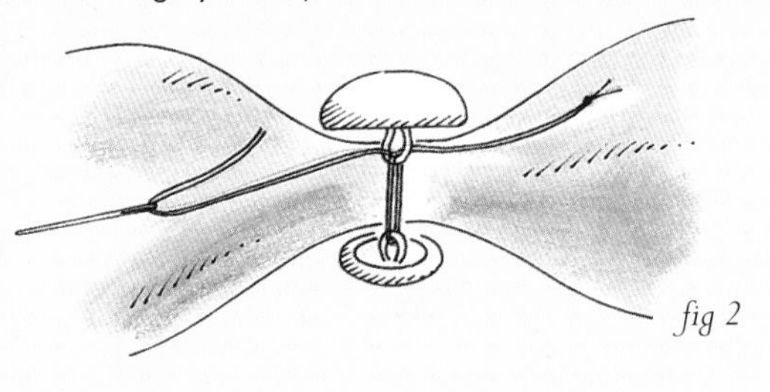

*fig 2*

# carnival of colour

## *decorative party fabrics* **for exotic effects**

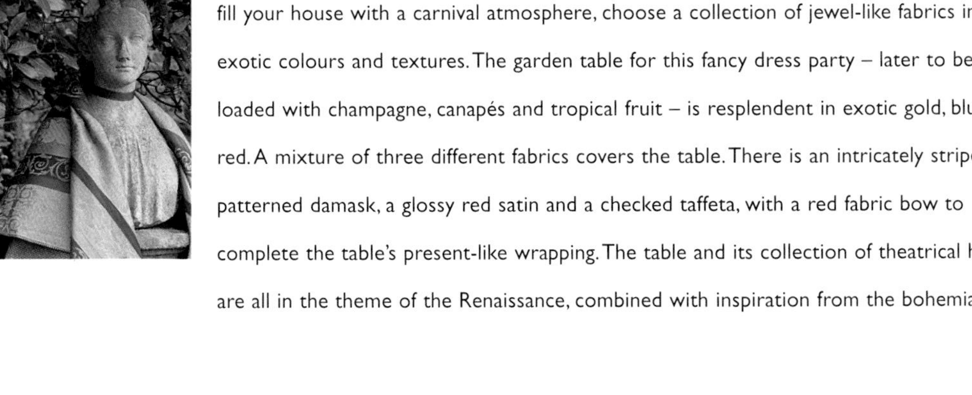

Parties held in the dark depths of winter should be as bright and colourful as possible. To fill your house with a carnival atmosphere, choose a collection of jewel-like fabrics in exotic colours and textures. The garden table for this fancy dress party – later to be loaded with champagne, canapés and tropical fruit – is resplendent in exotic gold, blue and red. A mixture of three different fabrics covers the table. There is an intricately striped and patterned damask, a glossy red satin and a checked taffeta, with a red fabric bow to complete the table's present-like wrapping. The table and its collection of theatrical hats are all in the theme of the Renaissance, combined with inspiration from the bohemian East.

above & right

Jewel-like fabrics dress a garden for a carnival party.

# *all the trimmings*
## dressing the furniture

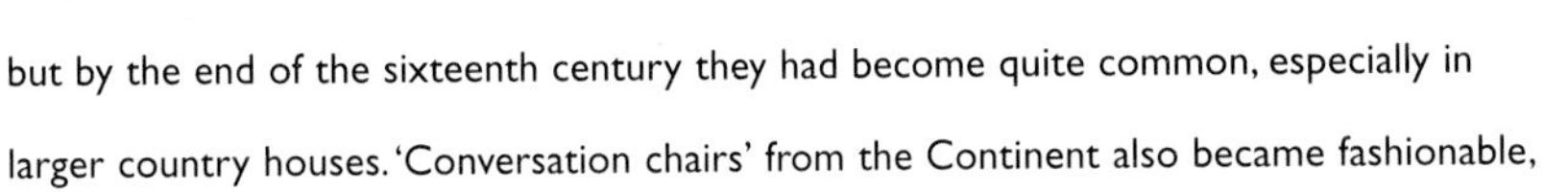

In medieval times chairs were a luxury, reserved for their owners and favoured guests only, but by the end of the sixteenth century they had become quite common, especially in larger country houses. 'Conversation chairs' from the Continent also became fashionable, with arms and low seats. Today, we have an ever-growing choice of chair designs, and fabrics with which to cover them, and our access to the choice thankfully does not depend on courtier status. Dress up your 'conversation chairs' with rich brocades and taffetas to rival the mansions of the sixteenth century. Raid market stalls and haberdasheries for sumptuous trimmings of fringing and ribbons. Here, striped silk is draped over a tired sofa, heaped with silk cushions edged in gold fringing and tied with green ribbons. A leafy velvet armchair is piled with soft velvet cushions in crimson and green and a stool is covered in rumpled crimson damask. Make sure the rest of the room lives up to this opulence with fabric wall coverings, decorated screens, decorative lampshades and crowds of glinting ornaments.

Pleated taffeta ribbon trims a woven paisley throw. The pleated silk lampshade has a gathered silk ribbon along the edge.

**See page 154 for frilled lampshade.**

left

A sofa is dressed up in bold striped silk throws and piled with cushions.

**See pages 182 for throws and 158–60 for cushions.**

far right

A skirted damask stool cover is ruched up at the four corners to reveal pretty gilded legs.

**See page 181 for ruched footstool cover.**

right

A damask chair cover with a decorative monk's hood dresses up an ordinary director's chair.

**See page 176 for director's chair with hood.**

# *couture dressing* **for winter baby baskets**

Red is often mistakenly thought to be an angry colour, but shades of it can be very comforting, unless you happen to be a Taurus. Line moses baskets in deep rose-red velvet, softer reds and burnt sienna, and in shiny red silks – the colour is strong and reassuring to a baby, and the feel of the fabrics suitably gentle.

When the baby has outgrown the basket it can be kept for the next offspring, or used for all manner of occupants, from dolls to teddies. The linings can be easily detached for cleaning. Make beautiful plain or quilted coverlets in the same fabric, or mix velvet with silk. Add pretty scalloped and frilled edgings and trim with silk and velvet ribbons.

### *materials*

Moses basket, paper and pencil, main fabric, contrast fabric, polyester wadding

### *measuring & cutting out the basic basket liner (figs 1 & 2)*

Make the base template by standing the basket on a sheet of paper and drawing around it. The template should be approximately 1.5cm larger all round than the inside. To make the quilt pattern, cut 20cm off the top end and add on an extra 2.5cm around the remaining edges.

For the sides, cut a long strip of paper, length 'a' and the same width as the highest point of the basket, 'c'. Tape it around the basket and cut the top edge to match the curve. Split it at the centre of each side to make separate patterns for the top and bottom parts, then add an extra 4cm along the top edges, and 2cm to each end.

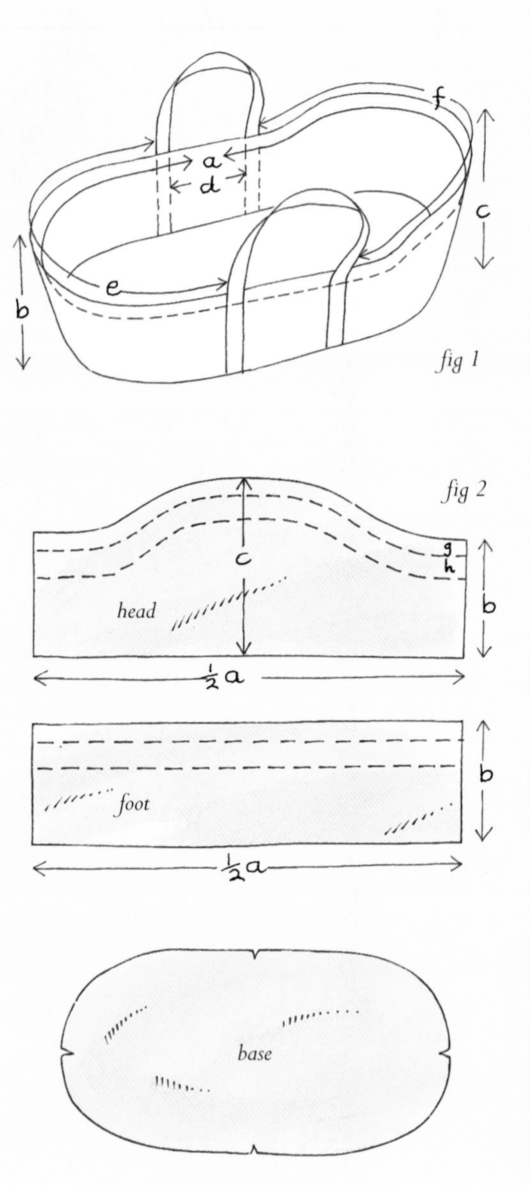


*fig 1*

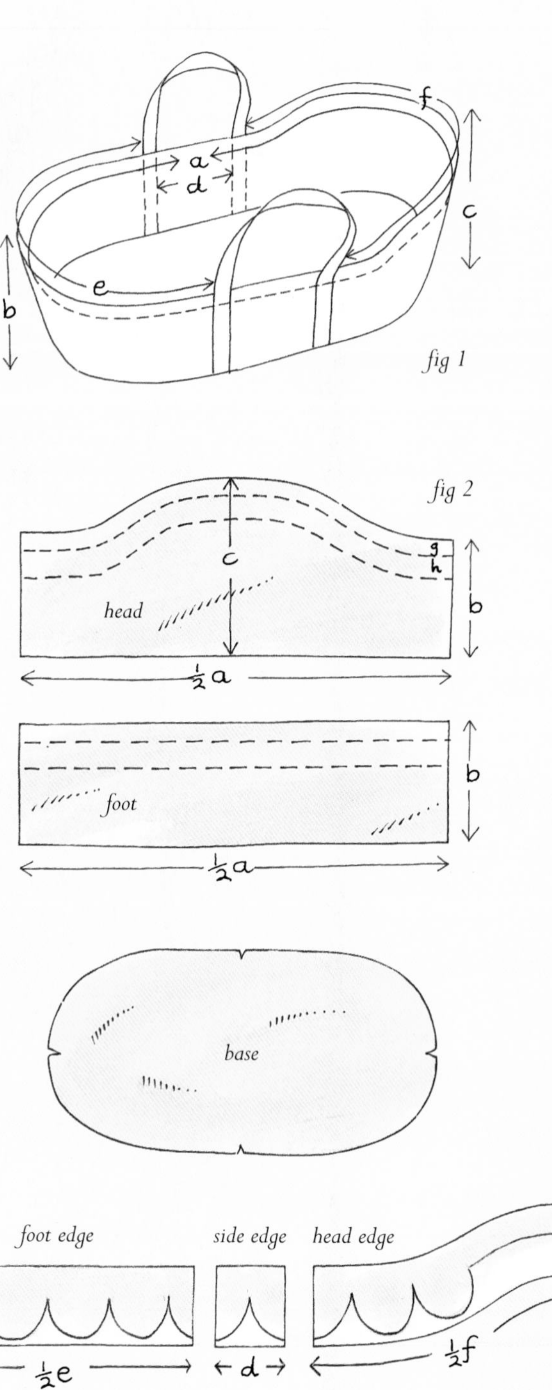


*fig 2*

### *lining*

Head: cut one piece as template. Notch the centre bottom edge

Foot: cut one piece as template. Notch the centre bottom edge

Base: cut one piece as template. Notch the centre sides, and top and bottom

Plain edge: cut two 8cm strips of fabric to fit around the head and foot, using the upper edge of the lining templates (indicated by line 'g') as a guide

Frill: cut four pieces 15cm-wide strips; 1 = 2e, 1 = 2f and 2 = 2d

Ties: cut four strips: width = 13cm, length = 50cm

Scallops: cut three 15cm-wide strips of paper to fit around the head and foot, using the upper edge of the lining templates (indicated by line 'h') as a guide. These should correspond to lines 'd', 'e' and 'f', so that the scallops will fit around the handles. Mark the cutting line as shown on the pattern *(fig 2)* and add on 1.5cm all round each piece

Cut two foot edge pieces, two head edge pieces and four side pieces.

### *making up*

**1** Join the two side lining pieces together at the short edges, with right sides facing, leaving a 1.5cm seam allowance. Press under 1cm along the top edge. Pin the lower edge to the base with right sides together. Match the notches at the centre head and foot, and align the side seams with the side notches on the base. Continue pinning, making two small pleats on either side of the head in the centre to take in the surplus fabric, and another two at the foot as necessary *(fig 3)*. Stitch, 1.5cm from the edge.

### *for a plain edge*

**2** Sew the two strips together along the short ends with right sides facing to form a loop, then press the seams flat. Make a 1cm double hem along the lower edge. Pin and stitch the strip to the top of the lining, with right sides facing, matching the seams. This will form a tight, narrow band that will hold the lining in place around the top edge and fit behind the handles.

*fig 3*

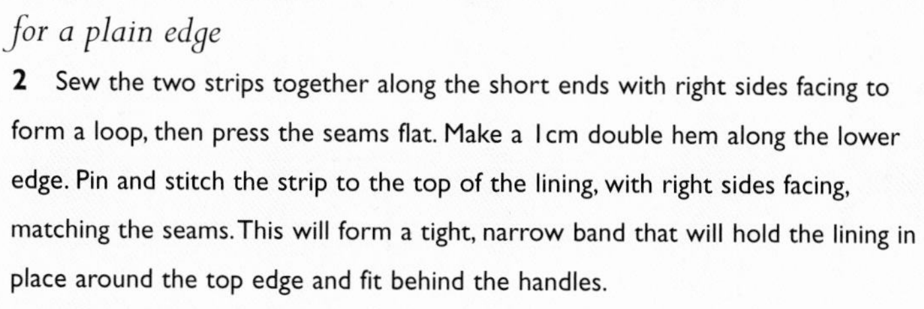

*for a frilled edge*

**2** The frill is made in four parts, so that it can fit around the handles. Make a narrow double hem along the short and lower edges of each piece. Notch the centre top edge of the two longer pieces. Sew a zigzag gathering thread (see p.142) along the raw edges.

**3** Place the lining, the right way up, inside the basket. Pin the raw edges of the frills in place on top, bottom and sides. Attach them with right sides facing to the underneath side of the neatened edge of the liner, matching the notches at top and bottom *(fig 4)*.

**4** Remove the lining from the basket and pull up the gathering threads to fit. Adjust the fullness so that it lies evenly and stitch down, over the threads. Trim the seam allowance to 6mm, then turn over 1.5cm all around the top edge to cover the raw edges. Top stitch, close to the folded edge.

**5** Make up the ties as on p.144. Fold in half, then sew two to each sides at the handle spaces. Place the finished lining in the basket and tie in place.

*for a scalloped edge*

**6** With right sides facing, pin the pieces together in pairs and stitch the scallop lines around the sides and lower edge of each. Trim, clip the curves (see p.139) and turn right side out. Pin the four sections to the turned-back seam allowance of the basket, as for the frilled edge, stitch in place and trim the seam allowance to 6mm. Turn over a further 1.5cm and top stitch.

*quilt (figs 1 and 5)*

Front: cut one piece from main fabric as template
Back: cut one piece from contrast fabric as template
Border: cut one piece, width (x) = 18cm, length = width of top
Wadding: cut one piece, 1.5cm smaller all round than the template

*making up*

**7** Turn under a 1cm single hem along one long side of the border. With right sides together, pin the raw edge to the top edge of the quilt top and stitch, 1cm from the edge.

**8** Baste the wadding to the wrong side of the back. With the border sandwiched between the two layers *(fig 6)*, pin the quilt top to the back with right sides facing. Stitch around the sides and curved bottom edge, leaving a 1cm seam allowance. Turn right side out and turn the border over to the front. The quilt can be finished with machine quilting, or with a scalloped edging or frill tucked under the border piece before it is stitched down.

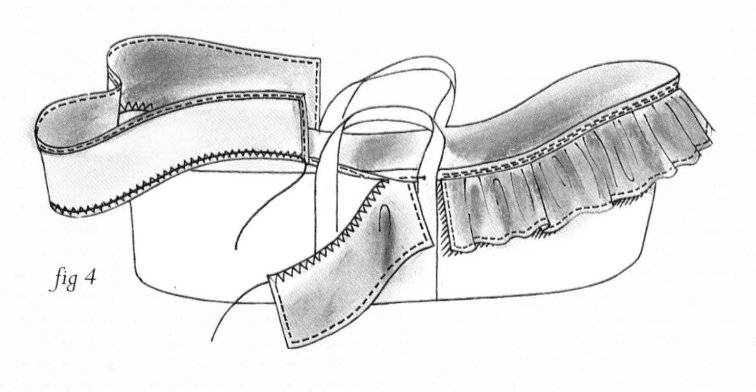

*fig 4*

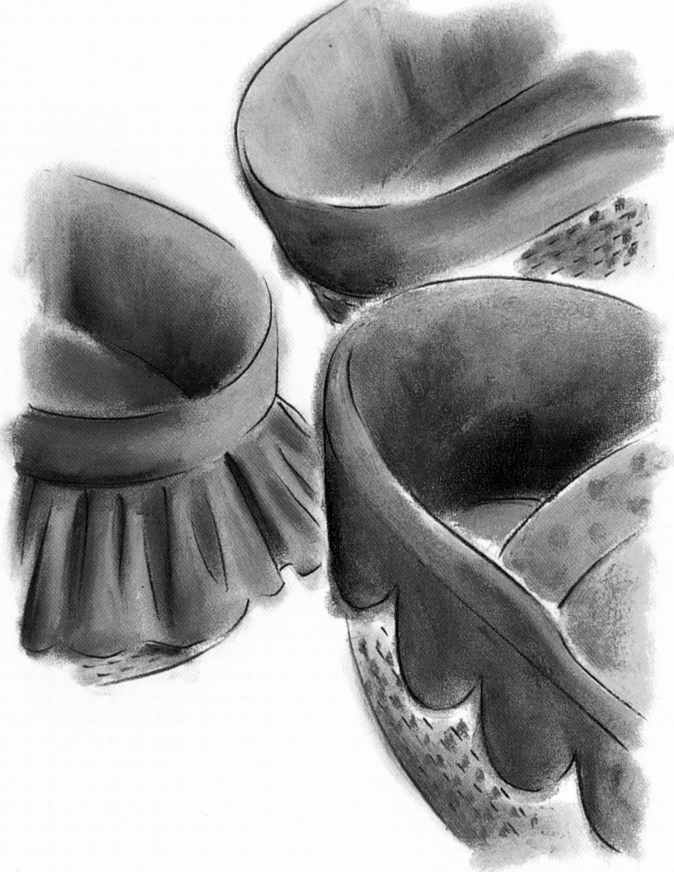

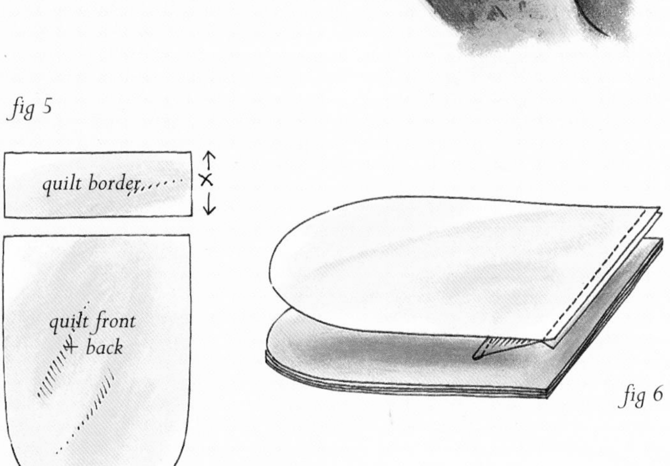


*fig 5*

*fig 6*

A pile of Renaissance-style cushions are covered in printed and cut furnishing velvets and damask, richly trimmed with tassels, cords and beads.

**See pages 158–60 for cushions.**

# renaissance

## *tapestry & tassels*
## for sumptuous dining-rooms

In the sixteenth century dress became wildly extravagant. Rich men spent huge amounts on velvet suits trimmed with silver, silk hats – worn indoors as well as out – and jewellery. Epaulettes were coming in, leg-of-mutton sleeves were all the rage, not to mention cloaks faced with gold or silver lace or even embroidered with pearls, and always elaborately lined. Men wore earrings, ladies wore hooped or padded skirts and scented gloves. Ruffs and feathers were everywhere, as were jewelled slippers and silk stockings. Houses too were beginning to reflect the tastes of their owners. Rich tapestries hung on the walls, beds became four-postered kingdoms, embroidered cushions and bolsters came into their own and Turkish rugs had even begun to infiltrate great halls. Life was becoming more comfortable, and warmer, than it had ever been before.

Just a pile of Renaissance-style cushions or some sumptuous curtains introduces a glimpse of this splendid age into your house, without having to sacrifice the central heating! Choose rich brocades and fringe them with home-made tassels or braided edging. Glossy cord piping is effective on velvet cushions, and you could also use lengths of black lace or raw silk off-cuts. Raid boxes of remnants in fabric shops for brocade, velvet and taffeta (remnant boxes are always full of treasures that can spark off ideas). Use your finds all over the house – not just for cushions, but also for chair-arm covers, curtain tie-backs, pelmets and placemats. Then take advantage of the wider variety of colours available today and mix the traditionally sombre, if rich, sixteenth-century mixtures of bronze, beige, purple, black and dark red with vibrant modern shades.

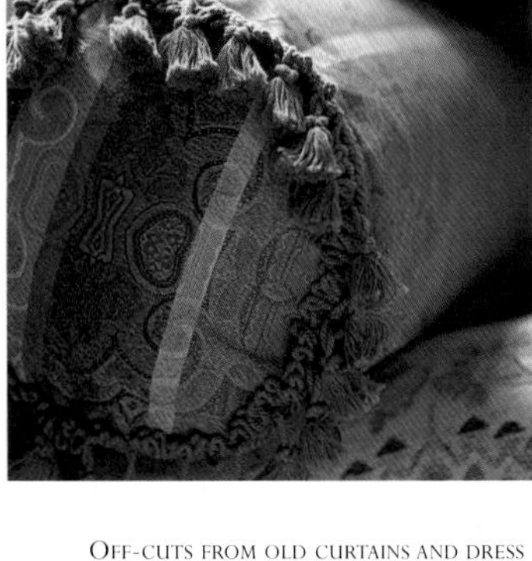

Off-cuts from old curtains and dress fabrics are used in details around the room, such as this flat-ended bolster.

**See page 163 for flat-ended bolster.**

# *fabric finery*
## for bedrooms & ensuite bathrooms

Far too often bathrooms are sad affairs, a functional appendage, a den of damp towels and too many half-empty jars of miracle creams. The experts unanimously advise that the best cure for stress is to take frequent aromatherapy baths by candlelight, while sipping a glass of Veuve Clicquot to the strains of Bach. None of which is an attractive prospect in a quick-shower-and-out-style *salle de bain*. So look to your bathrooms and transform them into royal boudoirs to help you survive in the cruel world.

The era that perfected the art of boudoir decoration was the eighteenth century, when women did not merely dress for a party, they armed themselves with the accessories of beauty to do battle in the ballroom. Follow their lead by decorating a chilly tiled bathroom with due care and attention. A discreet red and yellow screen makes a snug corner for the bath; full curtains and wall-drapes in sensuous soft red toiles and rich prints taken from antique documents are chosen for their rich glowing colours. The use of fabric on the walls not only looks sumptuous, it also makes the room physically warmer by retaining the heat. The fabric can be made into floor-to-ceiling panels and stapled to batons fixed to the walls, or attached with braids and pretty ribbons.

below

Richly decorated details make a transformation. A textured throw fixed to a curtain rail with special metal clips creates a splendid entrance. The fine muslin curtains edged with red bobbles echo the colour of the table cover.

left

Not just a place to wash, but a boudoir to languish in. This bathroom is transformed with the use of fabric on the walls and screen.

**See page 143 for fabric-covered panels.**

**For stool seat see page 55.**

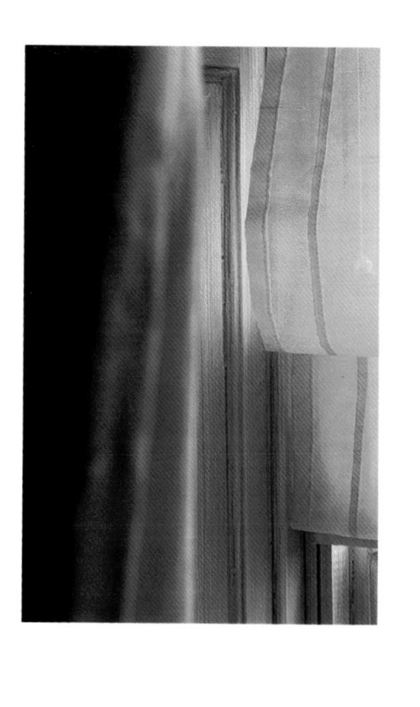

# *golden hazy days* **in the living-room**

On the whole, richly woven furnishing fabrics are expensive. If your resources do not quite stretch that far, the secret is to do what is known as a Scarlett O'Hara and turn old curtains, for example, to new uses. Second-hand curtain shops are a rich source of extravagant fabrics, as are textile galleries, charity shops, second-hand clothes shops and even street markets. Alternatively, search out attractive but less expensive printed fabrics, such as toiles de Jouy and faded florals, plain silk linings and Indian printed silks in exuberant dyes.

The desk chair shown here is covered with a woven damask akin to a sumptuous discarded golden curtain found in a grand house, shaped with a priestly cloak decoration at the back. The cover beautifully disguises the fact that the chair is a modern affair which would look ugly in this living-room-cum-study. The rest of the room is adorned in splendid fabrics. Moss green slubbed silk curtains look even more luxurious with a loose-flowing layer of brilliant yellow silk under-curtains, which share the same curtain pole. Translucent, golden yellow roman blinds made of an organza-type material filter out the grey days of winter and create an uncanny sunny ambience. They are also a superb alternative to net curtains as they are almost invisible, yet create privacy between you and the outside. The sofa is resplendent in gold, white, pink and green brocade. A hand-woven rug is slung over a screen to bring a sense of warm luxury to the room. Rather than letting the side down, the chair, in the spotlight of the winter sun, is a focal point.

above

A YELLOW ROMAN BLIND CASTS A WARM GLOW OVER THE LIVING-ROOM WHEN THE MORNING SUN SHINES THROUGH. IT ALSO SERVES TO BLOCK A MISERABLE VIEW OF THE RAIN AND WIND OUTSIDE WITHOUT DARKENING THE ROOM.

**See pages 146–7 for roman blind.**

left

THE CURTAINS ARE MADE UP OF TWO DIFFERENT WEIGHTS OF SILK IN CONTRASTING COLOURS – BRIGHT, SUNNY YELLOW AND MOSS GREEN.

**See pages 148–52 for curtains.**

right

A golden damask monk's chair cover is the focal point of this room. The desk is positioned near the window both for inspiration and light. Silk under-curtains filter the harsher rays of the winter sun and help ward off draughts.

**See pages 176 for director's chair with hood and 148–52 for curtains.**

# *my lady's chamber*
## the making of a bedroom

In the sixteenth century, when the four-poster bed arrived on the scene, the bedroom was one of the most splendid rooms in the house. The bed's tester roof, from which the curtains hung supported by posts at each corner, was often a wonderful tapestry. Headboards were huge and extravagantly carved, sometimes with little nooks for candles, and mattresses were stuffed with wool or feathers.

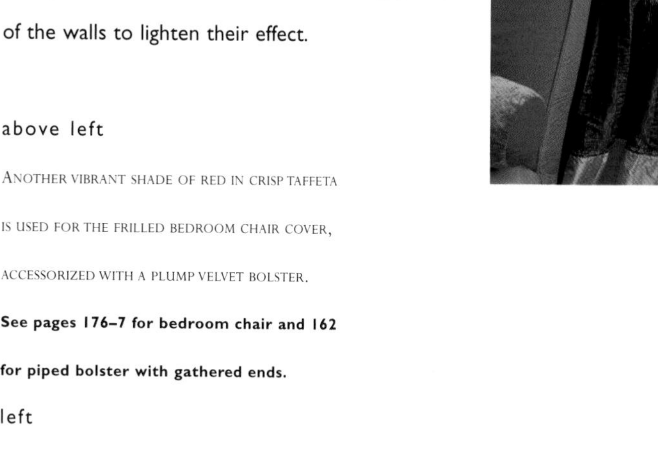

The role of the bedroom has not diminished, but the bed's structure has become less important than the sum of its coverings. Here, an old nineteenth-century walnut base is used for a bed, dressed in a rich array of Indian embroidered fabrics and a double-sided fabric throw boldly striped in velvet and silk. The polished wooden floorboards are covered with Oriental rugs for warmth. Too much wood can be gloomy, but this room has tall windows that bathe it in light. The crinkled, red silk curtains and roman blind are edged in Eastern striped silks in exotic colours. A mirror between the two windows gives the feeling of more light and space, and the white ceiling above the cornice breaks the strong yellow of the walls to lighten their effect.

above left

Another vibrant shade of red in crisp taffeta is used for the frilled bedroom chair cover, accessorized with a plump velvet bolster.

**See pages 176–7 for bedroom chair and 162 for piped bolster with gathered ends.**

left

In one corner is a comfy reading chair, covered in a sturdy weave in the rich colours of the room.

**See pages 178–80 for loose covers.**

Stateliness and exotic Eastern influences make for a sumptuous mixture in a bedroom. The crinkle-effect silk ballroom curtains are edged in stripes of exotic colours and gathered up with exquisite tasselled tie-backs. The moses basket is lined in taffeta with a scalloped velvet coverlet.

**See pages 128–9 for moses baskets.**

# *techniques & projects*

*Anyone who is familiar with basic sewing and dressmaking should have no problems undertaking any of the projects in this book. This section introduces the special techniques which will give a professional finish to your work, and includes clear and detailed explanations of how to make all the various soft furnishings featured, from a simple napkin or pillowcase to a loose cover for an armchair.*

# *basic techniques*

### seams

Careful preparation is needed to produce an accurate seam. Pin the two sides of the fabric at 5–10cm intervals, with the pins at right angles to the edge. Tack together with a contrasting thread, just inside the seam line. If the fabric is liable to fray, neaten the raw edges with a zigzag stitch before seaming.

### plain seam

Pin and tack the two pieces with right sides facing and raw edges level, then machine along the seam allowance. Secure each end of the seam with a few reverse stitches. Unpick the tacking and press open from the back *(fig 1)*.

### corners

To sew around a right-angled corner, lift the presser foot, leaving the needle down. Turn the fabric through 90 degrees, lower the foot and continue. Clip the seam allowance before turning right side out. On sharp corners, work one or two stitches across the point. Cut across the allowance, then trim back either side. For inside corners, snip into the allowance, to within 2mm of the stitching *(fig 2)*.

### curved seams

To reduce bulk, trim the seam allowance back to 6mm. For an outside curve, cut a series of regularly spaced notches to within 2mm of the stitching so that the seam will lie flat when pressed open. On an inside curve, clip the allowance *(fig 3)*.

### french seam

The second line of stitching on this double seam encloses the raw edges, which makes it hard-wearing and suitable for fabrics where a seam allowance would show through. With wrong sides facing, pin and stitch 6mm from the edge. Trim to 3mm, then refold with right sides together. Sew again, 8mm from the edge *(fig 4)*.

### flat fell seam

This strong double seam is reversible and will stand up to hard wear and washing. With wrong sides facing, stitch 1.5cm from the edge. Press the allowance to one side. Trim the lower edge to 5mm. Press under 3mm along the upper edge. Fold the upper edge over the lower edge and stitch down close to the fold *(fig 5)*.

### slip stitch

This makes a neat join between two folded edges. The needle passes through the folds so that only a small amount of thread shows. Butt the edges together and bring the needle through one fold and into the opposite side. Make a 6mm stitch down inside the fold, bring the needle out and back into the other edge *(fig 6)*.

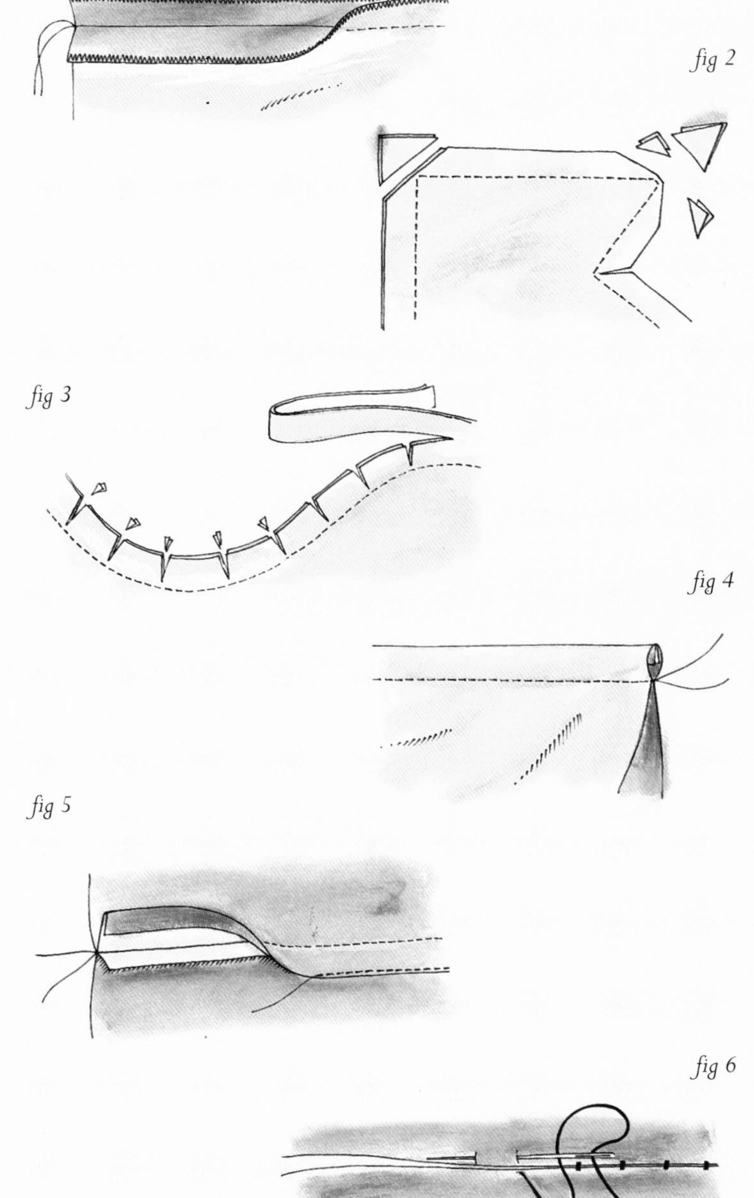

*fig 1*

*fig 2*

*fig 3*

*fig 4*

*fig 5*

*fig 6*

## hems

The way in which an edge is finished depends on the weight of the fabric. A thick material should only have a single hem with one turning. A double hem with one narrow and one deep turning is suited to most materials, whilst a hem which has two equal turnings is used to give a firmer edge or for sheer fabrics *(fig 1)*. Most hems can be machine stitched, but curtains should always be turned up by hand.

*fig 1*

### single hem

Zigzag the edge, or trim with pinking shears. Turn up to the right length, pin and stitch. To sew by hand, use herringbone stitch: starting at the left-hand side, take the needle diagonally upwards. Make a short horizontal stitch into the main fabric, from right to left. Take the needle down to the right and make the next horizontal stitch through the hem *(fig 2)*. Continue to the end.

*fig 2*

### double hem

Turn up to the right length. Press under 6mm along the raw edge and pin. Sew by hand with hemming stitch: work from right to left, picking up two or three threads from the wrong side for each small stitch *(fig 3)*. Do not pull the thread too tight.

*fig 3*

## mitring

When two hems meet at a corner, the surplus fabric can be neatened with a mitre. For a single hem, press under the turning along each side and unfold. Fold over the corner at a 45-degree angle, so that the creases line up to form a square *(fig 4)*, then refold. Slip stitch the folded edges. For a double hem, press under both turnings. Undo the second fold and turn in as above. Refold into a mitre *(fig 5)*.

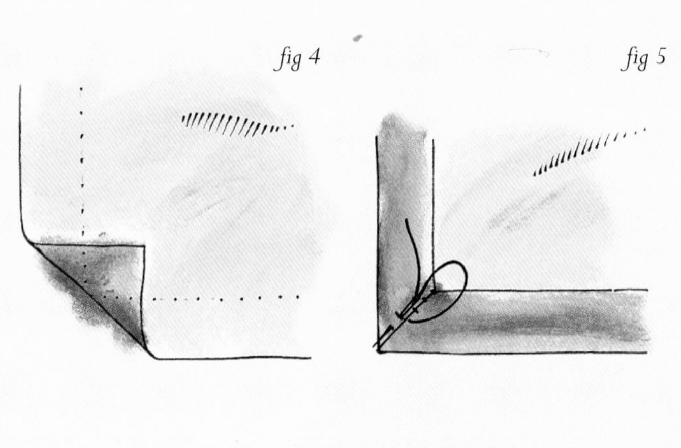


## binding

Binding is used to finish the edges of thick or quilted fabrics. Straight sides can be bound with fabric cut along the grain, but the flexibility of bias binding is needed on a curve. Ready-made bindings are available, but it is easy to make your own. Cut the strips twice the finished width plus 12mm for the turnings.

### cutting bias strips

Chalk a diagonal line across the fabric at 45 degrees to the edge. Mark a series of lines parallel to the diagonal, the required width apart, and cut along these lines. Join the strips together at right angles, 6mm from the edge *(fig 6)*. Press open and trim the corners.

To make a long strip, cut a 30 x 60cm rectangle. Cut off one corner at 45 degrees and sew one straight side to the opposite short edge of the rectangle. Rule a series of lines parallel to the diagonal edge *(fig 7)*. With right sides facing, match 'a' to 'b', pin and stitch. Turn right side out and cut along the now continuous line *(fig 8)*.

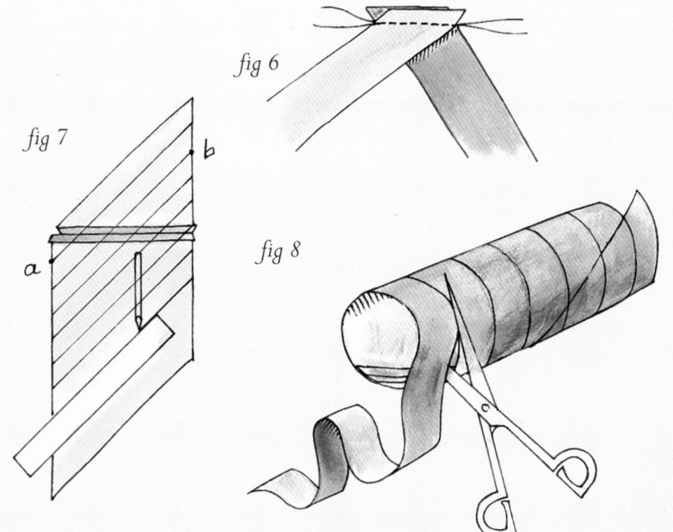

### attaching binding

Press under 6mm along each long edge, then press in half lengthways with wrong sides together. Fold over the edge of the fabric and pin, mitring corners and easing curves. Machine or slip stitch, close to the outer fold, making sure that the stitching goes through all the layers *(fig 9)*.

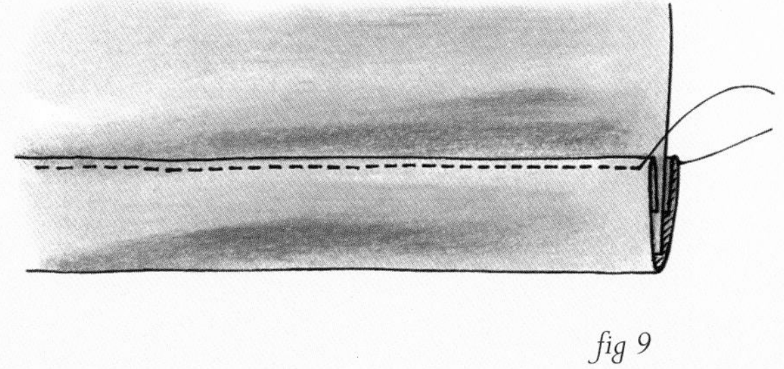

*fig 9*

## piping

Piping cord, covered with a bias fabric strip, is sewn into a seam as reinforcement and decoration. On loose covers it is used to outline the shape of a chair, and a round of contrast piping adds visual interest to a cushion cover. The cord can be bought in several thicknesses and should be boiled before use if it is not preshrunk.

### covering the cord

Cut a bias strip to the required length: the total length of the seams, plus an extra 5cm for each seam and join. The width of the strip should equal the circumference of the cord, plus 3cm. With the right side facing outwards, fold the strip around the cord and pin. Stitch in place, using a zipper or cording foot *(fig 10)*.

*fig 10*

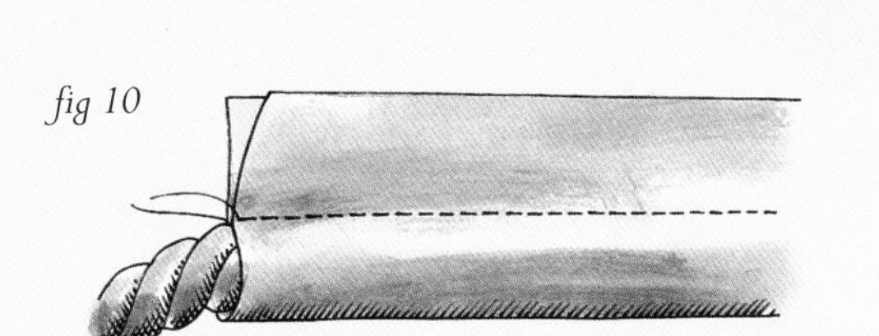

### piping a seam

Pin the piping to the right side of the fabric, matching the raw edges. Tack and stitch with a zipper foot. Clip into the seam allowance at any corners, and stitch around it in a curve, not at an angle. Notch the allowance on both piping and main fabric around a curved edge *(fig 11)*. Place the second piece of fabric right sides facing, matching the edges. Pin and stitch just inside the previous stitch line.

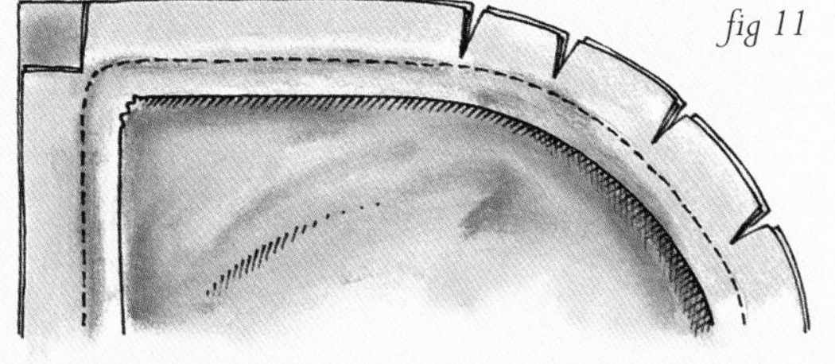
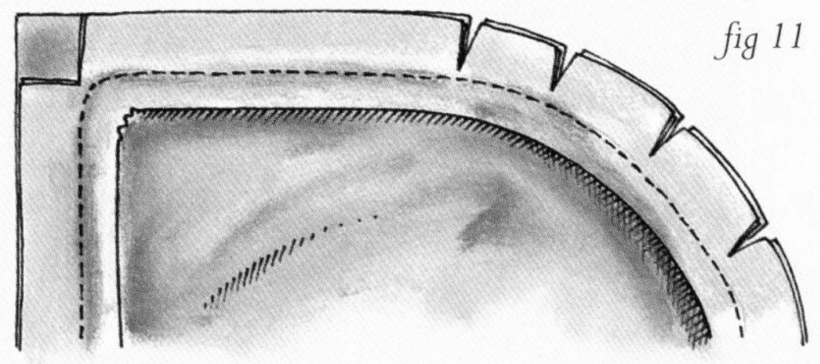

*fig 11*

### making a round of piping

A continuous length of piping, such as that on a cushion cover, has to have an inconspicuous join. This should be positioned next to a seam line if possible. Sew the piping in place, leaving 5cm unstitched on either side of the join. Unpick the stitching that encloses the cord for 3cm at each end. Trim the cord so that the ends butt together and bind with sewing thread. Trim the bias strip so that one end overlaps the other by 15mm. Turn under 5mm at this end and fold over the raw end *(fig 12)*. Slip stitch the join and finish stitching the seam line.

*fig 12*

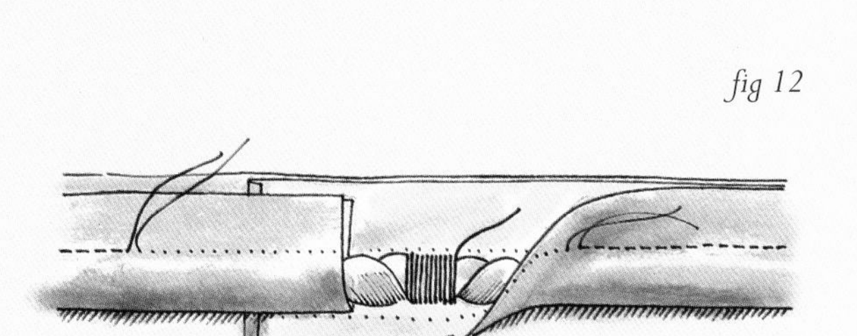

### decorative cords

Decorative silky cords are sewn by hand along a finished seam. Use matching thread and stitch through a few strands at the back of the cord. Cord cannot be joined neatly, so when it is applied to a cushion cover, the two ends are concealed within the seam. Allow an extra 5cm of cord and leave a 3cm gap in the stitching. Partially unravel one end of the cord and insert it into the gap *(fig 13)*. Stitch the rest around the edge and unravel the remaining end so that it lies flat. Tuck it into the gap next to the first end, then stitch securely in place.

*fig 13*

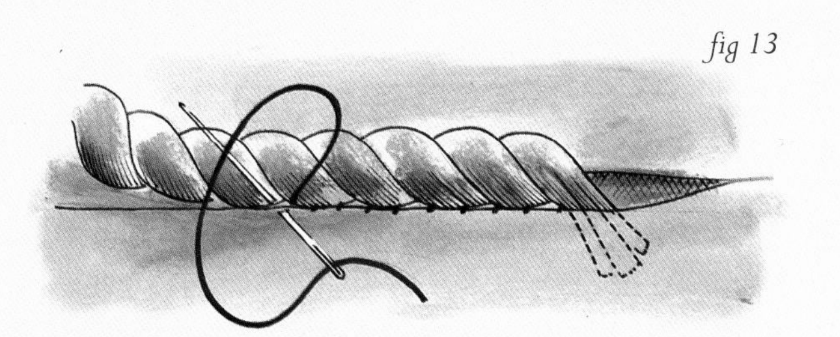

## braids and fringes

Woven braids and fringes and ready-made trims may be attached by hand or machine. If the trimming does not fray, the ends can be joined with a narrow seam; otherwise they should be overlapped and hidden inside the seam *(fig 1)*. Allow an extra 5cm at each end for this. When a fringe is used to border a throw, make it reversible by turning up a single hem on the right side and stitching the trimming to conceal the raw edge.

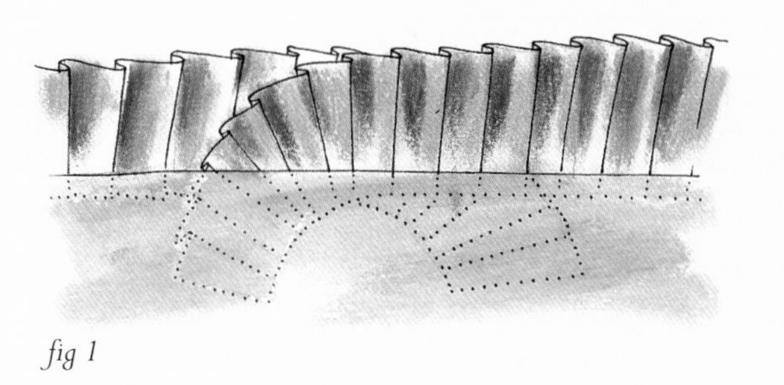
*fig 1*

## gathers and pleats

Gathered and pleated ruffles have many applications; they can soften the edge of a blind, add a formal border to a loose cover, or a flouncy skirt to a tablecloth. They may be double for extra fullness – simply cut the strip to twice the required width and fold in half – or single, with a narrow hem along the lower edge. Join the fabric with a plain seam for a double frill or a flat fell seam for a single frill.

### gathering

Fabric is drawn up with a thread sewn along one edge. With a lightweight fabric, run two parallel rows of long straight machine stitch, or use a double length of thread to sew a running stitch. On a heavy fabric or for a long length, use zigzag gathering to prevent the thread from breaking. Set the machine to a long narrow satin stitch and sew just inside the seam allowance. Secure a length of buttonhole thread around a pin at the start. Hold this under the presser foot as you sew, so that it is couched down by the zigzag *(fig 2)*, then pull up the gathers.

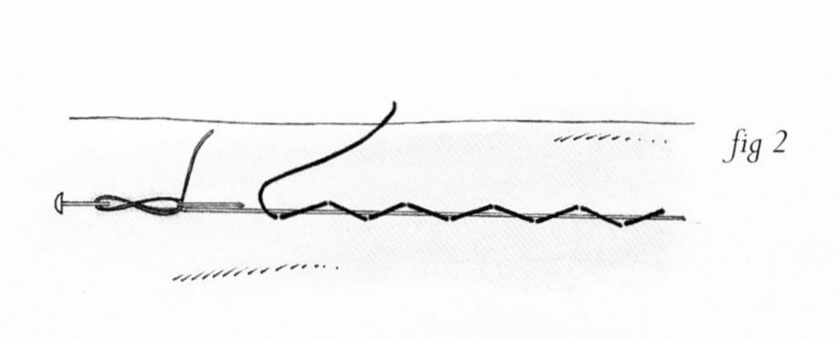
*fig 2*

### attaching gathers

It is important that the gathering is distributed equally. When a frill is to go on to a single edge, fold it in half, then quarters. Mark these divisions with notches at the top. Do the same with the lower edge of the main fabric. Sew a gathering thread along each quarter of the frill, and with right sides facing, pin to the main fabric, so that the notches match. Draw up each thread to length, adjust the gathers so that they are even, and pin *(fig 3)*. Knot the gathering threads before sewing. Neaten the raw edges with a zigzag.

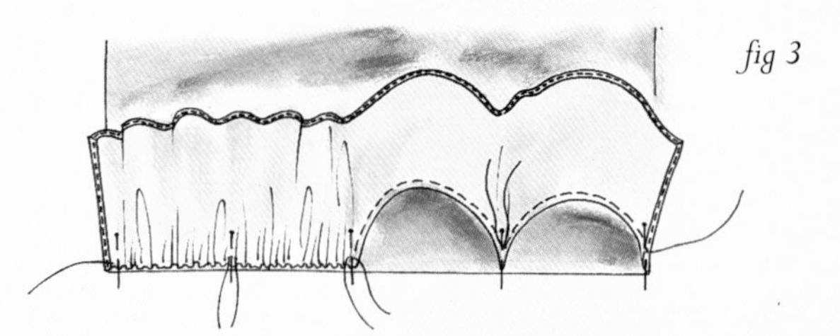
*fig 3*

This method is also used for a continuous frill. For a square, eg a cushion cover, the frill is folded into four, and one quarter sewn to each side. For a rectangle – a pillowcase or tablecloth – add the four sides and divide by eight. Make notches this distance apart around the perimeter, starting at one corner. Fold the frill into eighths, and notch the top edge. Make a gather between each pair of notches, and pin *(fig 4)*. Allow extra fullness at each corner. A frill is attached to a valance by measuring the sides and bottom edge in the same way.

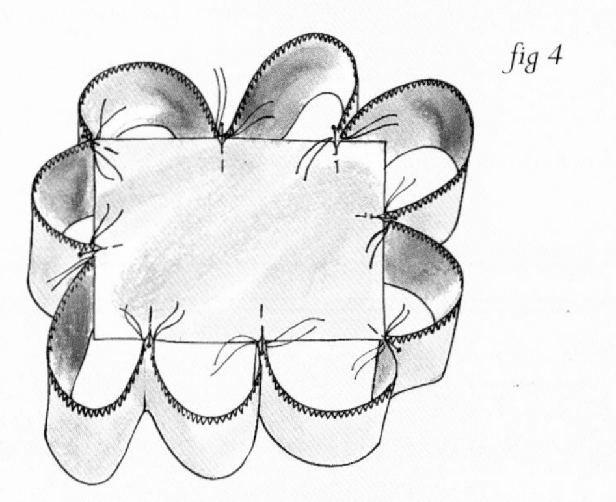
*fig 4*

### self-bound ruffle

Conceal the raw edges of the frill to give a neat finish to a cot drape or curtain. Trim the gathered edge back to 6mm and press under 5mm along the seam allowance of the main fabric. Fold the allowance over the gathers and slip or machine stitch in place *(fig 5)*.

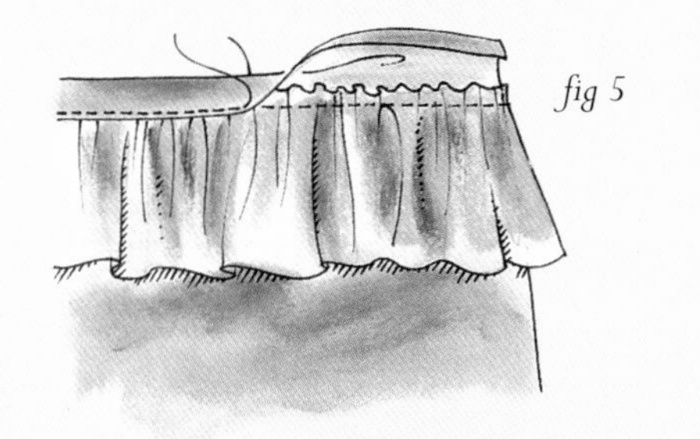
*fig 5*

## pleating

A strip of fabric for a pleated edge must be cut across the width of the fabric, following the grain, so that it will hang straight. Ensure that any joins lie at the back of a fold and that the pleats line up with the corners on chairs or valances.

### knife pleats

Cut a strip of fabric twice the finished length. With tailor's chalk, mark a series of lines the same width apart as one pleat. Match points 'a' to points 'c' so that all the pleats lie in the same direction *(fig 6)*. Pin, then tack in place along the top edge.

### box pleats

Two knife pleats folded towards each other form a box pleat – allow three times the finished length for a frill. Chalk parallel lines at right angles to the edge so that the distance between them is half the finished width of the pleat. Matching 'a' to 'c', then 'e' to 'c', pin each pleat *(fig 7)*, then tack along the top edge.

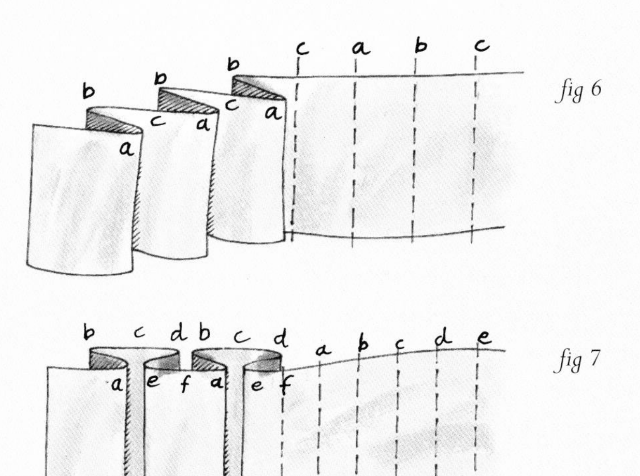

*fig 6*

*fig 7*

## fabric panels

There are several quick methods of using lengths of fabric which involve little sewing and which give instant results. A hemmed rectangle can be draped over a curtain pole as a swag, or pinned at ceiling height to cover a wall.

### matching patterned fabrics

When patterned fabrics are joined, the design has to match up horizontally across the seam. Ensure that the pattern starts at the same point on each piece. Press under the seam allowance along one side. Pin to the second length so that the motifs match. Tack together with ladder stitch: bring the needle through one fold and into the other side. Make a 1cm stitch, parallel to the folded edge. Take the needle back into the fold. Make a 1cm stitch inside, and continue down the seam *(fig 8)*. Place right sides together and machine stitch along the tacked line.

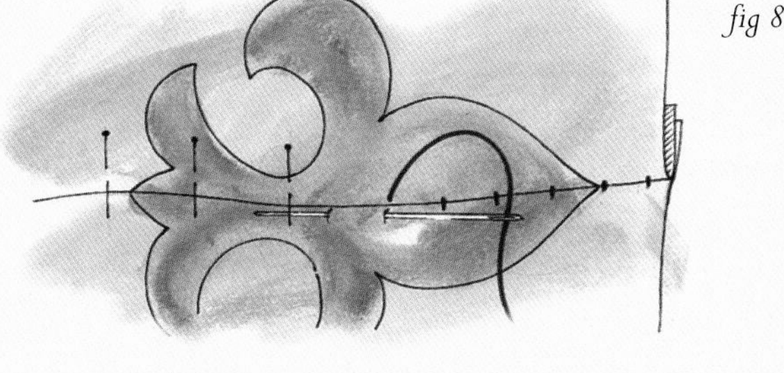

*fig 8*

### joining fabric lengths

To avoid an intrusive centre seam, cut the second piece of fabric lengthways into two panels and sew one to either side of the main piece *(fig 9)*.

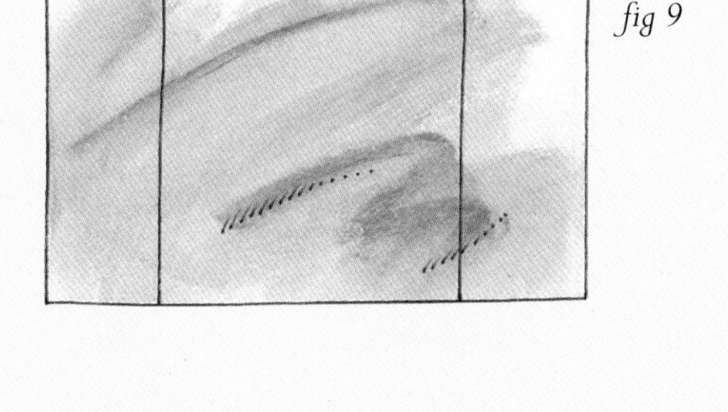

*fig 9*

### bagging

To make reversible panels, pin the two pieces with right sides facing. For a throw, sew around all four sides, leaving a 25cm gap at one edge. Clip the corners, turn right side out and slip stitch the gap. For curtains, sew the side and bottom edges, clip the corners and turn through. Finish the top edge with header tape or loops.

### fabric-covered panels

Fabric can simply be stretched over a screen or padded bedhead. Cut out a piece 5cm larger all round than the area to be covered. Staple to the centre of each side, leaving a margin of 5cm and keeping it taut. Working outwards, secure at 10cm intervals, checking that the grain is not distorted *(fig 10)*. Trim surplus fabric and glue braid around the edge to conceal the raw edges.

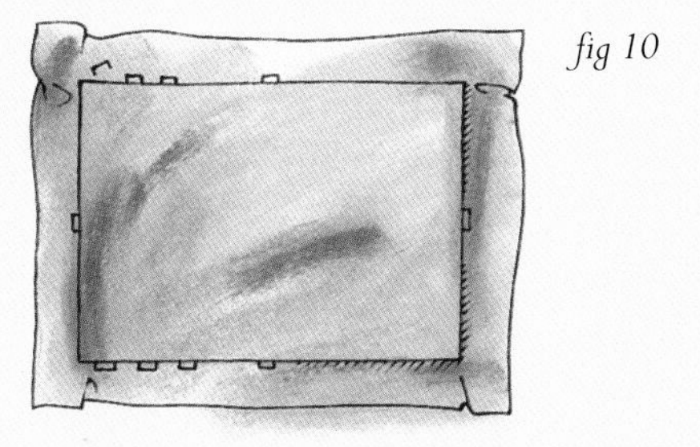

*fig 10*

## fastenings

Fastenings can be hidden away, like a practical zip at the back of a cushion cover, or, like ties or bows, made into a decoration in their own right.

### zips

Metal and nylon zips are available in various lengths, weights and colours for all purposes. The length is always measured along the teeth. Use a zipper foot to sew in place, stitching 3mm from the teeth.

#### inserting a zip in a plain seam

Tack the two sides together along the seam allowance. Machine stitch at each end, leaving a central gap 1cm longer than the zip. Work a few reverse stitches to reinforce either end of the stitching. Press open and place the zip, face down, along the tacked seam. Pin and tack, then stitch in place from the right side *(fig 1)*.

#### inserting a zip in a piped seam

Seam the two sides to the point where the zip is to be inserted. Open the zip and, with right sides facing, tack and sew one side along the piped edge, so that the teeth lie next to the cord *(fig 2)*. Turn the seam allowance to the wrong side and close the zip. Press under the allowance on the other side of the seam, and line up the folded edge with the piping. Tack the second side of the zip to the inside of the fold, and sew in place 6mm from edge and across the end *(fig 3)*.

### ties

For each tie, cut a strip of fabric, measuring the same as the finished length and twice the finished width, with 1cm added on all round.

For narrow ties press under 1cm along each edge including the ends, then press in half lengthways, right sides out. Tack, then machine stitch all round, 3mm from the edge *(fig 4)*.

For wide ties fold in half lengthways with right sides together, and stitch the long edge. Press so the seam lies down the centre, then sew across one end, straight or diagonally *(fig 5)*. Trim excess fabric and clip corners. Turn right side out, press.

### bows

An ornamental bow is made from four separate pieces. Detailed measurements are given with projects, but follow this method to make a bow of any size *(fig 6)*.

Main part: width = 2b, length = 2a, plus 1.5cm all round

Tails: cut two, width = 2d, length = c, plus 1.5cm all round

Centre: width = e, length = b, plus 1.5cm all round

Fold the main part in half lengthways with right sides together and join the long edges. Turn right side out and press with the seam centred on the back. Do the same with the centre piece. Turn the ends of the main part to the middle and sew two gathering threads through all the layers *(fig 7)*. Draw up and secure. Make up the tails as for a wide tie above. Press and sew to the back of the main part, either side of the gathers *(fig 8)*. Stitch the centre around the gathers and over the tails, securing at the back.

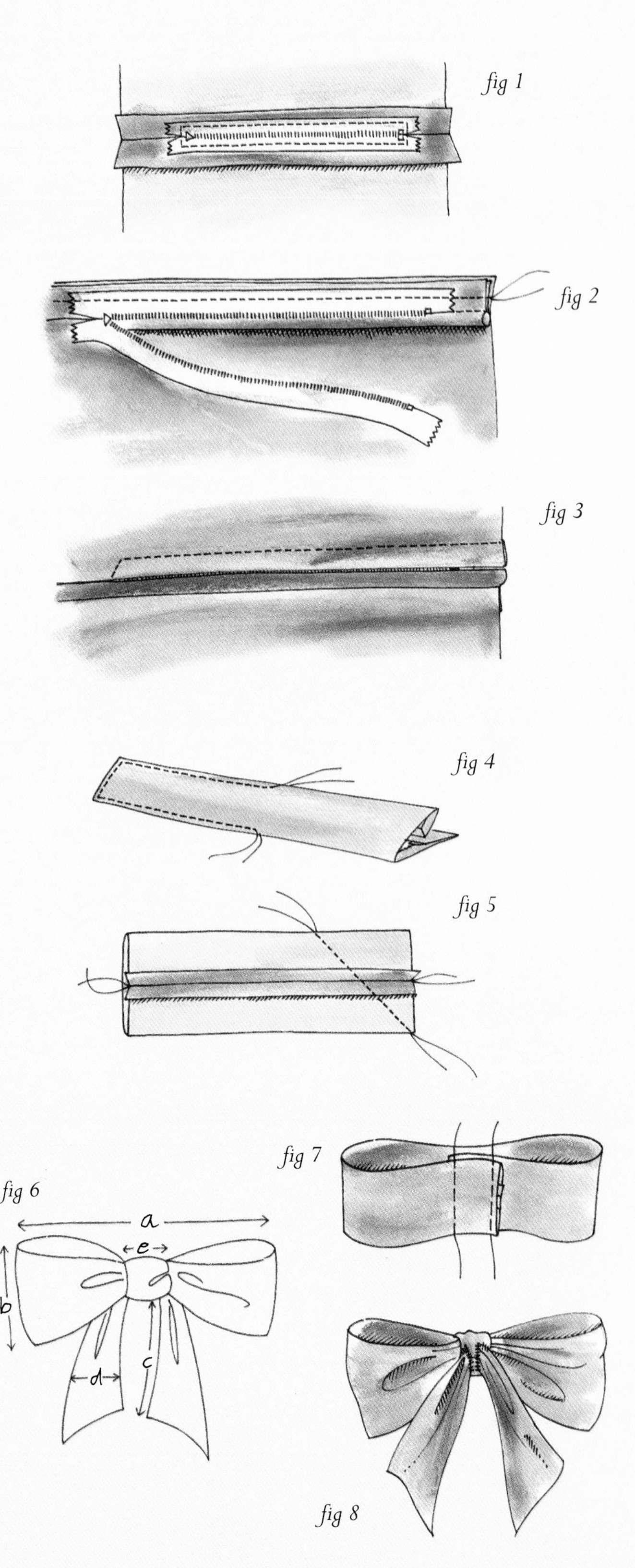


*fig 1* *fig 2* *fig 3* *fig 4* *fig 5* *fig 6* *fig 7* *fig 8*

# *blinds*

*Curtains, blinds, pelmets and valances can be used in combination, not just for privacy and insulation from sound and darkness, but to add drama, life and light. Creating your own is sometimes seen as a daunting task, but it can be as simple as sewing lengths of tape to the top of a hemmed panel.*

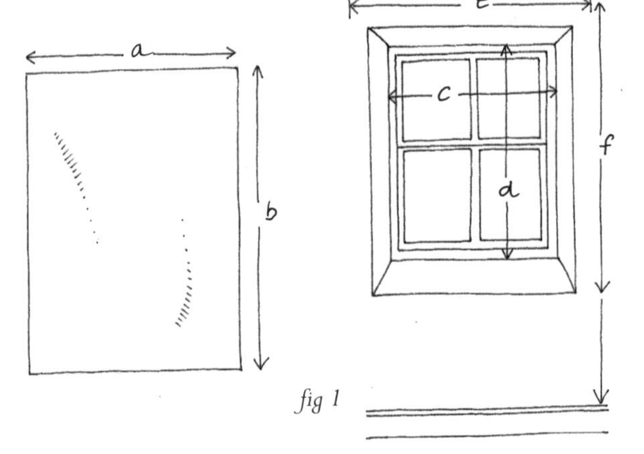


*fig 1*

Blinds can be used on their own for an uncluttered look, or hung behind co-ordinating curtains. Unlined swedish-style blinds roll up from the lower edge where a dowel supports the hem, and work well with patterned or semi-sheer fabrics as there are no rods to show through. Roman blinds are drawn up into pleats by a system of cords which run through rows of small rings fixed to the reverse side. Those stitched directly to the fabric give a soft, unstructured look; on wooden rods the cloth falls into more formal pleats. When choosing fabric, bear in mind that a roman blind will be raised for much of the day; large repeats may not work well when folded.

Swedish and roman blinds suit both large and small windows, but should not be wider than two metres, or the rods will bend under the weight of the fabric. A blind should ideally be cut from a single width of material. If fabrics have to be joined, sew half of the extra width to either side of the centre panel to avoid a seam in the middle. Using a contrasting colour for the two edges makes the additional fabric into a decorative feature. An ornamental finish such as a frill or a scalloped edging can be added to the bottom (see p.142), but position the first row of rings slightly higher than usual, so that the edge will show below the folds when the blind is drawn up.

### *measuring up* *(fig 1)*

Both types of blind are fixed with velcro to a fabric-covered wooden batten which can be screwed directly inside the window recess, or mounted on the wall above the window using angle brackets. Decide where you want your blind to hang before working out the finished width and length (a & b). The lining and main fabrics must be cut accurately along the grain, so that the blind will hang straight.

For a blind that fits within the window, a = the width of the recess (c) and b = the length from the top of the recess to the sill (d).

For a blind that lies outside the window, a = the width of the window frame plus the desired distance at each side (e), and b = the length from the top of the batten including the desired height of blind above window to the desired length below the sill (f).

## swedish blind

### *materials*

Main fabric, 1cm-diameter dowelling rod (length = a - 1cm), 2cm-wide velcro (length = a - 1cm), fine cotton piping cord, (length = 6b + a), 2 glass or metal rings 3cm in diameter, 40 x 2cm strips of leather or woven tape

For mounting: wooden batten 5 x 2.5cm (1cm shorter than finished width) extra fabric to cover batten, staple gun, 2 x 1cm screw eyes, tacks, hammer, cleat

### *measuring & cutting out* *(fig 1)*

Main fabric: width = a + 6cm, length = b + 16cm

### *making up*

**1** Press under and stitch a 3cm double hem along each side of the blind. Make a 3cm double hem along the lower edge. Insert the rod through this channel and slip stitch the ends to hold it in place *(fig 2)*.

**2** At the top edge, press a 2cm turning to the wrong side. Pin the hooked side of the velcro strip so that it conceals the raw edge and stitch it in place *(fig 3)*.

### *mounting & cording*

**3** Cover the batten with fabric to match the blind, neatening the corners like a parcel. Staple the other side of the velcro to one narrow side and screw the two eyes under at points 5cm in from each edge *(fig 4)*. Mount the batten so that the velcro faces into the room.

*fig 2*

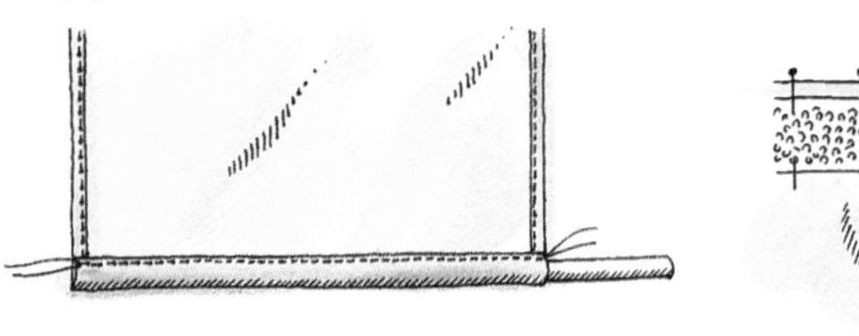

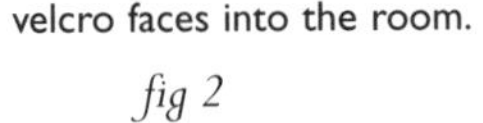

*fig 3*

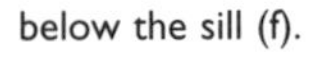

*fig 4*

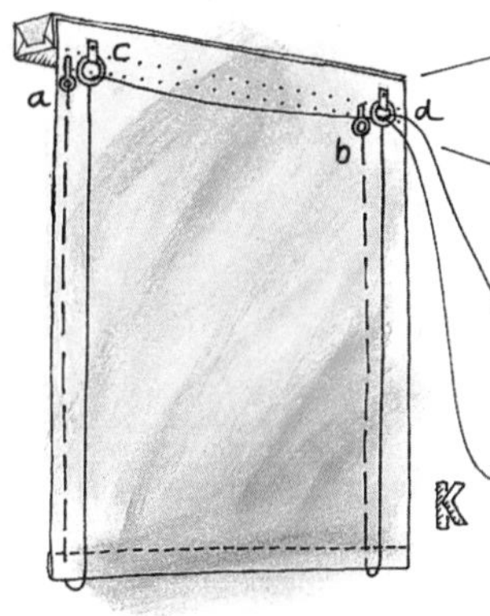

*fig 5*

*fig 5a*

**4** Attach the blind to the batten, matching the velcro strips. Cut the tape or leather strip in half and thread each piece through one of the rings *(fig 5a)*. Fix one to each side of the blind heading, 5cm in from the edge *(fig 5)*.

**5** Tie one end of the cord to the screw eye at 'a', then bring the other end under the blind and back up through loop 'c' at the front. Tie the other end securely to the second screw eye at 'b', then thread the double cord forward through loop 'd' at the front to form the pull *(fig 5)*. Screw the cleat to the wall at the right-hand side at windowsill level.

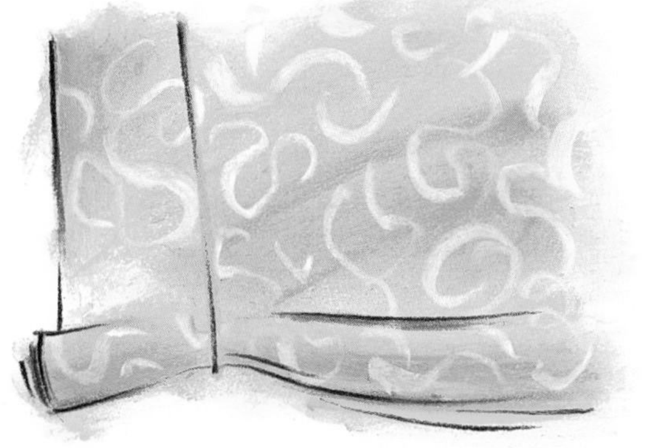

## roman blinds

Decide how many folds your blind is to have; depending on the proportions of the window, there are usually four or five. Deduct 5cm (z) from the finished length, to allow space for it to be drawn up, and calculate the length between the rods or rings.

### ● working out the distance between the folds

For a blind without rods: divide length 'x' by twice the number of folds plus one, to find length 'c'. The first row of loops will be this distance from the lower edge and subsequent rows will be 2c apart *(fig 6)*.

For a blind with rods: subtract 5cm for each rod from length 'x', then divide by twice the number of folds plus one for length 'c'. The first fold will be this distance from the lower edge and the following folds will be at 2c + 5cm intervals.

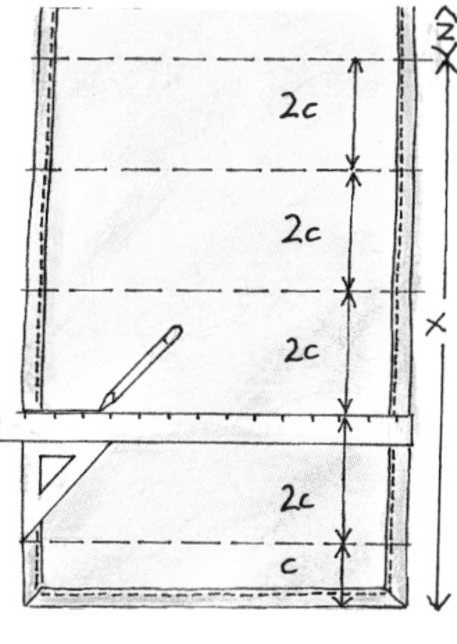


*fig 6*

## soft roman blind

This is the most basic roman blind which falls into loose folds. An unlined blind allows in some daylight, so select a lightweight fabric with a firm weave.

*materials*

Main fabric, approx 15 x 12mm rings, 1cm-diameter dowelling rod (length = a - 1cm), metre rule and set square, fade-away pen or chalk pencil

*measuring & cutting out (see fig 1)*

Main fabric: width = a + 4cm, length = b + 8cm

*fig 7*

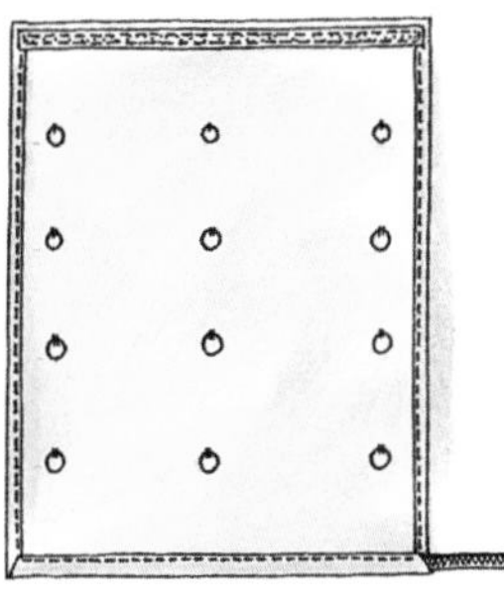

*making up*

**1** Press under and stitch down a 2cm double hem along the two sides of the blind. Make a 3cm double hem along the lower edge, mitring the corners (see p. 140). Insert the rod under the mitres, and slip stitch in place (see *fig 2*).

**2** Work out the distance between the rows of rings (see below left), then mark the fold lines on to the back of the blind using a set square and ruler *(fig 6)*. Take each measurement from the bottom edge to ensure the lines are parallel.

**3** Using matching thread, sew on the rings in rows of three, one 5cm in from each side edge and one in the centre *(fig 7)*. Finish the top edge of the blind with velcro as for step 2 of the Swedish Blind.

## formal roman blind

The more formal pleats of this blind are supported by a series of rods inserted into narrow channels made by folding and stitching the fabric. Stitch each line in the same direction so that the fabric does not pull.

*materials*

As for the Soft Roman Blind, plus 1cm-diameter dowelling rod (length = a - 1cm) for each channel, 2cm wooden lath (length = a - 1cm) instead of dowel for bottom channel

*measuring & cutting out (see fig 1)*

Width = a + 8cm

Length = b + 8cm, + 5cm for each rod channel

*making up*

**1** Press under and stitch a 2cm double hem along the two sides of the blind. Make a 3cm double hem along the bottom edge. Mitre, but do not stitch down the corners. Press, then place the blind face down on the work surface. Work out the distance between the rods and mark on the reverse side as for step 2 of the Soft Roman Blind.

**2** Fold along the first line and press lightly. Pin the two sides together at right angles to the fold and stitch 2.5cm from the fold *(fig 8)*. Repeat for the other channels.

**3** Insert one rod into each channel and slip stitch the open ends to keep them in place. Slip the lath into the bottom channel under the mitred corners, and slip stitch them together. Sew three rings to each channel, one 10cm in from each side and the third in the centre. Stitch them securely to the folded edge *(fig 9)*. Finish the top edge of the blind with velcro as for step 2 of the Swedish Blind.

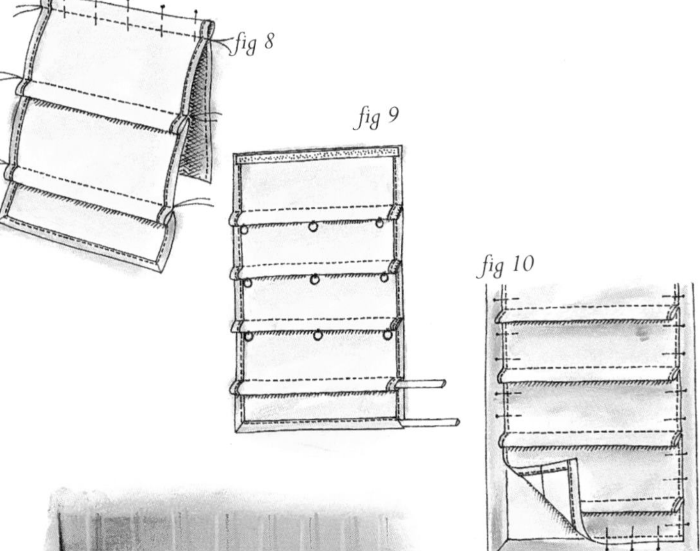

*fig 8*

*fig 9*

*fig 10*

## lined roman blind

The additional layer of fabric gives this blind a tailored appearance. The rods are attached to the lining, which is made in the same way as the formal blind. It is hand sewn on to the main fabric, so that no stitch lines are visible from the front.

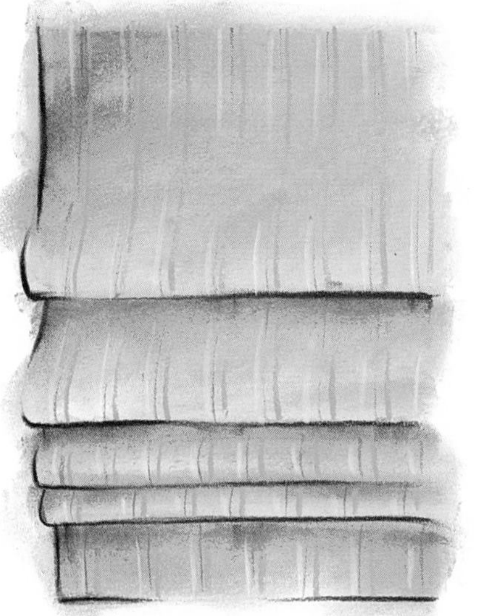

*materials*

As for the Soft Roman Blind, plus lining fabric

*measuring & cutting out (see fig 1)*

Main fabric: width = a + 12cm, length = b + 12cm

Lining: width = a = 6cm, length = b + 5cm for each channel

*making up*

**1** Press under, then pin and tack a single hem of 3cm along each side of the lining fabric. Mark and sew the stitching lines on the right side, as for steps 1 and 2 of the Formal Roman Blind.

**2** Press under a single hem of 6cm along each side and the lower edge of the main fabric, mitring the corners. Sew down by hand using herringbone stitch.

**3** Lay the main fabric face down on the work surface. Place the lining on top, with the channels facing upwards. Line up the corners and seams so that it is centred, and pin in place *(fig 10)*. Slip stitch the lining to the blind.

**4** Insert the rods and lath and finish as for step 3 of the Formal Roman Blind.

### ● cording and mounting roman blinds

The same technique is used for all three roman blind variations.

*materials*

Thin polyester cord (length = 6b + 2a), length of 5 x 2.5cm wooden batten (1cm shorter than finished width), 3 screw eyes, 2 angle brackets or 2 large screws, staple gun or hammer and tacks, cleat, wooden drop weight cord pull

*method*

Cover the batten and attach the velcro as for the Swedish Blind (see *fig 3*). Fix above the window or into the recess, using a spirit level to keep it straight. Screw the eyes to the underside so that they will line up with the rows of loops. Velcro the blind to the batten.

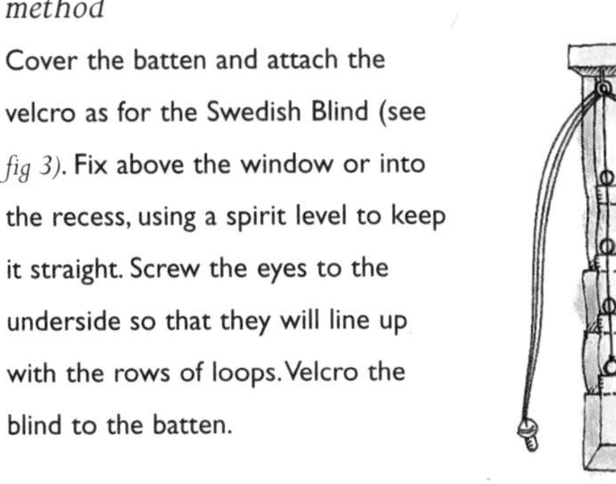

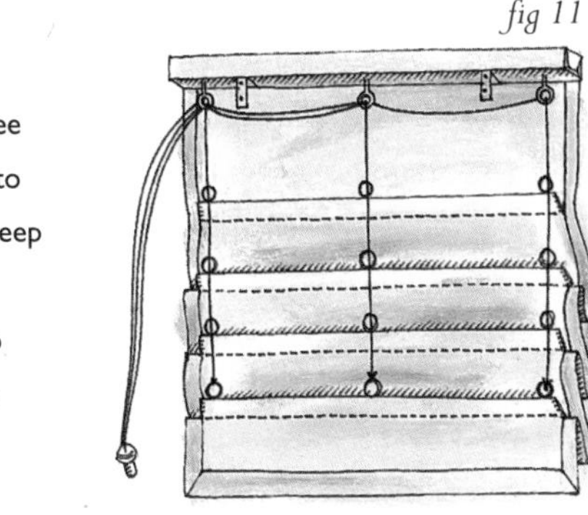

*fig 11*

*threading the cords (fig 11)*

Cut the cord into equal lengths. Standing between the window and the back of the blind, knot the cord securely to the first loop on the bottom rod, then thread it up the row and through the screw eye. Thread the middle cord in the same way and pass the end to the left and through the first screw eye. Do the same with the last cord, so that all the ends pass through the same screw eye. Knot the cords together at sill level and trim the ends even. Attach the drop weight.

# curtains

*When deciding which fabric and type of heading to use for curtains, bear in mind the proportions of the window and the size of the room. Brocade drapes with a pencil-pleat heading, topped by a matching shaped pelmet, may be ideal for a large, high-ceilinged drawing room, whilst short, café curtains will look pretty in a cottage dining room. Bedroom curtains should be lined to keep out the light in the early morning. Curtains are not just for windows; they can also be made to hang on a bedframe, or across a door opening or screen.*

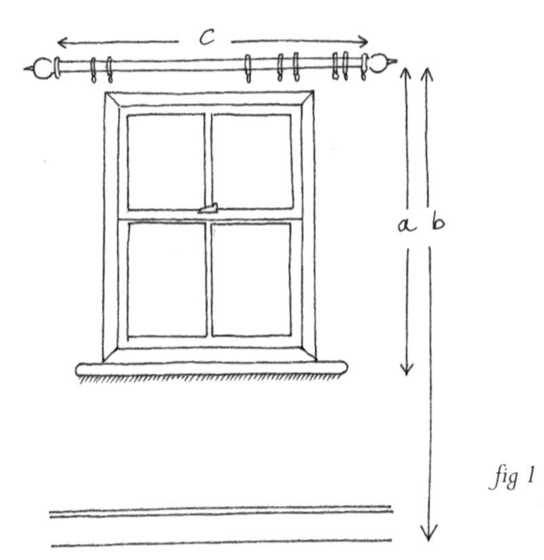


*fig 1*

### *tracks & poles*

The type of fitting – track, rod or pole – will influence the look of the finished curtain. Make sure it is at least 20cm longer than the width of the window so the curtains can clear the frame when they are drawn back.

Decorative poles, which are supported on brackets above the window, come in many styles: wrought iron with curled ends, wood with turned finials or shiny brass. Curtains can be hung directly on the pole with ties or loops, or using hooks attached to large rings that are threaded on to the pole.

Curtain tracks can be fixed to the wall or ceiling above the window and are attached at several points along their length to give adequate support. They usually lie near the wall, but deeper fittings are available to allow space for a blind to be fitted behind the curtains. An overlap arm in the centre will ensure that the curtains pull together neatly, and a track with a pull-cord system for heavyweight curtains will prevent soiling caused when they are drawn by hand.

### *measuring (fig 1)*

The fitting should be in place before you measure. Decide how long you want the curtains to be: above or below the windowsill, skimming or touching the floor, or somewhere in between. Then choose the heading. This will affect the fullness – a gathered, sheer fabric will require more widths than a lined panel, and a large-scale pattern may look more effective if it hangs flat.

### *calculating fabric amounts*

This may seem complicated, but the rules are straightforward. Reputable fabric suppliers usually have experienced staff who can help you work out how much fabric you need.

### *length*

The basic length is the distance between the fitting and the bottom of the curtain (a or b). To this are added the allowances for the heading and hem. If you are using patterned fabric, allow extra so the design lines up across the seams and both curtains in a pair will match. Measure the height of the repeat and add this measurement to each length.

### *width*

A curtain for a tall window will need to be fuller than one for a small window so the fabric can hang in proper folds. Multiply the length of the track (c) by the fullness needed for the chosen heading (see headings p.150). Divide this figure by the fabric width: most fabrics are a standard 120cm wide, but check first. This gives the measurement for a single curtain; divide by two to find the number of widths for a pair.

Multiply the curtain length by the number of widths to find the total amount.

The measurement for lining is the same as for the main fabric, but need not include any allowance made for pattern repeats or headers.

### *cutting out & joining*

All cut edges must be straight so that the curtains will hang properly. Lay the fabric flat on a clean surface, measure the length accurately and use sharp, long-bladed shears to cut out. For plain fabrics cut carefully across the weave – it may help to pull out a single thread to achieve a straight line. Follow the pattern lines on printed fabrics, marking a chalk guideline with a ruler and set square if necessary. When making a pair of curtains, any half widths to be added should be sewn to the outside edge of the main pieces.

Always cut off the selvedges before joining fabric widths to remove any lettering and to prevent pulling. For lined curtains use a flat open seam; if they are to remain unlined, use a double seam which conceals the raw edges. Pin plain fabrics together with right sides facing and stitch along the seam line. Stripes and checks have to be matched up first. Patterned fabrics are more complicated as they must line up horizontally across the join (see p.143). When cutting the lengths, ensure that the pattern starts at the same point at the top of each drop.

## unlined curtains

An unlined curtain is simply a rectangular piece of fabric which has been hemmed and mitred around three sides, then finished along the top edge with a heading.

### *measuring & cutting out* *(see fig 1)*

Calculate the amount of fabric (see left). Add 12cm to the finished width for side turnings, and 16cm to the length for the hem, plus the heading allowance.

### *making up*

**1** With right sides together, join the widths of fabric with a french or flat fell seam (see p.139). Press under a 3cm double hem along each side and an 8cm double hem on the lower edge.

### *mitring the corner*

**2** Mark three points with pins; one at the corner, one on the inside edge of the side turning where it meets the hem, and the corresponding point on the hem *(fig 2)*. Unfold all the creases, then refold so there is a single turning along both edges. Fold the corner inwards so that all three points line up *(fig 3)* and refold the side and hem to form a mitre. Insert a curtain weight if required, then slip stitch the two sides together *(fig 4)*, from the corner to the inner edge.

**3** Hand or machine stitch the side and hem turnings. Press the heading allowance to the wrong side and finish with your chosen heading.

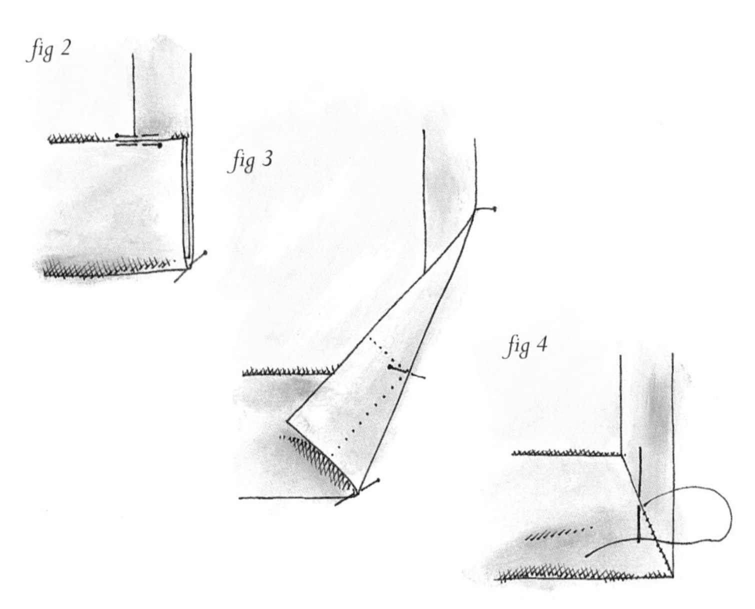


## lined curtains

A lining is needed when making curtains from thicker fabric. As well as improving the way the material drapes, it will provide insulation and prevent fading. If a curtain is to be seen from both the front and back – a bed hanging for example – sew the two sides together using the bagging technique to make it reversible (see p.143).

## loose-lined curtains

These curtains have a separate layer of fabric joined to the main fabric along the sides and the top edge, while the two hems remain separate.

### *measuring & cutting out* *(see fig 1)*

Add a seam allowance of 3cm to the finished width of the main fabric. Add a 10cm hem, and a heading allowance to the length. Cut the lining so that it is 10cm shorter and 6cm narrower than the main fabric.

### *making up*

**1** Join widths as required with a 1.5cm flat seam and press open. Fold both lining and main fabric in half along the top edge and mark the centre points.

**2** Matching the top and each side edge and with right sides together, join the lining to the main fabric along the sides, taking a 1.5cm seam allowance. Stitch to a point 15cm above the bottom edge of the lining. Turn right side out and line up the two centre points at the top. The side seams should now lie 2cm in from the outer edges. Press the seam allowance towards the centre.

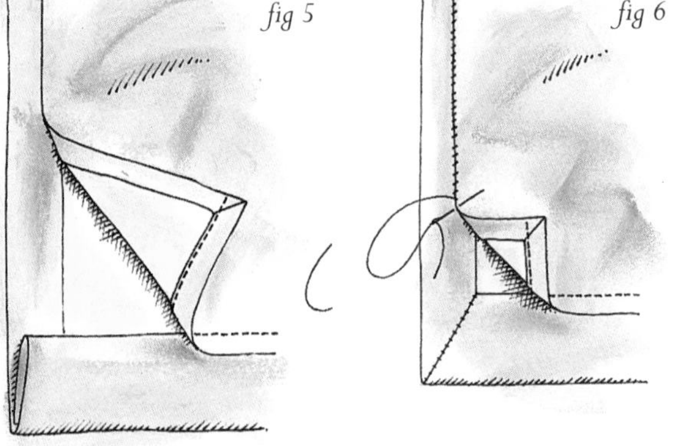


**3** Press under a 3cm double hem on the lining *(fig 5)*. Mark the corners and the points where the side and hem meet and mitre as in step 2 of the Unlined Curtain. Join the corners with slip stitch, then machine stitch the hem.

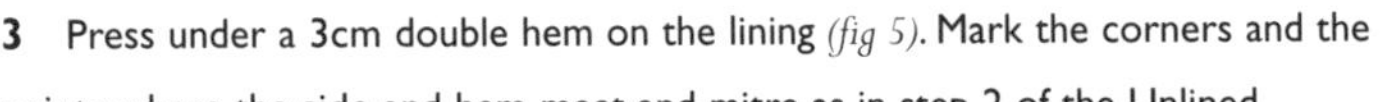

**4** Press under a 6cm double hem along the lower edge of the main curtain *(fig 5)*, then mitre the corners as before. Inserting a weight inside each improves the way the curtain hangs. Slip stitch the hem, then slip stitch the loose edges of the lining to the sides of the main curtain *(fig 6)*. Press the heading allowance to the wrong side and finish with your chosen heading.

## decorative headings

Curtain hooks and tracks are the traditional way of hanging curtains, but there are many quicker and less formal ways of attaching lined or unlined curtains to poles and rings using matching or contrasting ties, loops and tapes.

## cased heading

This heading slots over a curtain wire or café rod and is suitable for sheer fabrics, such as voile or muslin, and lightweight cottons.

*measuring & cutting out*

Allow up to three times the width of the finished curtain, depending on the weight of the fabric, and add 12cm to the finished length (more for a thick pole).

*making the heading*

Press under and pin a double 6cm hem along the top edge. Machine stitch a line 3cm from the top, then a second line 2.5cm further down to form the casing (*fig 7*). Slot the curtain on to the rod and fix in place. Use this method to cover a screen by making a second channel along the hem, with or without a frill.

*fig 7*

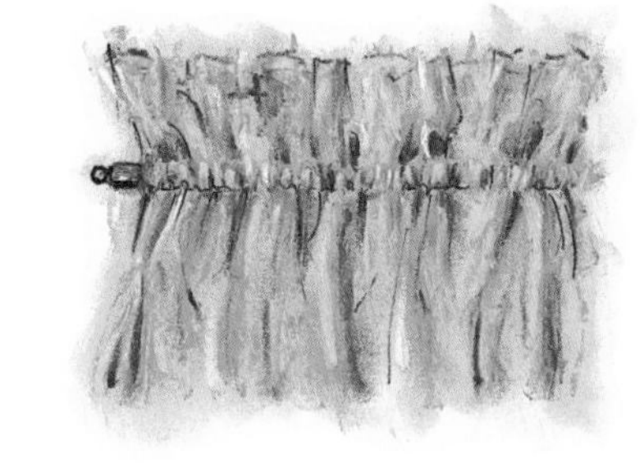

## tape ties on straight heading

Ties can be fixed to curtain rings or directly to a pole. The heading hem will turn towards the front of the curtain when it is hung.

*measuring & cutting out*

Use 40cm lengths of 1cm-wide cotton tape to make the ties. Divide the width of the curtain by the number of ties to make sure they are spaced evenly. They should be 12–15cm apart. Add a heading allowance of 6cm to the finished length.

*making the heading*

Press under a 3cm double hem along the top edge. Fold the first tie in half and slip the folded edge under the hem, 2cm in from the outside edge. Pin the hem in place and add the other ties at regular intervals. Top stitch the hem, securing the ties as you sew (*fig 8*).

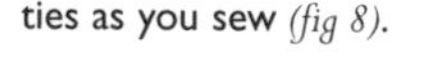

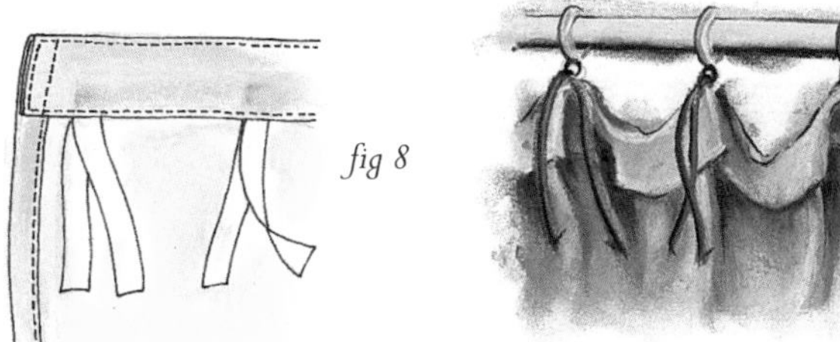

*fig 8*

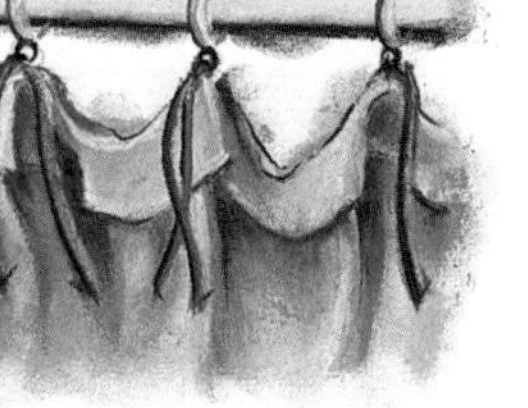

## fabric ties on pleated heading

This softly pleated heading works best on sheer fabrics.

*measuring & cutting out*

The pleats are 12–15cm apart (distance 'a' on *fig 9*). Work out how many pleats will fit along the finished width, and add 10cm for each. Add a 16cm heading allowance to the finished length.

*making the heading*

Press under and stitch an 8cm double hem along the top edge. With a pin, mark a point which lies ½a from the top left corner. Mark a second point 10cm (z) away. Bring the two points together and pin at the top edge to make a pleat. Repeat at regular intervals (distance a) along the top edge (*fig 9*). Catch each pleat into position with a few secure stitches. Make a 2 x 25cm narrow fabric tie (see p.144) for each pleat. Fold in half and stitch in place.

*fig 9*

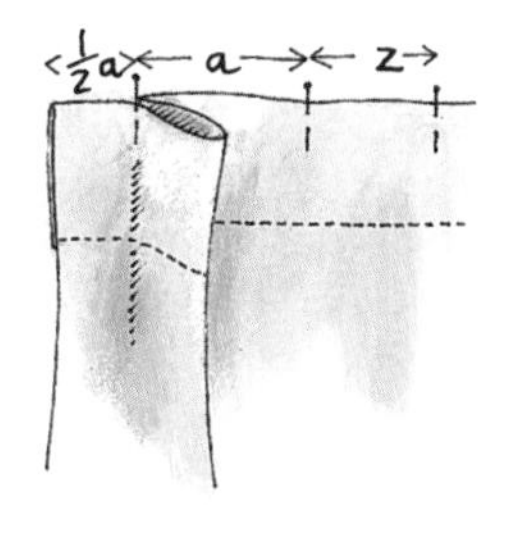


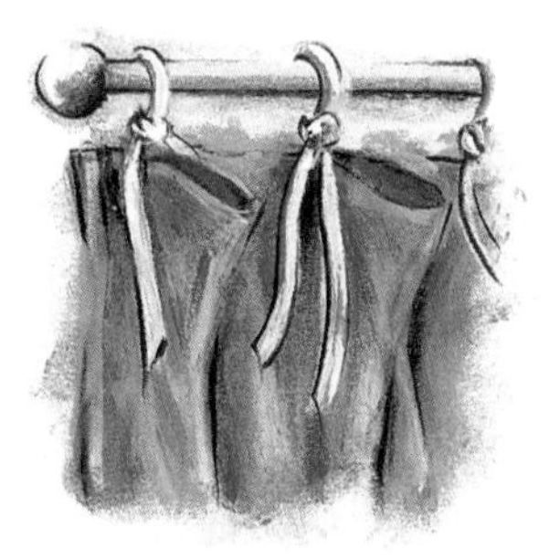

## buttoned loops

These can be used to fasten curtains to a pole or to a fixed structure such as a bedframe.

*measuring & cutting out*

Work out the spacing as for the tape ties above. Depending on the thickness of the fabric and the size of the pole or frame, the finished loops should be about 3cm wide and 12cm long. Add a 4cm heading allowance to the finished length. For each loop, cut a strip of fabric twice the finished length plus 5cm by twice the finished width plus 3cm.

*fig 10*

*making up the loops*

With wrong sides facing, stitch the long edges together, taking a 1.5cm seam allowance. Press the seam open so it lies along the centre and stitch along the top of the tube, 1cm in from the edge (*fig 10*). Clip the corners, turn right side out and press. Make a buttonhole parallel to the closed edge on each loop.

*making the heading*

Press a 2cm double hem to the wrong side along the top edge. With the seamed side of the loops upwards, slip the first loop under

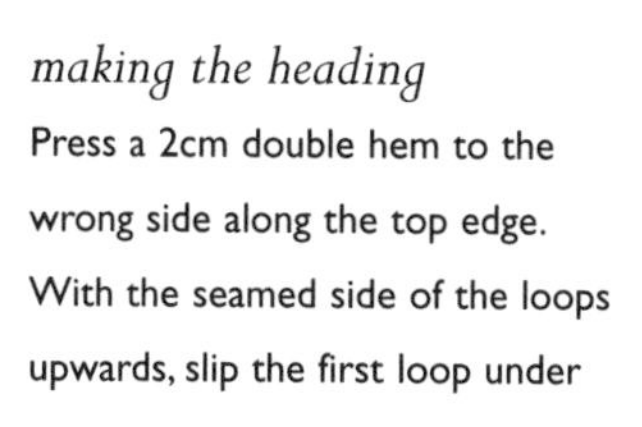

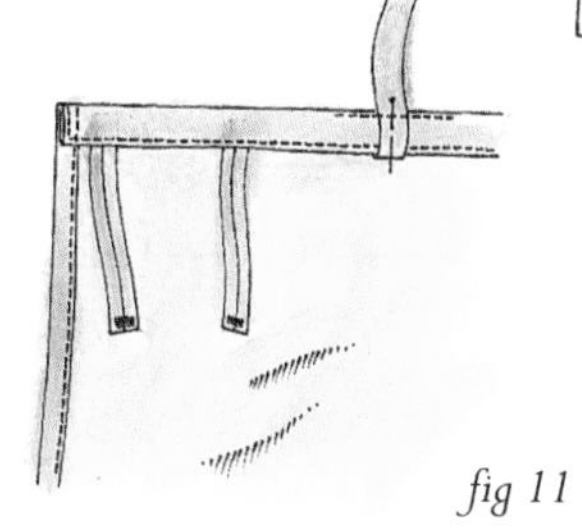

*fig 11*

the fold and pin. Pin the other loops at regular intervals, then stitch the hem down. Turn the loops upwards and pin *(fig 11)*, then top stitch along the upper edge to hold them upright. Sew a button to the base of each loop on the right side.

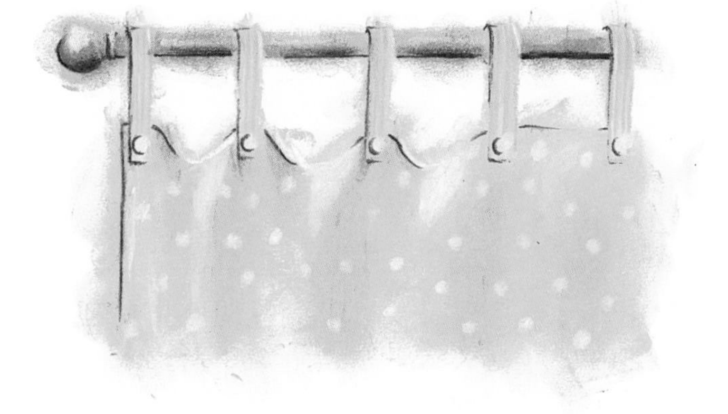

## heading tapes

Heading tape is used both to gather a curtain and as a support for the hooks which attach the drapes to the track or to the rings on a pole. It comes in various weights and has continuous thick threads woven through it which can be pulled up to give the curtain its fullness, or left flat. Standard 3cm tape is used for finer fabrics and you should allow 1½ to 2 times the width of the finished curtain. Pencil tape, 7.5cm wide, gathers up into narrow pleats and is suitable for heavier lined curtains, which should be 2½ times the finished width. Always use metal hooks, which are stronger and last longer. Slot one hook into the loop nearest each edge of the curtain, then at 8cm intervals in between.

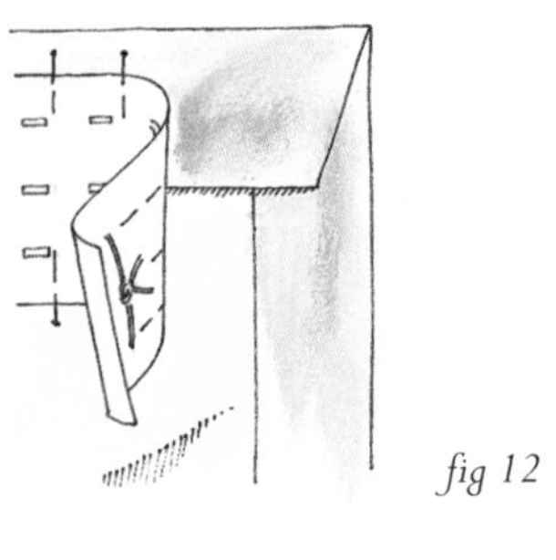

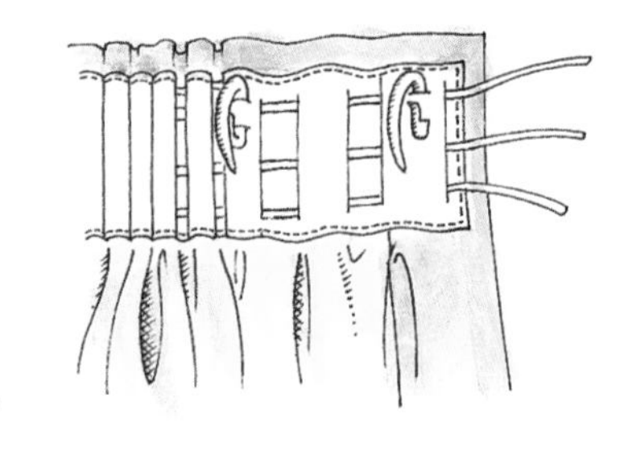

*fig 12*

### *sewing on the tape*

Leave a heading allowance of 3cm at the top edge, and press to the wrong side. Press the corners under at a slight angle. Cut the tape to the same measurement as the finished width of the curtain. At one end, knot the cords firmly together on the wrong side and trim. Turn under 1cm at each end and pin the tape along the top edge, 1cm down from the fold *(fig 12)*. Stitch in place. Pull up the gathering threads and knot to secure the heading. Do not cut the loose ends – wrap them around a small piece of card and conceal it behind the heading when the curtains are hung.

## gathered heading

A ruffled edge can be created simply by stitching the tape further down from the top of the curtain.

### *measuring & cutting out*

Allow 2½ times the finished width of the curtain and add a heading allowance of twice the desired depth of the frill plus 2cm to the finished length.

### *making the heading*

Fold the allowance in half, turning the corners under at a slight angle, and stitch the tape so that it covers the lower edge *(fig 13)*.

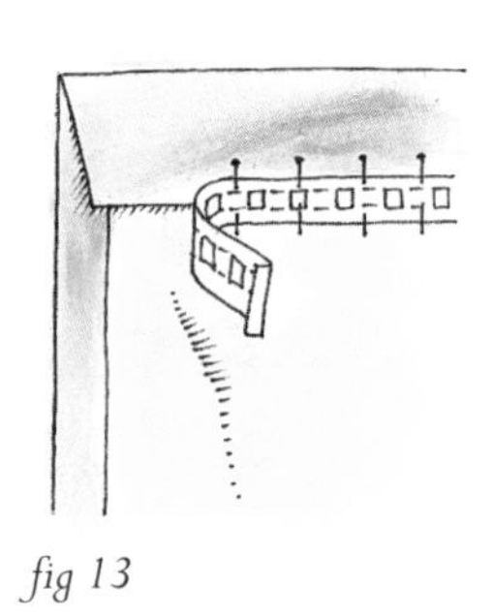

*fig 13*

## buttoned pleats

These hand-stitched box pleats are held in place on the reverse side by flat header tape.

### *measuring & cutting out*

The pleats are made at approximately 15cm intervals (distance 'a' below). Work out how many will fit along the finished width of your curtain and add 12cm of fabric for each pleat.

### *making the heading*

Fold and pin a series of 12cm box pleats (see p.143), leaving distance 'a' between them, and tack in place 12cm from the top edge. Hand or machine stitch a length of 3cm heading tape over the tacking line, ensuring that it is parallel to the top *(fig 14)*. Finish by sewing a button to the front of each pleat. This heading works well on heavyweight unlined fabrics, such as tweed; unravel the threads 2cm along each edge to make a narrow fringe.

*fig 14*

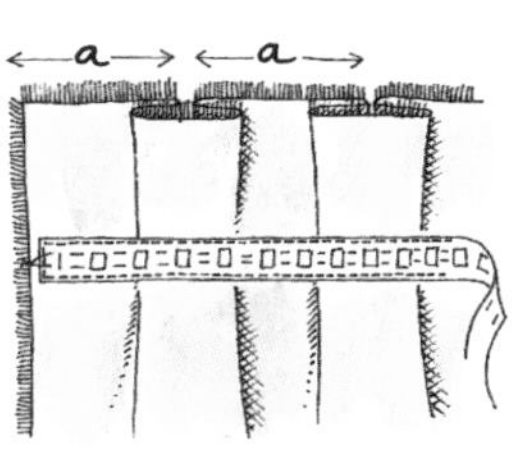


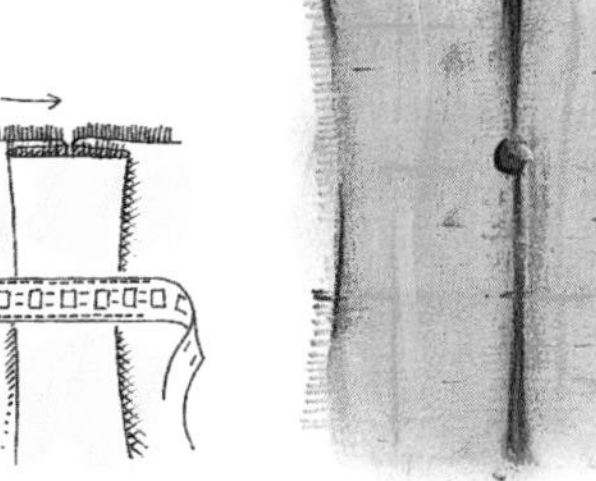

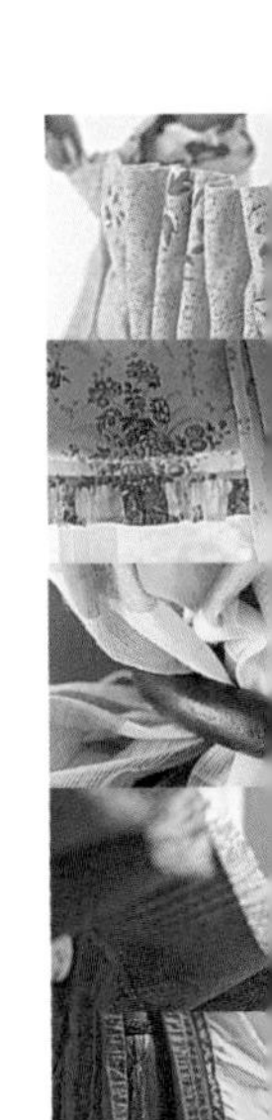

**fall-back frill**

A contrasting piece of fabric sewn along the top of a curtain makes an attractive frilled heading.

*measuring & cutting out*

Decide how deep the frill should be and cut a strip of fabric twice this width plus 3cm, and the same length as the curtain width. Add a heading allowance of 2cm to the finished length of the curtain.

*making up*

Fold the frill piece with right sides together and seam the short ends, leaving a seam allowance of 1.5cm. Clip the corners, turn right side out and press. Sew the header tape 2cm down from the top edge of the curtain. Pin the open edge of the frill to the wrong side of the curtain top *(fig 15)* and stitch the two together with a 1.5cm seam. Turn the frill over to the right side and press the top edge before drawing up the header tape.

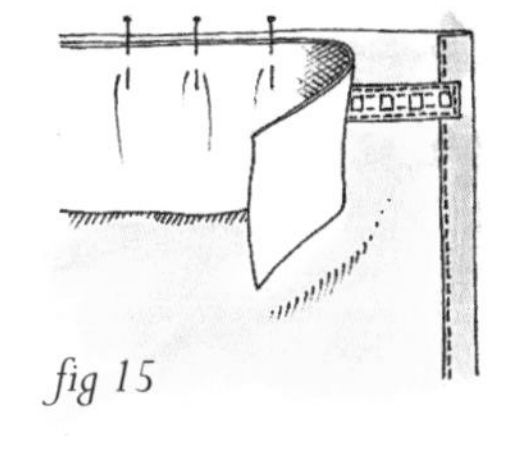

*fig 15*

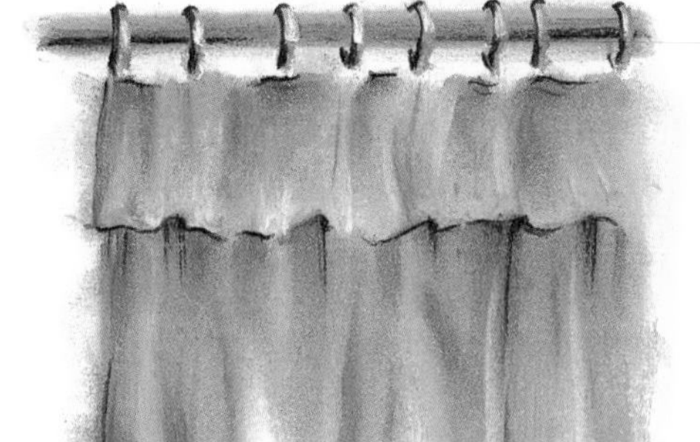

# *pelmets & swags*

*Pelmets and swags provide a decorative frame for the top of a window, and can conceal the track or batten below. Depending on how they are sited, they can also give the illusion that a window is taller or wider than it is. Straight or gathered box pelmets are attached with velcro to a wooden shelf above the window. A straight pelmet can be made from a single strip of fabric, or given a decorative chevron edging.*

*fig 1*

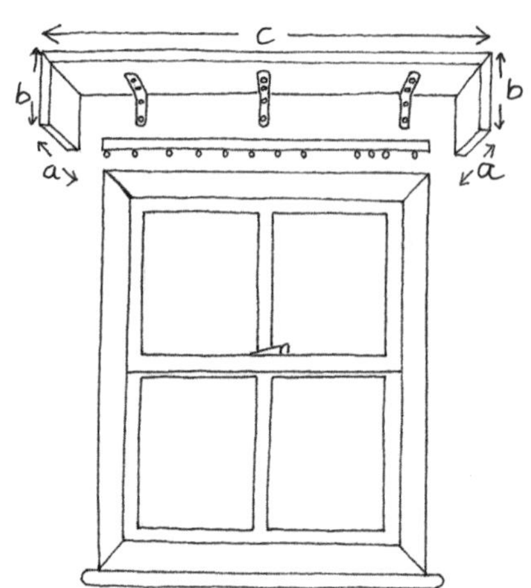


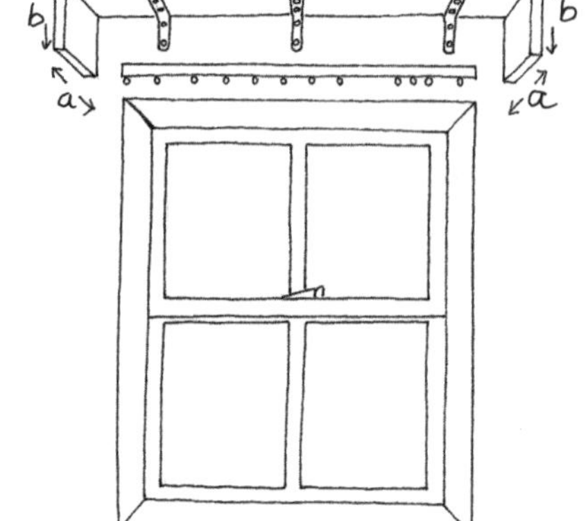

*fig 2*

## gathered box pelmet

This pelmet is in effect a short version of the curtains and is usually made to match. Curtain weights can be sewn inside the bottom corners so that it hangs close to the wall. For a lightweight fabric which does not need to be lined, allow an extra half width. Double-hem the sides and lower edge, then follow the method from step 2.

*making the shelf (fig 1)*

Cut the shelf from 2cm plywood and fix to the wall with three or four angle brackets. It should be long enough to give 8cm clearance at each end of the track (c) and can be 12–20cm wide (a), depending on the size of the window. The side panels are screwed to each end of the board. They help the pelmet hang straight and keep it clear of the curtains. Cut a strip of velcro equal to length 2a + c and staple it around the top edge of the shelf *(fig 2)*.

*materials*

Main fabric, lining fabric, header tape (length = length of finished valance), 3cm-wide velcro strip equal to length of finished pelmet, wooden pelmet shelf

*measuring & cutting out*

Cut main fabric and lining alike: length = 2 x length of finished pelmet, width = required depth, plus 1.5cm seam allowance all round

*making up*

**1** Pin the lining and main fabric together with right sides together and stitch around the sides and lower edge. Clip the corners, turn right side out and press.

**2** Press the seam allowance along the top edge to the wrong side and sew the header tape 1cm down from the folded edge. Draw it up so that the valance fits exactly around the shelf and knot the cords.

**3** Hand stitch the hooked side of the velcro over the header tape and fix the pelmet in place.

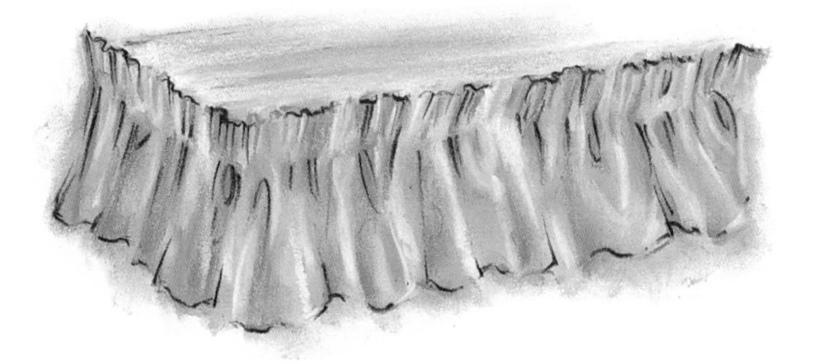

## ruffled pelmet

This simplest of all pelmets is fixed directly to the wall. The jaunty frill created by the cased heading contrasts particularly well with the straight lines of a swedish blind.

### *materials*

Main fabric, 3cm-diameter wooden pole, 2 large screws and rawlplugs, drill and screwdriver

### *measuring & cutting out*

Cut one rectangle: width = 3 x length of pole, length = finished length (from top of frill) + 12cm

### *making up*

**1** Make a 1cm double hem along the two sides and the lower edge. Press under a 1cm allowance along the upper edge, then fold under a further 10cm and press. Pin the fold down and stitch a line 4cm down from the top edge. Stitch a second line to hold the folded edge down and to form the cased heading for the pole.

*fig 3* *fig 4*

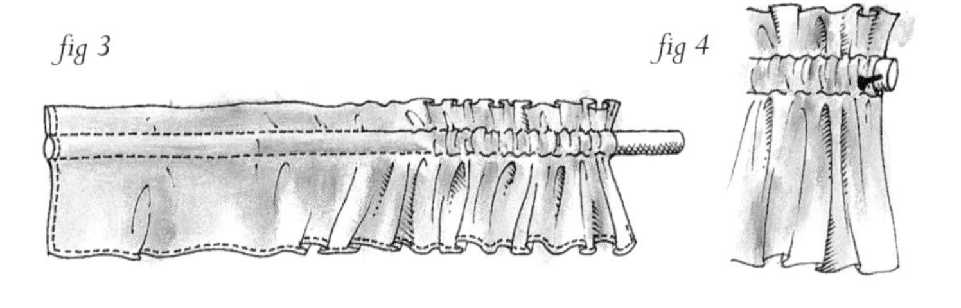

**2** Drill a hole 1cm from each end of the pole and slide the pelmet into place on the pole *(fig 3)*. Mark the position on the wall, drill two holes and fit rawlplugs. Ease back the casing at either end and screw the pelmet to the wall *(fig 4)*. Pull the loose fabric back to cover the ends of the pole, securing with a few stitches.

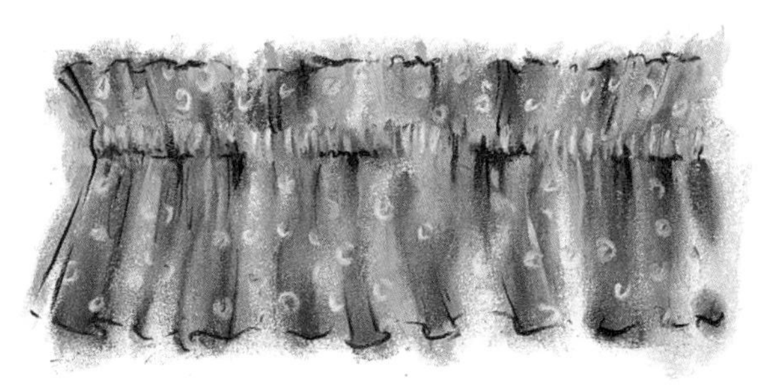

## swedish swags

This ingenious method of making swags involves the minimum of sewing, but produces a dramatic effect very quickly. They can be made with or without tails.

### *materials*

Main fabric, 2 small elastic bands, 2 large cup hooks

### *measuring & cutting out (figs 5 & 6)*

– for a swag with tails

Cut one rectangle: length = 2a + b + 2c, width = c, + 2cm hem allowance all round

– for a swag without tails

Cut one rectangle: length = 2c + b, width = c, + 2cm hem allowance all round

*fig 5*

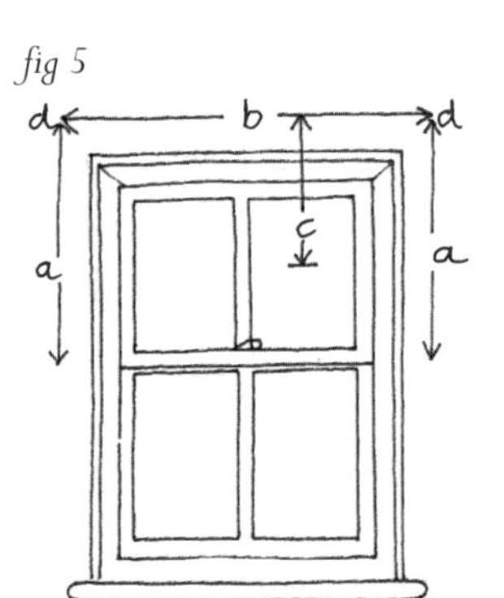


*fig 6*

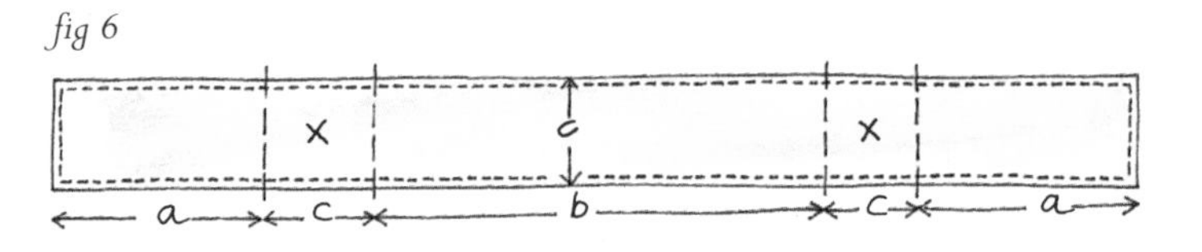


### *making up*

**1** Fix the two hooks into the wall above the window at points 'd' *(fig 5)*.

**2** Make a 1cm double hem around all four sides of the fabric. Mark the two points 'x' *(fig 6)* as shown. With one hand, pick up the fabric at 'x' and bunch it into a point with the other hand *(fig 7)*. Still holding it firmly, slip an elastic band over the point. Do the same at the other end.

**3** Slip the bunches over the hooks so that the tails hang down, and adjust so that the swag falls into regular folds.

*fig 7*

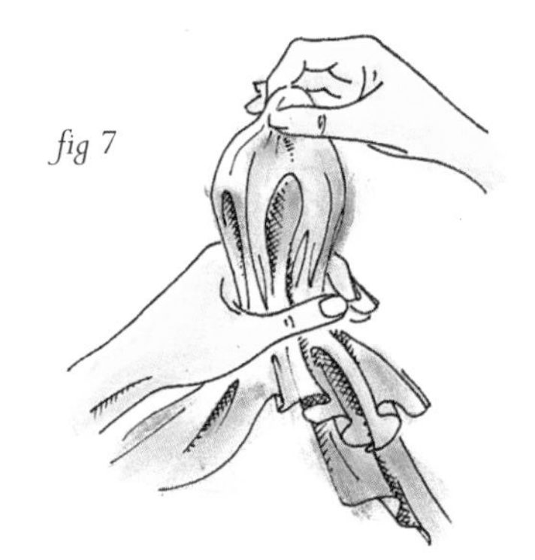

# lampshades

*There is a great art to making traditional lampshades, but equally effective results can be achieved quickly and simply by dressing up a ready-made shade. Always be sure to use the lightbulb wattage specified for the shade.*

*fig 1*

## handkerchief point lampshade

*materials*

Lampshade, main fabric, spray adhesive

*measuring & cutting out (fig 1)*

Shade cover: cut a bias strip, width = ½b + 5cm, length = c + 2cm

Top cover: cut a square, sides = 2b + d + 7cm. Mark and cut out a circle from the centre of the square, diameter = d - 2cm

Binding: cut a bias strip, width = 7cm, length = a + 2c

*making up*

**1** With right sides facing, join the short ends of the shade cover with a 1cm flat seam and press open. Spray a light coat of adhesive on to the lower half of the lampshade and slip the shade cover over *(fig 2)*. Smooth the fabric in place. Spray the inside edge of the lampshade and turn under the surplus fabric.

**2** Make a 1cm double hem around the four sides of the top cover. Join the short ends of the binding with right sides facing and press open.

**3** With right sides together, pin the binding around the edge of the cut-out circle in the top cover. Clip into the curves so they fit neatly, and stitch together 1cm from the edge *(fig 3)*. Press the seam allowance towards the centre. Spray adhesive to the top inside edge of the shade and stick the lower edge of the binding in place, so the handkerchief drapes over the shade.

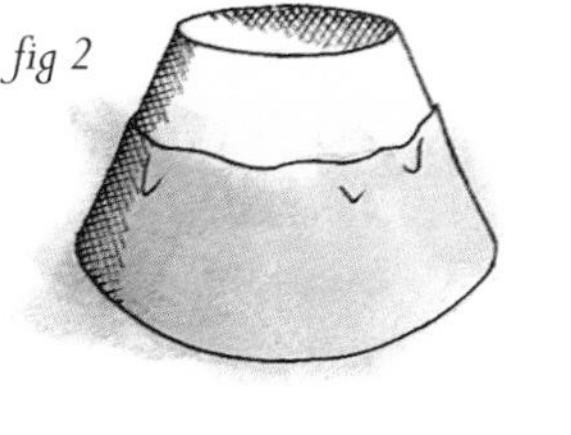

*fig 2*

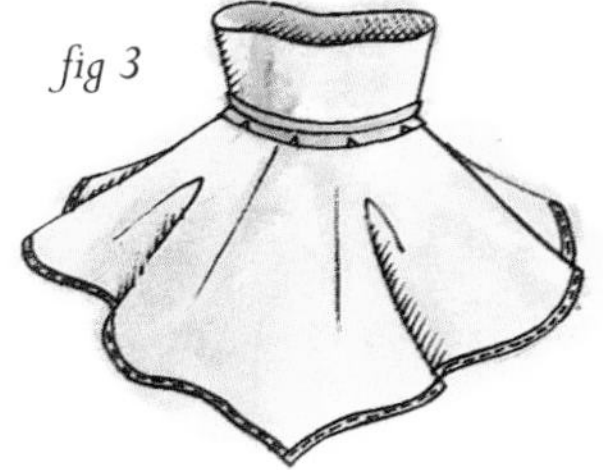

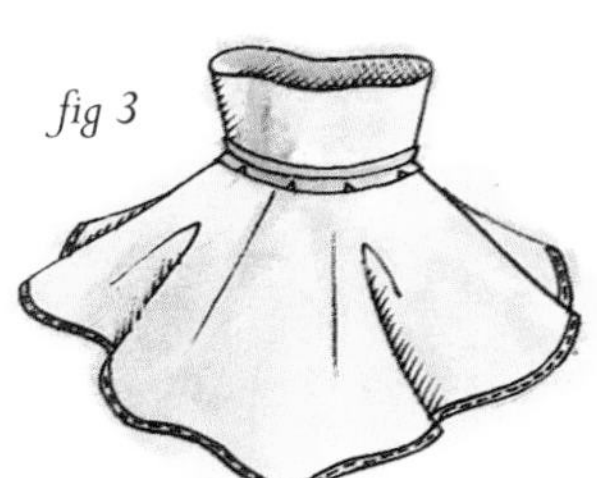

*fig 3*

## frilled lampshade

*materials*

Lampshade, main fabric, fabric glue

*measuring & cutting out (fig 1)*

Shade: width = b + 3cm, length = c + 5cm

Frill: width = 6cm, length = 2c

Binding: width = 5cm, length = a + 2cm

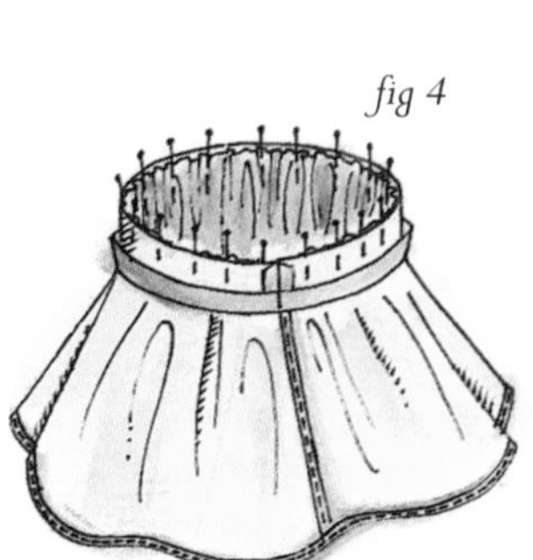

*fig 4*

*making up*

**1** Join the short edges of the binding with a 1cm flat seam. Press open, then press in half lengthways. Press under 1cm around one edge.

**2** Join the short edges of the shade with a french seam and double hem the lower edge. Sew a gathering thread 1cm from the top and draw up to fit the binding.

**3** With right sides facing, pin and stitch the gathers to the raw edge of the binding, distributing them evenly *(fig 4)*. Fold the binding along the pressed line and slip stitch to the wrong side.

**4** Join the frill into a loop and make a narrow double hem along each edge. Gather down the centre and draw up to fit around the hem of the shade. Pin, then stitch in place over the gathering line. Remove the gathering thread. Glue top and bottom edges to the card shade.

## gathered lampshade

*materials*

Lampshade, main fabric, narrow curtain header tape (length = 1½c + 4cm), spray adhesive, fabric glue

*measuring & cutting out (fig 1)*

Shade cover: cut a bias strip, width = ½b + 6cm, length = c + 2cm

Top cover: width = b + 5cm, length = 1½c + 2cm

*fig 5*

*making up*

**1** Cover the shade as for step 1 of the Handkerchief Point Shade.

**2** With right sides together, join the two short ends of the top cover. Make a narrow double hem along the lower edge. Press under 2cm along the top edge. Sew header tape to the wrong side, 1cm from the fold *(fig 5)*. Draw up to fit the shade, and secure.

**3** Glue the top cover in place at the top edge. Gather parts of the lower edge and stab stitch to the shade at various points for a random, ruched effect.

# *pillowcases*

*Pillowcases must be easy to put on and take off and should be made from fabric such as cotton sheeting or linen that will stand up to frequent laundering. Purely decorative pillowcases can be made out of light- to medium-weight fabrics of any description. The 'housewife' cover has an inner flap to hold the pillow in place, and more decorative versions can be made with scallops, frills or contrast edges.*

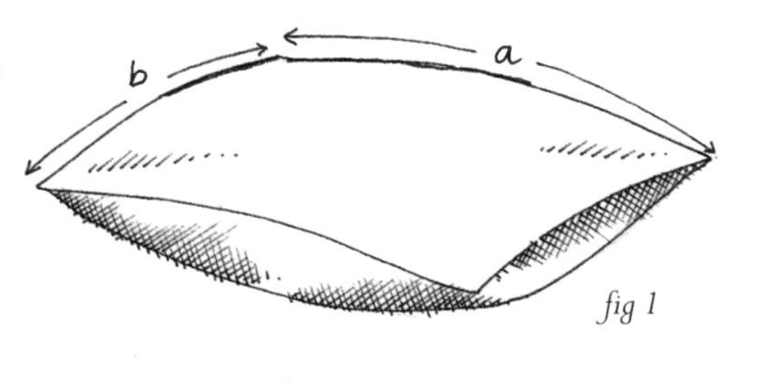


*fig 1*

## basic housewife

*materials*

Main fabric

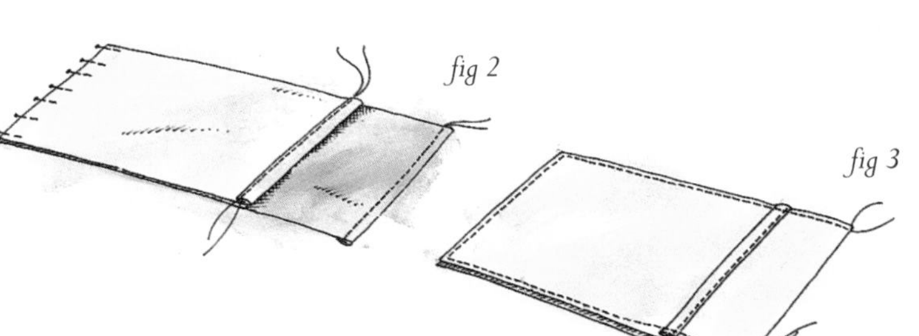

*fig 2*

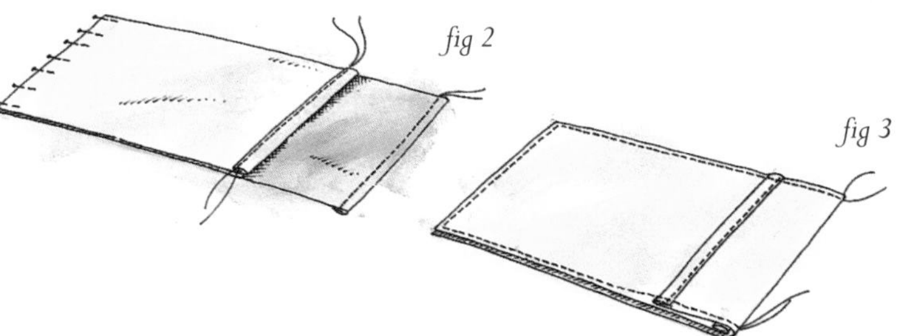

*fig 3*

*measuring & cutting out (fig 1)*

Front: cut one rectangle, length = a + 20cm, width = b, + 1.5cm all round

Back: cut one rectangle, length = a, width = b, + 1.5cm all round

*making up*

**1** Make a narrow double hem at one short end of both pieces. With right sides facing, pin them together along the unhemmed ends *(fig 2)*.

**2** Fold the flap over so that it lies across the hemmed end of the back piece and pin the two sides together. Stitch around the three unhemmed edges, leaving a 1.5cm seam allowance *(fig 3)*.

**3** Trim the seam allowance and zigzag the edges to make the seam more durable. Turn right side out, ease out the corners, and press.

## decorative housewife

The contrasting flap lies across the front of the pillowcase and can be trimmed with buttons or a lace edging.

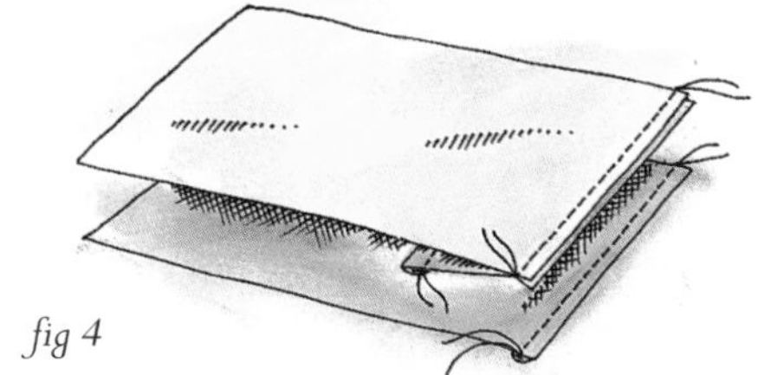

*fig 4*

*measuring & cutting out (fig 1)*

Front and back: cut two rectangles, length = a, width = b, + 1.5cm all round

Flap: cut one rectangle, length = 23cm, width = b, + 1.5cm all round

*making up*

**1** Make a double hem along one short edge of the front piece. Make a narrow double hem along one long edge of the flap.

**2** With right sides facing, pin the flap to one short edge of the back and stitch along the seam allowance. With right sides together, pin, then stitch the sides and lower edge to the front, so that the flap is sandwiched between the two main pieces *(fig 4)*. Finish as for step 3 above.

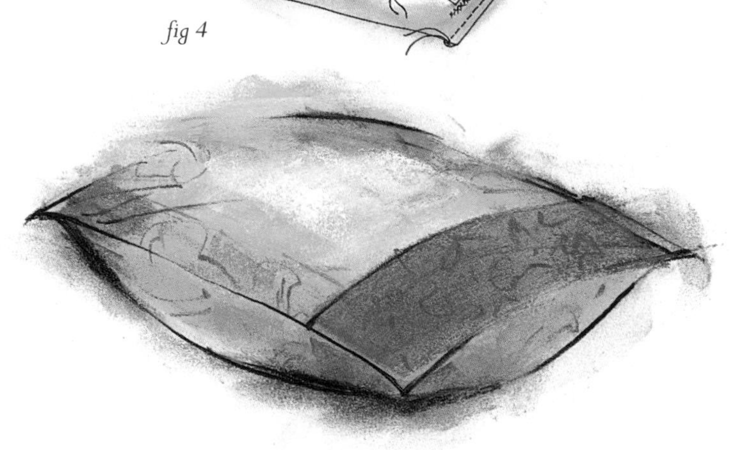

## oxford pillowcase

This cover has an integral flap like the Basic Housewife and the border is defined by a round of stitching within the outer edge.

### *materials*

Main fabric, ruler, dressmaker's pen or chalk pencil

### *measuring & cutting out* *(see fig 1)*

Front: cut one rectangle, length = a + 30cm, width = b, + 6.5cm all round

Back: cut one rectangle, length = a + 6.5cm, width = b + 13cm

### *making up*

**1** Sew a narrow double hem at one short end of each piece. With right sides facing, pin the front and back along the unhemmed short edges *(see fig 2)*.

**2** Make the flap by folding over the surplus fabric from the front, 6cm from the hemmed edge of the back piece. Pin the two sides together *(fig 5)*. Stitch around the three unhemmed edges, leaving a 1.5cm seam allowance.

**3** Turn right side out, ease out the corners, and press. On the right side mark a rectangle 5cm in from the edge, using a dressmaker's pen or chalk pencil. Stitch over this line to form the border *(fig 6)*, but be careful not to catch the open end in the stitching.

## scalloped-edge pillowcase

This attractive pillowcase may look complicated to make, but it is simply a variation on the Oxford Pillowcase. To make larger scallops, add extra fabric to the 5cm margin. A cushion cover can be made in the same way. Cut a square of paper to the finished size and draw on the scallops. Use this as a template for the front and make a vent opening at the back (see p.159). Omit the inner stitch line and make a fibre-filled pad the same shape, to fit inside.

### *materials*

As for the Oxford Pillowcase, plus large sheet of paper, pair of compasses

### *making up*

**1** Make up the pillowcase as for steps 1 and 2 above.

**2** Cut a piece of paper the same size as the pillow, plus 5cm all round. Draw a line 5cm in from each edge and using a pair of compasses, draw a series of semi-circles within this border *(fig 7)*.

**3** Pin the paper pattern to the pillowcase and draw around it. Remove and place a pin across each scallop to keep the two layers together, and stitch over the line *(fig 8)*. Clip the curves, trim the seam allowances, turn right side out and press. On the right side mark a rectangle 5cm in from the edge. Stitch over this line to form the border *(fig 9)*.

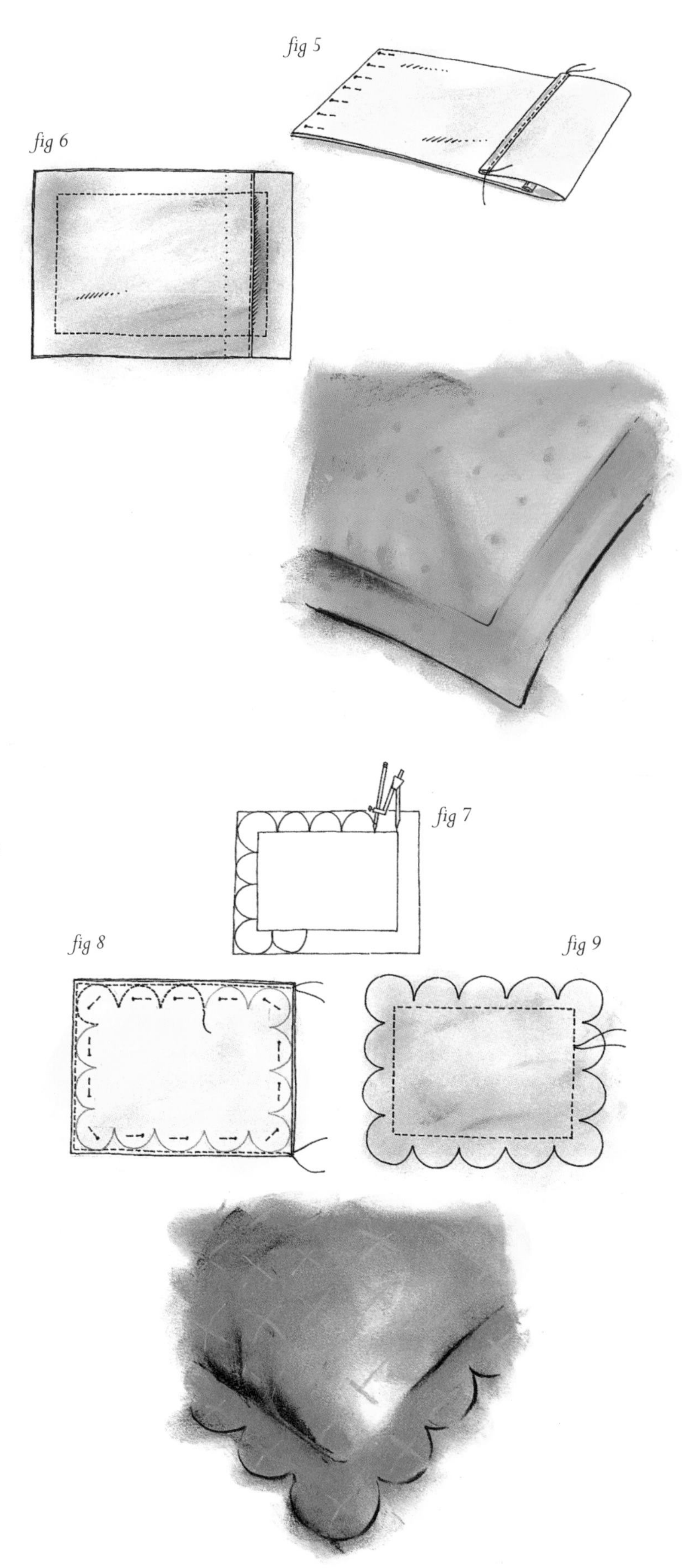

## pillowcase with ruffled edge

A frilled edge adds an extravagant touch to a plain pillowcase. You can use the same method to make a border from gathered broderie anglaise.

### *materials*

Main fabric, frill fabric

### *measuring & cutting out* (*see fig 1*)

Front: cut two rectangles, length = a, width = b, + 1.5cm all round

Flap: cut one rectangle, length = 20cm, width = b, + 1.5cm all round

Frill: cut one strip, length = 4 x a + b, + 5cm all round, width = 20cm

### *making up*

**1** Make up the frill and attach it to the front piece, ensuring that the fullness is distributed evenly (*fig 10*).

**2** Sew a 2.5cm double hem along one short edge of the back piece and, with right sides facing, pin the other three sides to the front piece (*fig 11*).

**3** Neaten one long edge of the flap with a narrow hem. With the right side facing down, pin the unhemmed edges to the open end of the pillowcase (*fig 12*). Sew around all four sides 1.5cm from the edge. Trim and zigzag the seam allowances. Turn right side out and press.

*fig 10*

*fig 11*

*fig 12*

## buttoned pillowcase

This open-ended case resembles a large rectangular cushion cover in construction and buttons together along the band. This extra border piece hangs over the edge of the pillow, so that it is not uncomfortable to sleep on.

### *materials*

Main fabric, band fabric, buttons

### *measuring & cutting out* (*see fig 1*)

Main piece: cut one rectangle, width = a, length = 2 x b, + 3cm all round

Band: cut one strip, width = 30cm, length + 2 x b, + 3cm all round

### *making up*

**1** Press the band in half lengthways, with wrong sides together. Stitch a 1cm single hem along one long edge. With right sides facing, pin the band to one side of the main piece (*fig 13*). Stitch, leaving a 1.5cm seam allowance.

**2** Press the seam towards the band, then fold in half widthways. Pin the two raw edges and stitch along the seam allowance (*fig 14*). Press open the seam on the band. Trim the surplus fabric on the main cover and zigzag the edge.

**3** Fold the hemmed edge of the band to the wrong side along the crease, to conceal the seam below. Pin in place (*fig 15*). Turn the cover right side out and stitch the band just inside the seam. You can also topstitch the open edge.

**4** Mark the button positions on the band and make machine buttonholes on the top side of the front band. Sew the buttons in place (*fig 16*).

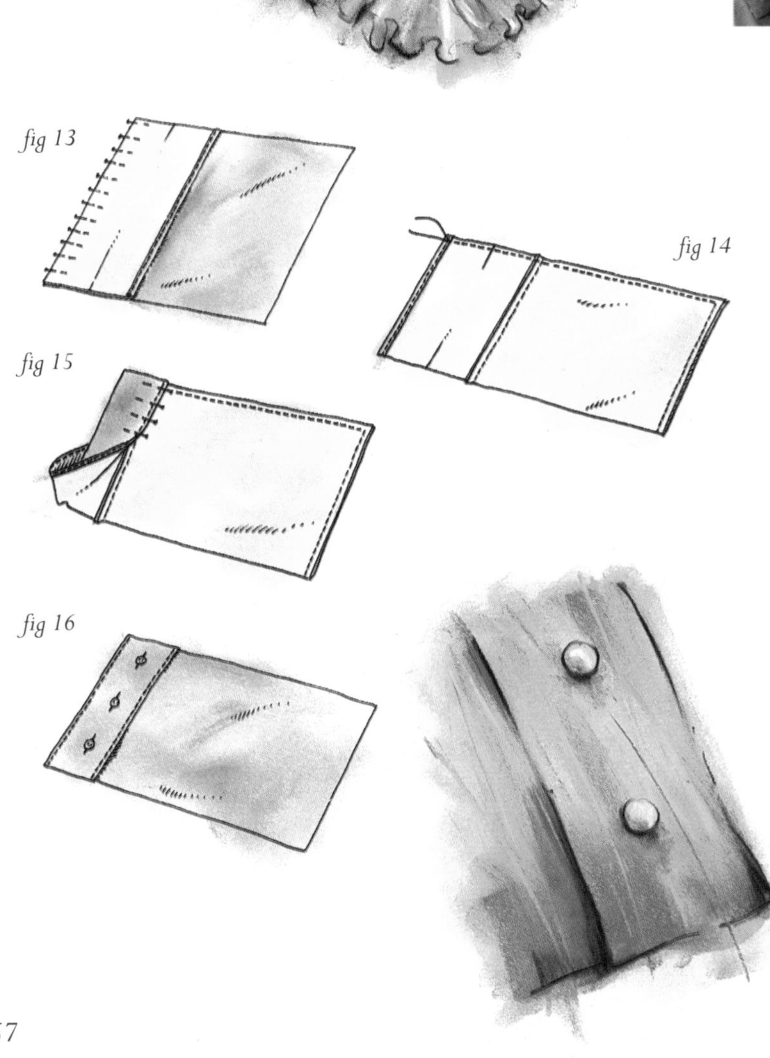

*fig 13*

*fig 14*

*fig 15*

*fig 16*

# cushions

*Cushions may be sumptuous, sophisticated or informal – the variations of shape, size, borders and trimmings are endless. This section introduces the basic elements – fastenings, fillings and edgings – that can be put together in any combination to make a highly individual cushion cover.*

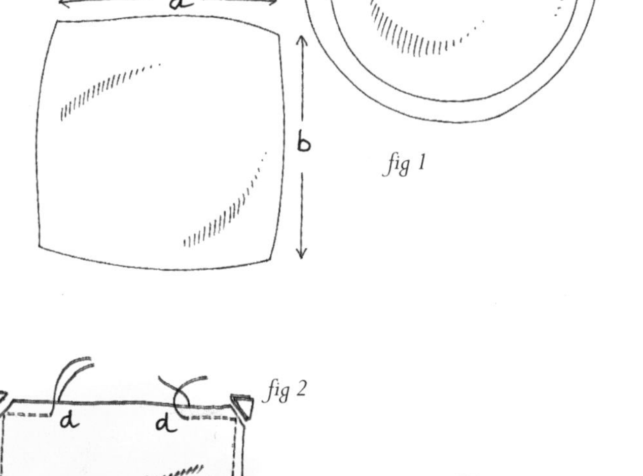


fig 1

fig 2

fig 3

## basic slip-stitched cover

The quickest way to close a cover is by hand, with a line of slip stitch. This gives an inconspicuous finish on all fabrics and is the neatest way to finish a piped cover, but the seam will have to be unpicked and resewn for cleaning.

*materials*

Main fabric, cushion pad

*measuring & cutting out (fig 1)*

Front and back: cut two alike, width = a, length = b, or circumference = c, plus 1.5cm all round

*making up*

**1** Pin, then stitch the two pieces together along three sides from 'd' to 'd' *(fig 2)*.

**2** Press the seam allowances along the open edge lightly to the wrong side, then clip the corners and turn the cover right side out.

**3** Insert the cushion pad, easing it into the four corners and slip stitch the opening neatly together with matching thread *(fig 3)*.

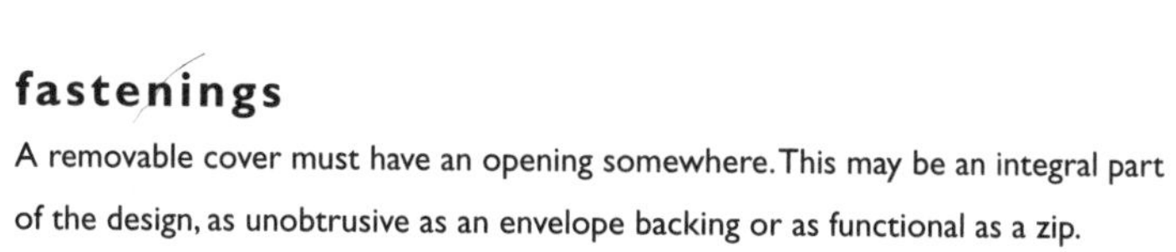

## fastenings

A removable cover must have an opening somewhere. This may be an integral part of the design, as unobtrusive as an envelope backing or as functional as a zip.

## open-ended cover

This slip-on cover looks particularly effective used over a contrasting plain cushion and kept in place with ties or bows.

*materials*

Main fabric, ruler

*measuring & cutting out (fig 1)*

Front and back: cut two rectangles, width = a + 11.5cm, length = b + 1.5cm

*making up*

**1** Sew a narrow double hem along one short end of each piece. With right sides facing, pin and stitch around the other three sides, 1.5cm in from the edge *(fig 4)*.

fig 4

fig 5

**2** Turn 10cm to the wrong side around the open edge. Check with a ruler that it is level, and press. Pin *(fig 5)*, then stitch in place close to the edge of the hem.

## envelope or vent back

The cushion back is made from two overlapping pieces and the cushion pad is slipped between them. This finish can be used on a cushion of any shape, and can be made more decorative by adding ties or buttons before making up.

### *measuring & cutting out* *(see fig 1)*

For a square cushion:

Front: cut one square, width = a, length = b, + 1.5cm all round

Back: cut two rectangles, width = ½a + 10cm, length = b, + 1.5cm all round

For a round cushion:

Front: cut one circle, diameter = c + 1.5cm all round

Back: cut two part circles. To make the template, fold the paper pattern for the front piece in half along the diameter and unfold. Draw a line 11.5cm from the fold and cut along this line

### *making up*

**1** Make a narrow double hem along one long edge of each rectangular back piece or along each straight edge for a round cushion.

**2** Lay the front piece the right way up, then place one back piece right side down along the right-hand side, matching the outside edge. Place the second piece to the left so that the hemmed edges overlap *(fig 6)*. Pin and stitch around all sides, leaving a 1.5cm allowance. Clip corners or curves, turn right side out and press.

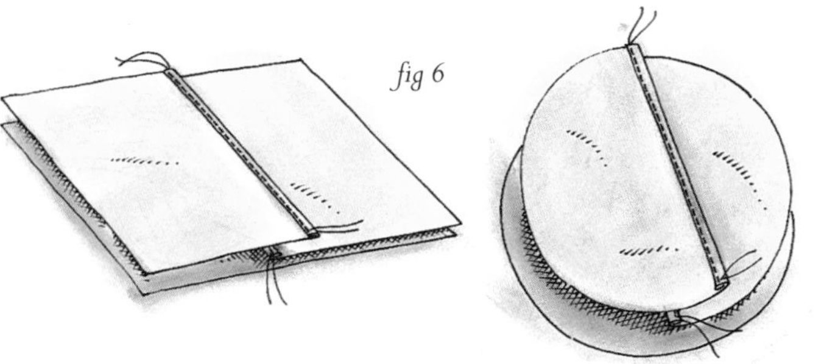

*fig 6*

## zips

A zip is the most usual way of fastening a cushion cover that will have a lot of use. It should be 6cm shorter than the side where it is attached – this may be along the length or across the width depending on the shape. Patterned fabrics should be matched on either side of the opening, and if the fabric has a large-scale repeat it is best to set the zip close to one side.

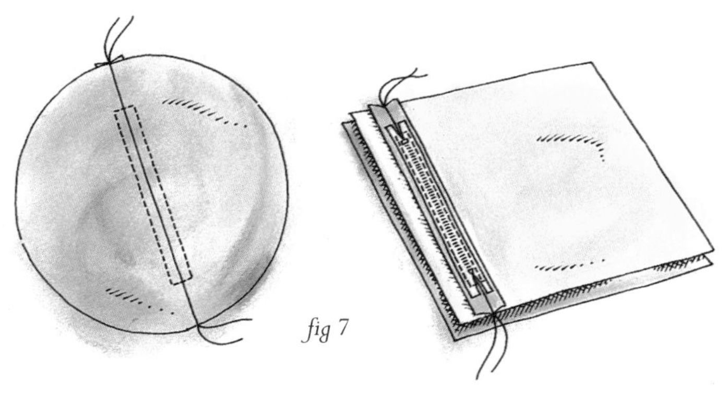

*fig 7*

There is a special technique for sewing a zip into a piped seam (see p.144), but for most square or rectangular cushions it can be placed at the centre back. For a round cushion, the zip should always lie across the centre back; it would distort the shape if sewn into the seam *(see fig 7)*.

### *measuring & cutting out* *(see fig 1)*

For a square or rectangular cushion:

Front: cut one piece, width = a, length = b, + 1.5cm all round

Back: cut two pieces, width = ½a + 7cm, length = b, + 1.5cm

For a round cushion:

Front: cut one circle, diameter = c + 3cm

Back: cut two semicircles, radius = ½c, + 1.5cm all round

### *making up*

**1** With right sides facing, pin and tack the two back sections along the seam line. Machine stitch a short seam at each end, leaving a central opening for the zip. Reverse the stitching at the start and finish of the stitch line to reinforce. Press open and insert the zip following the instructions on p. 144 (see *fig 1*).

**2** Leaving the zip partly open, pin the back to the front with right sides together and stitch all around the outside edge, leaving a seam allowance of 1.5cm. Clip the corners or the curves. Turn right side out and press, then insert the pad.

## fillings

Ready-made pads – square, round and bolster-shaped – are available in many sizes. They are stuffed with feathers, which are soft and long-lasting, or hypo-allergenic synthetic wadding, which has the advantage of being fully washable. You can, where necessary, make a specially shaped pad from calico and stuff it with fibrefill.

## edgings

There are many edgings that can be used to embellish a plain square or round cushion. Some, such as gathered or pleated frills, piping and some ready-made fringes, are sewn between the front and back pieces as the cover is being assembled, but others – cord and braid – are sewn by hand to the completed cover (see pp.141–3).

### piping

Piping cord can be covered in fabric that matches or contrasts with the main cover. Make a length equal to the perimeter plus 5cm, and tack in place on the right side of the front piece so that the join lies in the centre of one edge. Clip the corners for a square; for a circle clip into the seam allowance all round *(fig 8)*. With right sides facing, pin and stitch the back piece (or pieces) in position, using a zipper foot to sew close to the stitching.

*fig 8*

### frills

Cushion frills can have a hemmed or bound edge (see p.142), but the extra fabric in a reversible double frill gives the most effective finish. A wide frill measuring up to 10cm for a large cushion or 5cm for a smaller pad looks even more extravagant. For a full effect, allow twice the perimeter of the cushion pad, joining the fabric as necessary and pressing the seams flat. The same measurements and method are used for both square and round covers.

*making up*

**1** Pin the frill to the seam allowance on the front piece *(fig 9)*, following the technique on p.142 to ensure that the gathers are equally distributed. For a frilled and piped cushion, first apply the piping, then add the frill, remembering to use a zipper foot to sew close to the piping. Tack the frill along the seam line, using small stitches to keep it secure. Pin the gathers to the cushion front so that they do not get caught in the seam.

**2** Place the back piece face down on the front and pin, then tack in place. Machine stitch along the seam allowance, curving gently around the square corners. Clip the corners, turn right side out and press.

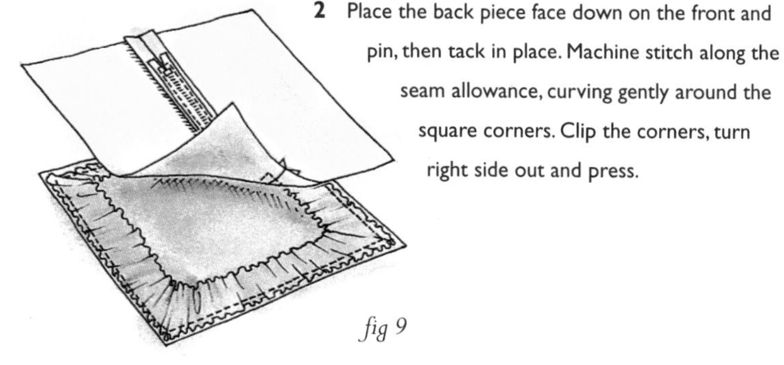

*fig 9*

## decorative fastenings

A slip-on cover must be held in place with ties or buttons. These decorative fastenings can also be used to add interest to a simple vent-back cushion cover.

### ties

The ties for an open-ended cover can be in matching or contrasting colours, with square or tapered ends. They can be threaded through specially made buttonholes either side of the opening *(fig 10)* or sewn on to the cover *(fig 11)*. See the method on p.144 for details of how to make ties from fabric, or try using woven braid or ribbon tied into bows. Ties for a vent back should be sewn in place before making up the cover *(fig 12)*.

*fig 11*

*fig 10*

*fig 12*

### buttons

Buttons can also be used to close a slip-on cover *(fig 13)* or to join the two sides of an envelope opening. The top layer of the back could be finished with a placket, like a shirt front *(fig 14)*. Buttons can also be used on the front of a cushion to give a padded, upholstered effect *(fig 15)*, if they are sewn through both sides of the cushion.

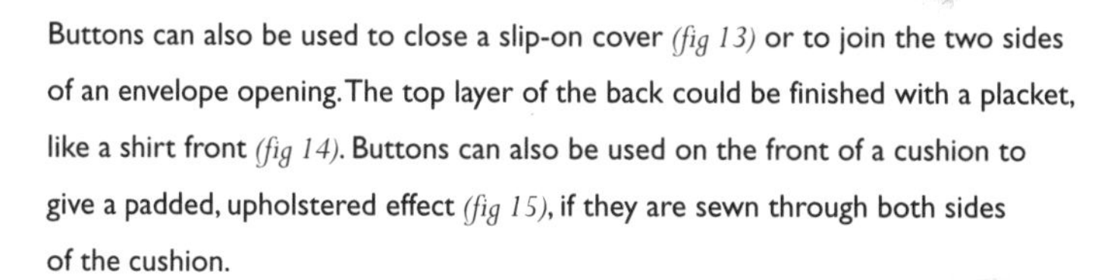

*fig 13*

*fig 14*

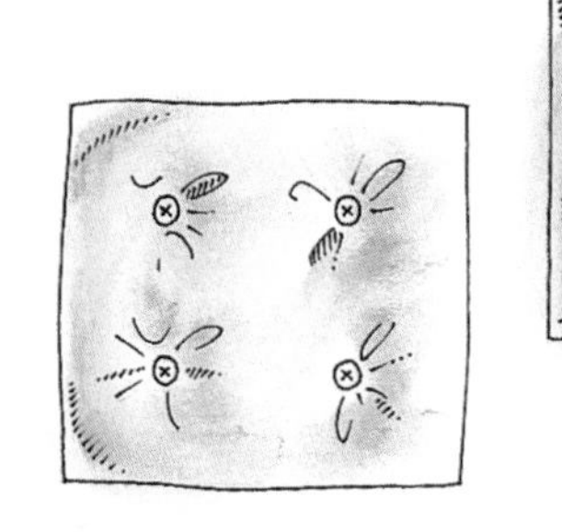

*fig 15*

# bolsters

*Upholstered bolster cushions have long been used to complement a chaise longue or day bed. The traditional cover is a tailored cylinder of fabric with piped, flat ends and a zip fastening, but more decorative versions have gathered ends trimmed with a button or tassel. Loosely tied ends, fastened with bows, are even less structured. None of these variations has to have a zip – a gathering thread can be temporarily undone if the cover needs to be removed for cleaning. Omit the seam allowances to create a really tight-fitting cover. A large bolster for a bed can be made in the same way by scaling up the fabric requirements.*

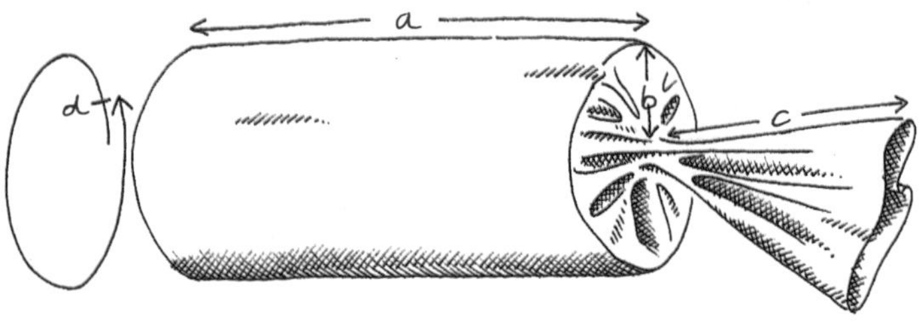

*fig 1*

## tied-end bolster

This informal cover is quick and easy to sew, as it is made from a single length of fabric.

### *materials*

Main fabric, buttonhole thread, bolster pad

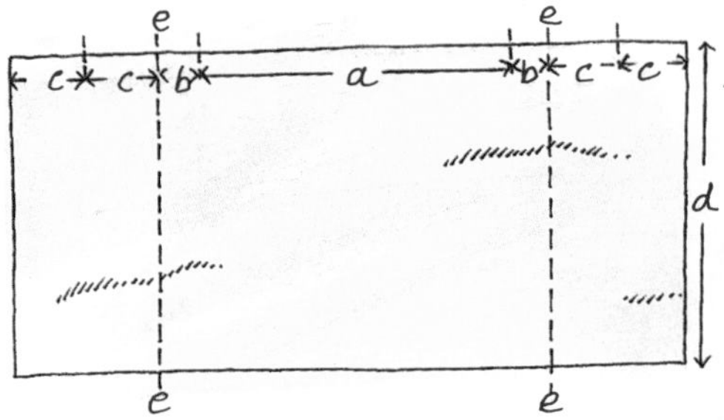

### *measuring & cutting out (figs 1 & 2)*

Main piece: cut one rectangle, width = a + 2b + 4c, length = d + 3cm

Ties: cut two strips, 6 x 60cm

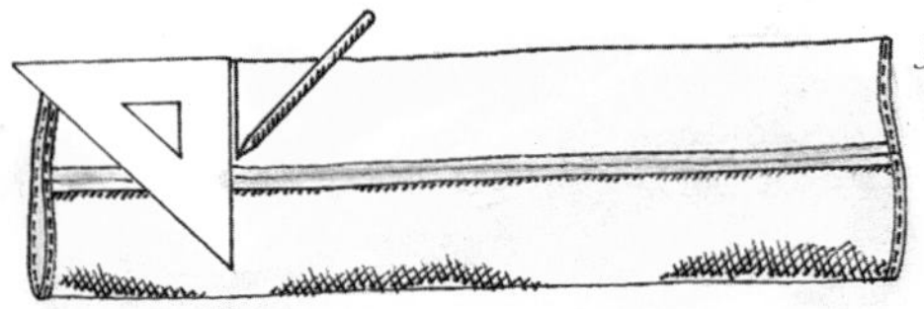

### *making up*

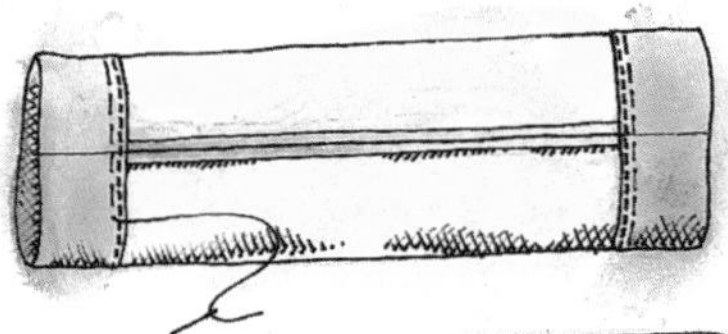

**1** With right sides facing, sew together the two long edges of the main fabric, leaving a 1.5cm allowance. Press the seam open. Make a narrow single hem around each open end.

**2** Using a chalk pencil, mark the two gathering lines (ee) where the ties will go, on to the wrong side of the fabric *(fig 3)*. Turn the surplus fabric at one open edge back to the wrong side so that the hem lines up with the marked line and tack in place. Do the same at the other end *(fig 4)*.

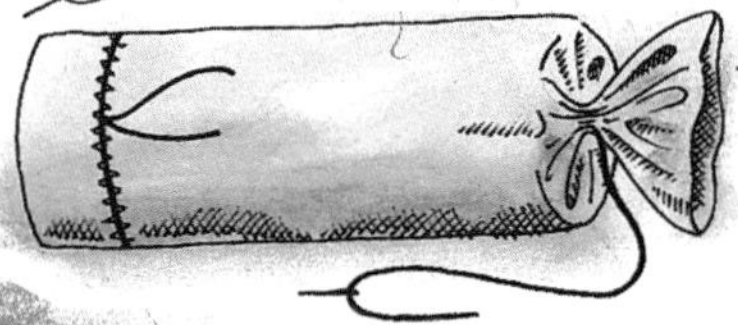

**3** Turn the cover right side out and sew a round of zigzag gathering (see p.142) over buttonhole thread on top of each tacked line. Insert the bolster pad so that it lies in the middle of the cylinder.

**4** Draw up both buttonhole threads tightly to enclose the pad and tie off securely. Sew the loose ends so that they are hidden inside the cover *(fig 5)*. The knot can then simply be unpicked if the cover has to be removed.

**5** Distribute the double gathers evenly to form a rosette shape. Make up the two ties (see p.144) and tie one in a bow at each end.

*fig 2*

*fig 3*

*fig 4*

*fig 5*

## piped bolster with gathered ends

The end pieces can be cut from matching or contrasting fabric, but look particularly dramatic when different textures and patterns are used.

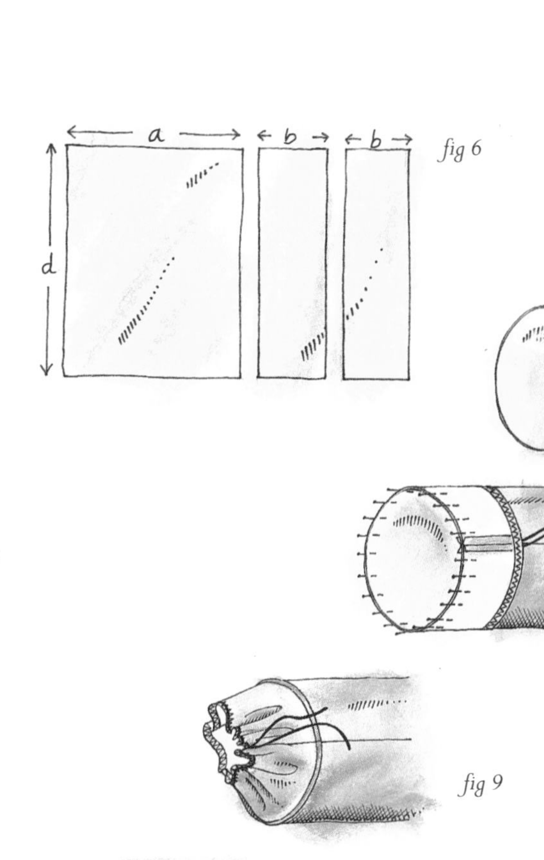


### *materials*

Main fabric, fabric for ends, piping and buttons, bolster pad, 2 self-cover buttons, piping cord, buttonhole thread

### *measuring & cutting out* *(see fig 1 & fig 6)*

Main piece: cut one piece, width = a, length (of circumference) = d + 1.5cm all round

End pieces: cut two pieces, length (of circumference) = d + 3cm, width = b + 1.5cm

Piping cord and bias strip to cover: length = 2d + 10cm

Buttons: cut two circles using the template supplied with the buttons

### *making up*

**1** With right sides facing, stitch the main piece together along 'a' to make a cylinder, leaving an allowance of 1.5cm. Press seam open and turn right side out.

**2** Cut the piping cord in half and cover it, then make up into two rounds, which fit exactly around the edges of the pad (see p.141). With the cut edges together, pin a round of piping along the seam line around each open end of the main piece, making sure that the joins match up. Stitch in place using a zipper foot *(fig 7)*.

**3** Pin the edges of one end piece to form a loop, with right sides facing. Stitch together, leaving a 1.5cm allowance and press open. Press a 1cm turning to the wrong side around one edge. On the right side, make a zigzag gathering line close to the raw edge (see p.142).

**4** With right sides facing, pin, then tack the cut edge to one end of the main piece *(fig 8)*, matching the seams. Sew in place, using a zipper foot so that the stitching lies close to the piping. Do the same at the other end.

**5** Insert the bolster pad and draw up the gathering thread tightly *(fig 9)*. Tie off and sew the loose ends back inside the cover. Cover the buttons and sew on securely so that they conceal the gathered ends *(fig 10)*.

## variations

For a more extravagant look, the ends can be made so that they are either gathered more fully or pleated. To do this, make the length of the strips twice the bolster's circumference. Make up the main part of the cover as for steps 1 and 2, then continue as follows.

### gathered end with extra fullness

**3** Stitch the short edges of one end piece to form a large loop, with right sides facing. Press open. Fold in half, then half again and mark the four creases with notches along one edge. On the right side, work four separate zigzag gathers (see p.142) between the notches, stitching close to the edge. Make a continuous zigzag gather around the other edge *(fig 11)*.

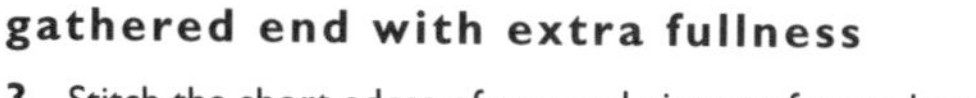

4 Mark quarter sections on the main cover in the same way. With right sides facing, pin together, matching the notches *(fig 12)*. Draw up the four gathering threads so that the ring of fabric fits the cushion tightly, then knot the ends. Pin the gathers, distributing them evenly *(fig 13)* and stitch close to the piping, using a zipper foot. Do the same with the other end and finish as in step 5, left.

### pleated end

3 With right sides facing, stitch the short edges of one end piece to form a large loop and press open. On the right side, make a line of zigzag gathering, 5mm in from one edge (see p.142). Divide the unstitched edge of the loop and one end of the cover into quarters as in step 4 above. With right sides facing, pin the loose fabric in place in a series of narrow, even pleats *(fig 14)*. Tack down, then stitch close to the piping using a zipper foot. Do the same with the other end and finish as for step 5, left.

## flat-ended bolster

This close-fitting cover is fastened with a zip. It can be trimmed with braid, cord or fringing, or finished with a round of piping at each end.

### *material*

Main fabric, bolster cushion pad, zip (6cm shorter than length of bolster), braid

### *measuring & cutting out* (*see fig 1 & fig 15*)

Main piece: cut one rectangle, width = a + 3cm, length (of circumference) = d + 4cm End pieces: cut two circles, diameter = 2b + 1.5cm all round

Braid: length = 2d + 4cm

### *making up*

1 Insert the zip (see p.144) so it is centred along the 'a' seam of the main fabric *(fig 16)*. Leave the zip partly open whilst putting the cover together. Clip 1cm into the seam allowance around each raw edge at 3cm intervals.

2 For a piped end only, make two notched rounds of piping and sew to the right side of the flat ends before sewing in place *(fig 17)*.

3 Make 1cm notches around the edge of each round end piece, snipping every 3cm. With right sides facing, pin, then tack the ends to the main cover. Stitch in place, leaving a 1.5cm seam allowance *(fig 18)*. Press lightly and turn right side out.

4 If trimming with braid, cord or fringing, cut the trim in two and slip stitch it in place around each edge using a matching sewing thread. Turn the braid under 1cm at each end and butt the folded edges together. Join them with slip stitch *(fig 19)*. Trim the other end of the bolster in the same way.

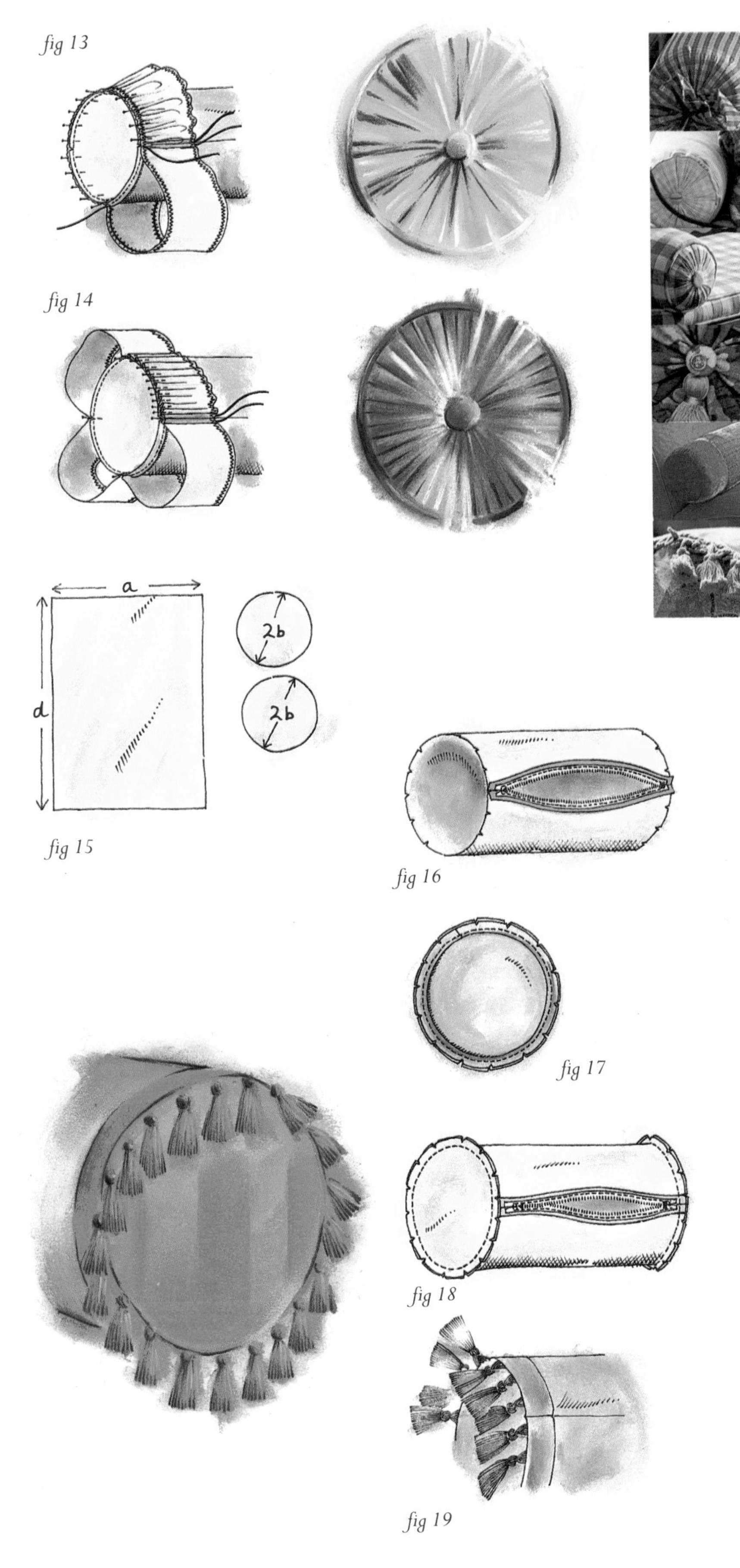


*fig 13*

*fig 14*

*fig 15*

*fig 16*

*fig 17*

*fig 18*

*fig 19*

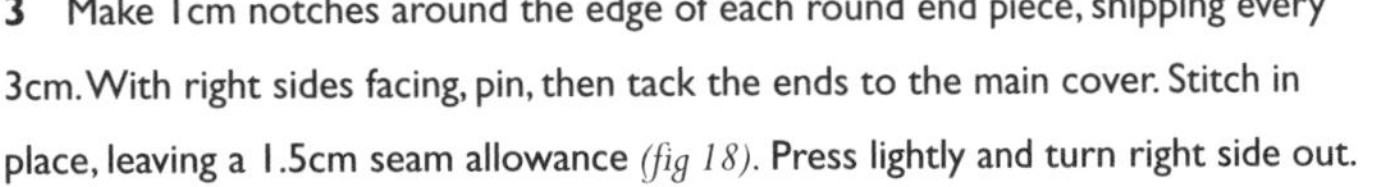

# cushions for seating

*Cushions add style, fun, colour and comfort to all forms of seating – armchairs, footstools, dining chairs, and benches – and can be made to suit your individual requirements. A cover which will undergo heavy use should be easily removable and made from hard-wearing fabric, without piping or intricate trimmings, whilst a decorative squab for an antique chair may be more ornate and fragile.*

*Ready-made pads can be adapted for seating, but upholstery foam is used for fitted or box cushions. Thin foam can be cut with long-bladed scissors, but the deeper type has to be ordered and cut to size. All foam or sponge fillings must conform to current safety regulations. For protection and to give a smooth finish to the finished cushion, the pad should first be covered with a close-fitting cotton lining. Make this by following the technique for the finished cover and slip stitch it in place.*

## gathered-corner cover

This is the simplest method of giving depth to a cover for a square or rectangular pad with a soft filling. Add sturdy fabric ties to hold the cushion in place on a chair seat or back.

### *materials*

Main fabric, ruler, tailor's chalk or dressmaker's pen, zip (10cm shorter than length of cushion pad), cushion pad

### *measuring & cutting out*

Front: cut one piece, the same size as the cushion, + 1.5cm all round

Back: cut one piece, width = width of front, length = length of front + 4cm for zip

### *making up*

**1** Cut the back into two pieces lengthways and insert the zip (see p.144). With wrong sides facing, stitch the two pieces together, 1.5cm from the edge.

**2** Draw the gathering line at each corner. Mark three points: one 5cm in from the end of each seam (a & b) and one which lies 2.5cm diagonally in from the corner (c). Join the marks with a shallow curve *(fig 1)*. These measurements can be scaled up for a larger cushion.

**3** Using a strong thread, hand stitch along this line and draw up the gathers *(fig 2)*. Wrap the thread around the gathered point and secure the ends. Repeat for each corner. Turn right side out and insert the pad, easing the cover smoothly over the corners *(fig 3)*. To secure the cushion to the back or seat of the chair, insert two ties (see p.144) into each corner of one side seam before sewing the back and front together.

a
c
b

*fig 1*

*fig 2*

*fig 3*

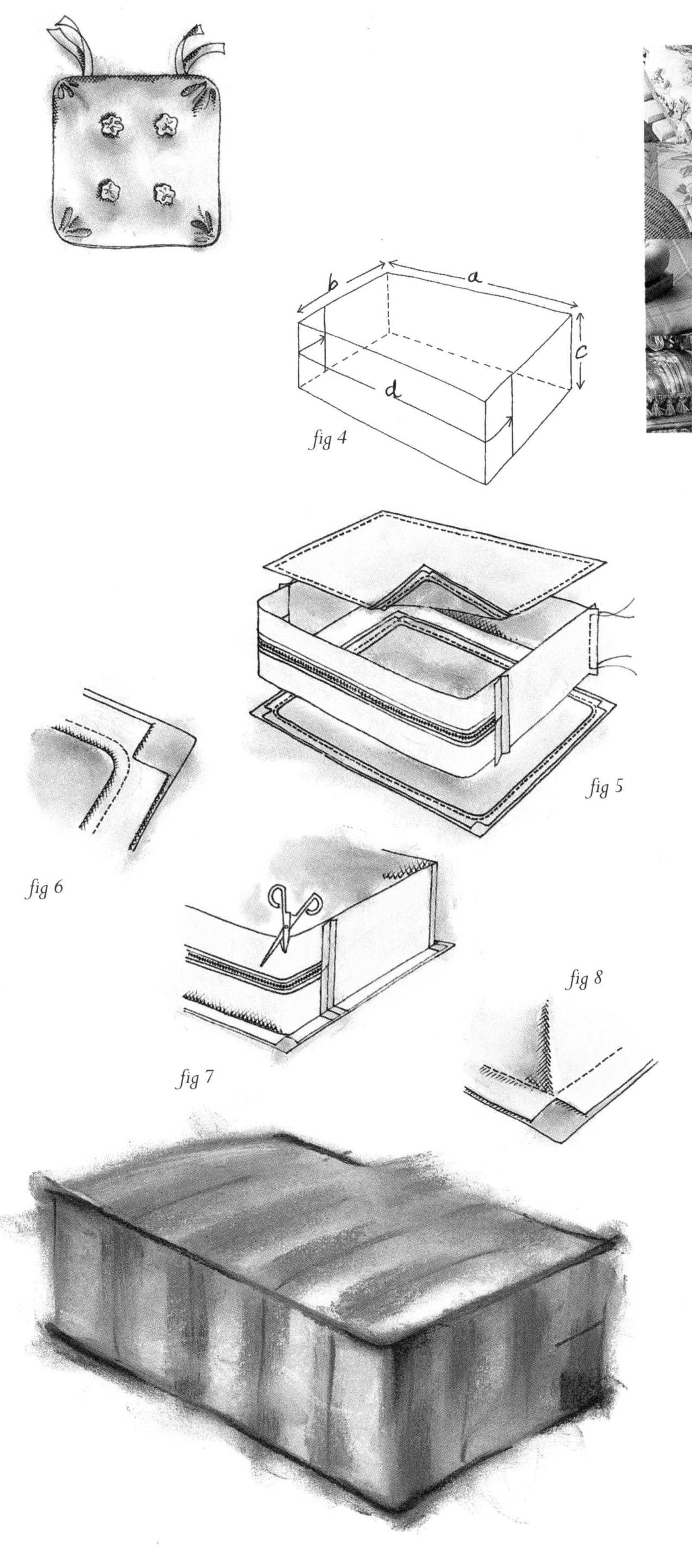


*fig 4*

*fig 5*

*fig 6*

*fig 7*

*fig 8*

## variation

A stylish upholstered look can be given to the finished cushion by attaching either 10cm circles cut from matching fabric or self-cover buttons sewn on through all layers (see *fig 2* on p. 121).

## fitted box cushion

Deep box cushions are ideal for window seats or day beds, but the same method can be used to make smaller versions to fit chairs and stools. The close-fitting cover is piped around the top and bottom to strengthen the seams and is fastened with a long zip which extends around the back corners.

### *materials*

Foam cushion pad covered with cotton slipcover, main fabric for cover and piping, heavy-duty zip (length of pad plus 16cm), piping cord (length = 2 x perimeter of cushion + 10cm)

### *measuring & cutting out (fig 4)*

Top and bottom: cut two pieces, width = a, length = b, + 1.5cm all round
Front gusset: cut one piece, width = a, length = c, + 1.5cm all round
Side gussets: cut two pieces, width = b - 10cm, length = c, + 1.5cm all round
Back gusset: cut one piece, length (d) = a + 20cm, width = c + 4cm, + 1.5cm all round

### *making up*

**1** Cut the back gusset in half lengthways. Following the method on p.144, stitch the zip in place between the two pieces at 'dd'.

**2** With right sides facing, pin the front, side and back gusset pieces together to form a loop. Slip over the pad to check the fit and adjust if necessary. Tack, then machine stitch the seams, leaving 1.5cm unsewn at each end of the two front seams *(fig 5)*. Press the seams open.

**3** Attach a round of piping to the outside edge of the top and bottom pieces (see p.141). Clip into the seam allowance of the piping at each corner *(fig 6)*.

**4** With right sides together, pin the gusset around the bottom piece, matching the front seams to the corners. Clip down to the seam at the back corners *(fig 7)*. Tack, then stitch the seam, using a zipper foot to sew close to the piping. Make an extra row of reinforcing stitches at each corner. Open the zip and attach the piped top piece in the same way, clipping the back corners first *(fig 8)*.

**5** Trim the seam allowance to 1cm and zigzag the raw edges to neaten and strengthen. Turn the cover right side out, easing the corners into shape. Insert the pad, ensuring that the seam allowances lie towards the gusset, and close the zip.

## fitted squabs

A squab cushion is cut to match the shape of a particular piece of furniture. It may be a feather-filled cushion which sits on a stool or in a favourite armchair or it may be tied on to an upright dining chair. The first step in making any fitted squab is to draw an accurate template of the seat.

## footstool squab

### *materials*

Pencil and paper, masking tape, upholstery foam 4cm deep, marker pen, cotton lining fabric, main fabric, cord (length = perimeter of seat top + 5cm)

### *making the template (fig 9)*

Tape a sheet of paper over the stool and smooth it down to reveal the shape of the top. Draw over this edge with a pencil, remove the paper from the stool and cut along the line. Lay the template back on the stool to check for accuracy.

### *measuring & cutting out*

Lining: cut two pieces the same shape as the template + 2.5cm all round

Top and bottom: cut two pieces the same shape as the template + 3.5cm all round

Pad: cut one piece the exact shape of the template

### *making up*

**1** Pin, then stitch the two lining pieces together, leaving a gap along one straight edge (aa), to insert the pad *(fig 10)*. Clip the curves and trim the seam allowance. Turn right side out, and put the foam in place. Slip stitch the opening *(fig 11)*.

**2** Join the main pieces together *(fig 10)*. Clip the curves, turn right side out and insert the covered pad. Slip stitch the opening, leaving a gap of 2cm. Attach the cord, following the method on p.141, concealing the ends inside the gap.

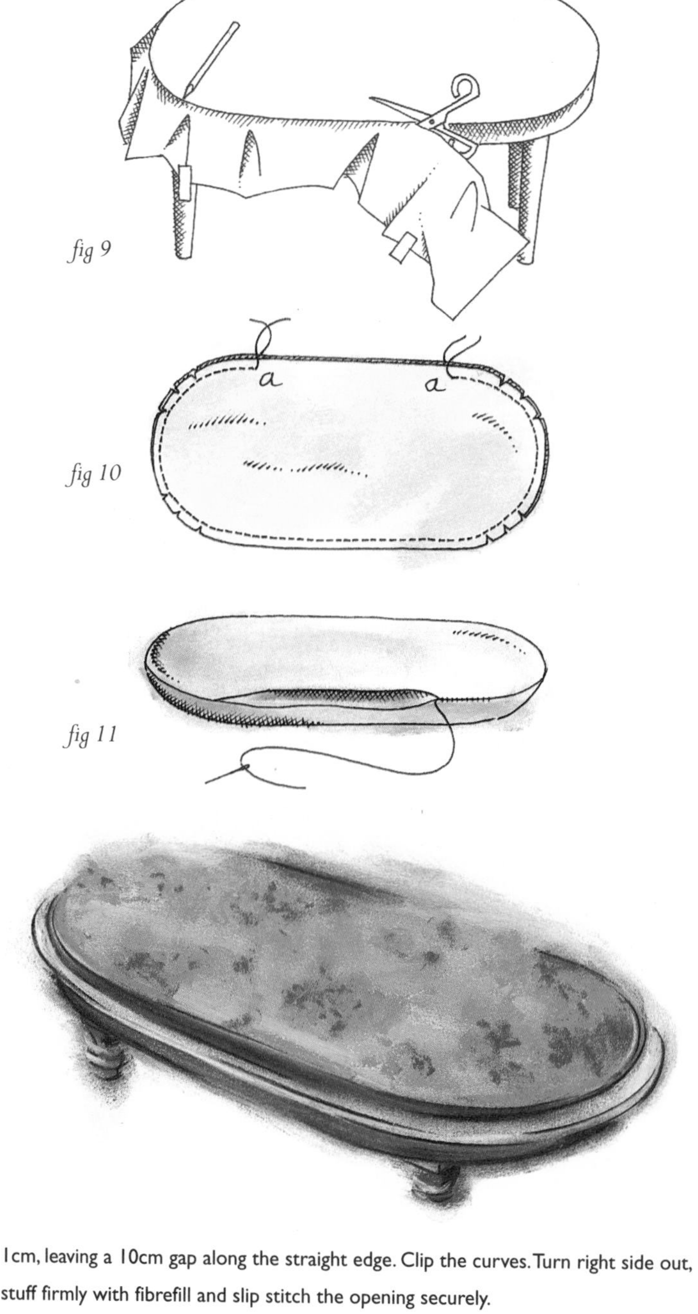


## frilled cushion for a basket chair

A basket chair requires a special cushion pad. This can easily be made from cotton lining or calico, cut to the shape of the seat (make a paper template as above). The plumper the cushion, the more luxurious it will appear, so stuff the pad well.

### *materials*

Polyester fibrefill, cotton lining fabric, main fabric

### *measuring & cutting out*

Lining: cut two pieces the same size as the template, + 1.5cm all round

Front and back: cut two pieces the same size as the template, + 2.5cm all round

Frill: cut one strip, 25cm wide by 2 x straight edge of cushion

### *making the cushion pad*

**1** Pin and stitch the two pieces of lining fabric together with a seam allowance of 1cm, leaving a 10cm gap along the straight edge. Clip the curves. Turn right side out, stuff firmly with fibrefill and slip stitch the opening securely.

### *making the cover*

**2** With right sides facing, fold the frill in half lengthways. Stitch together the two sides of each short end. Clip the corners, turn right side out and press, then stitch along the raw edges to secure.

**3** Place the cushion top right side up. Pin one end of the frill to each front corner, 1.5cm in from the sides, with the folded edge lying inwards. Arrange the fullness into evenly spaced box pleats (see p.143) and pin in place *(fig 12)*. Stitch in place 1.5cm from the edge.

**4** Press under the seam allowance along the straight edge of the back piece. Pin the front and back together with right sides facing. Sew around the outside seam line, taking care not to stitch into the frill. Clip the curves, turn right side out and press. Insert the pad and slip stitch the folded edge of the back to the frill along the stitched line *(fig 13)*.

## tie-on squab

The method for cutting a template for an upright chair is slightly more complicated, as it has to fit around the struts, but the technique is the same as for the stool. This version is piped, but alternative finishes include a gathered frill or sew-on braid or fringing. A zip could be inserted along the back seam if necessary, but a slip-stitched opening can easily be unpicked if the cover needs to be washed.

### *materials*

Pencil and paper, masking tape, upholstery foam (4cm deep), cotton lining fabric, main fabric, covered piping cord to fit perimeter of seat top + 5cm

### *making the template (fig 14)*

Smooth the paper over the seat to reveal the underlying shape. Snip around the struts and tape the paper in place securely. Draw around the outline and fold the paper in half. Cut out around the pencil line, then check against the seat. Mark the position of the ties on each side of the struts.

### *measuring & cutting out*

Pad: cut one piece the exact shape of the template
Lining: cut two pieces the same size as the template, + 2.5cm all round
Back and front: cut two pieces the same size as the template, + 3.5cm all round
Ties: cut four strips, 6 x 40cm

### *making up*

**1** Make the inner cover by sewing the two lining pieces together along the sides and front from 'b' to 'b' *(fig 15)*, leaving a 1.5cm seam allowance. Clip the corners and turn right side out. Insert the pad and slip stitch the opening.
**2** Transfer the tie position marks ('a' and 'b') to the main back piece. Sew a line of reinforcing stitches along the seam line from 'a' to 'b' at the corners of both the front and back pieces. Clip the seam allowance around the curves and corners. Make up the ties (see p.144) and pin, then stitch them to the back piece *(fig 15)*.
**3** Attach the covered piping to the main front piece *(fig 16)* so that the join lies at the centre back seam (see p.141). With right sides facing, stitch the front and back pieces together along the curved edges of the sides and front, using a zipper foot to sew close to the piping. Turn under and press the unstitched seam allowance on the back piece. Insert the pad and slip stitch the opening from 'b' to 'b' along the underside of the piping *(fig 17)*.

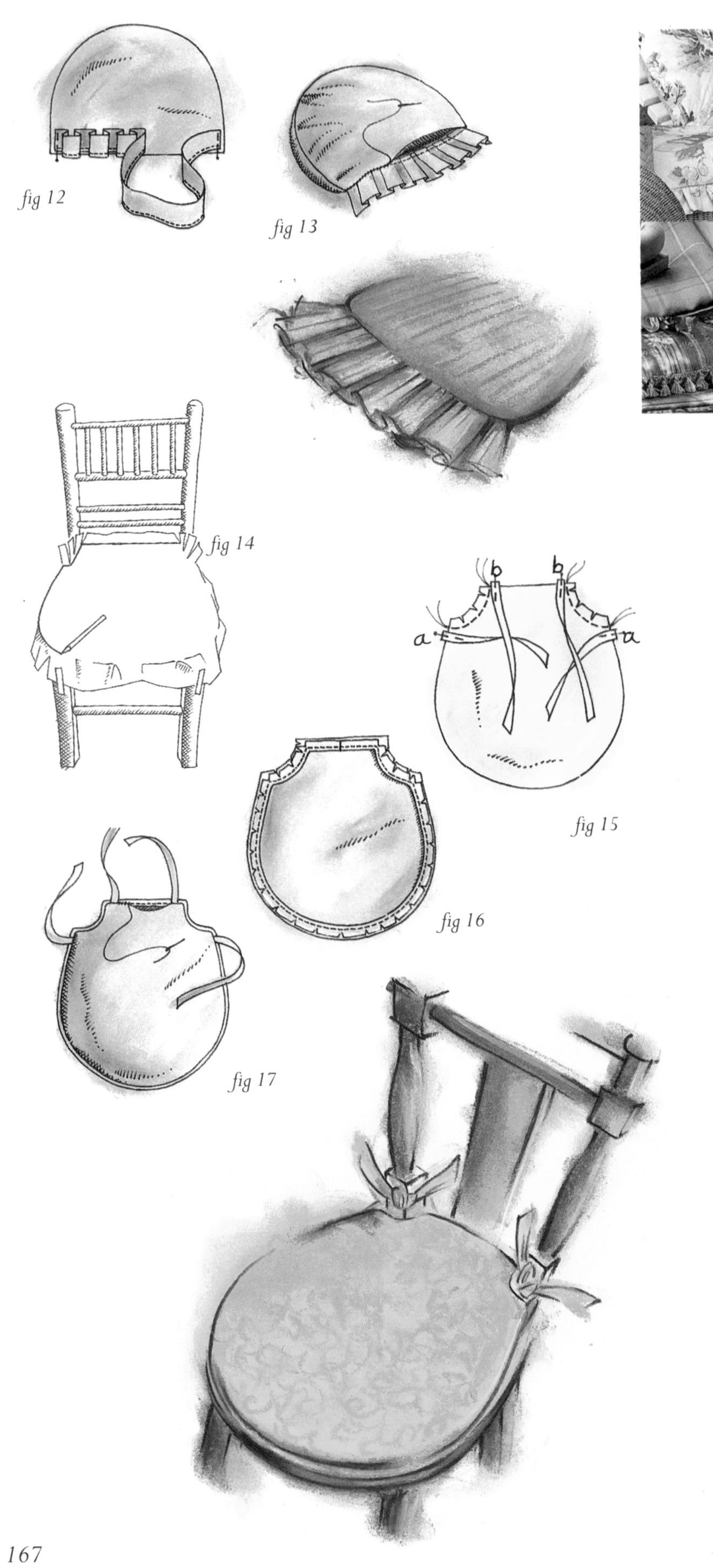

*fig 12*
*fig 13*
*fig 14*
*fig 15*
*fig 16*
*fig 17*

# loose covers

*Loose covers serve several purposes – they can protect upholstery, disguise a worn but comfortable armchair, or provide an effective update for an old wooden chair. All chairs vary in shape and proportion, so careful measurement is essential for a professional finish. When making a cover, you should start with a calico toile or preliminary version. Like a couturier designing a one-off garment, you can adjust this on the chair itself to achieve a perfect fit before cutting out the main fabric.*

## two-piece chair cover

This set is designed for a straight-backed dining chair; the fitted seat cover and separate back can be made up in any combination of fabrics and skirt lengths. The seat is held in place with either a cross-over tie or two bows.

### *materials*

Paper, pencil, masking tape, main fabric, cotton lining fabric

### *measuring & cutting out* *(figs 1, 2 & 3)*

Measure your chair and decide on the proportions: depth of the back (b) and frill (c) (8–10cm), skirt length (10–30cm), and the width and number of ties. Add a seam allowance of 1.5cm all round each piece.

Seat: make a template *(fig 2)*. Add an extra 5cm to 'f' and 'e', shown by the shaded area. Cut two pieces, one from main fabric and one from lining
Front skirt: cut one piece, width = 4e + 2f + 15cm, depth = g
Back skirt: cut one piece, width = 2d, depth = g
Ties: cut two or four, length = 75cm, width = 10-18cm
Back: cut two pieces, width = a + (z) 5-7cm, depending on the thickness of the chair, depth = b (half the height of the back)
Frill: cut one piece, width = 4a, depth = 2c. Notch the centre of one long side

### *making up the seat cover*

**1** Make a 1cm double hem along the side and bottom edges of the two skirt pieces. With right sides facing, pin the top corners of the back skirt to the seat back (along d), 1.5cm from the edges. Fold the skirt into knife pleats (see p.143), 4cm apart, along the unhemmed edge. Pin them in place as you go, then stitch down, 1.5cm from the edge.

**2** With right sides together, pin the top corners of the front skirt to the sides of the seat, 1.5cm down from the curves. Pin into equal pleats, making sure that the last fold at each corner lies 1.5cm from the adjacent side *(fig 4)*. Stitch together, clipping into the seam allowance of the skirt *(fig 5)*.

**3** Make up the ties as on p.144. Pin, wrong sides up, at points 'a' for a single tie and 'a' and 'b' for a double bow *(fig 6)*. Turn the ties back into the centre of the seat cover and with right sides facing, pin the lining to the seat, checking that the skirts and ties are not caught up.

*fig 1*

*fig 2*

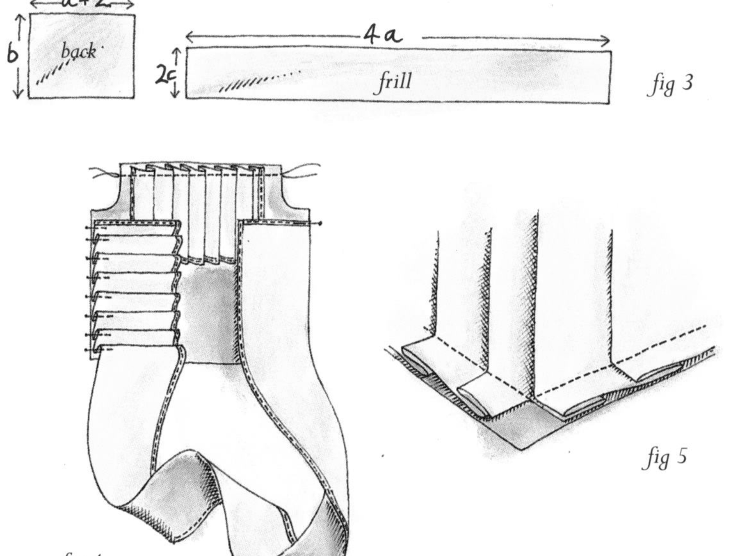


*fig 3*

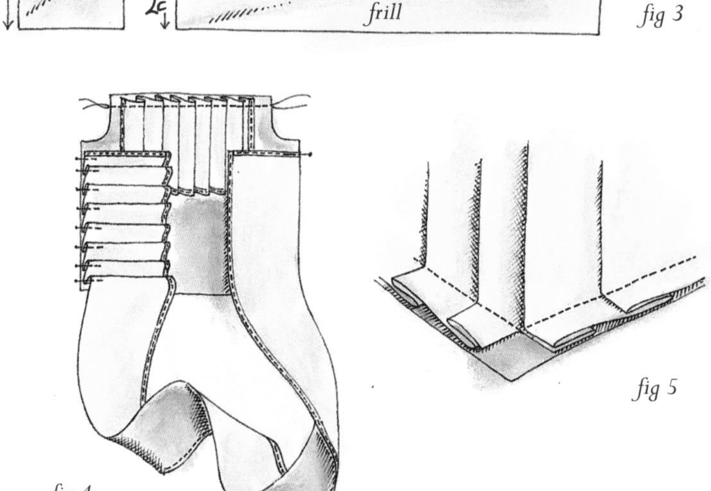

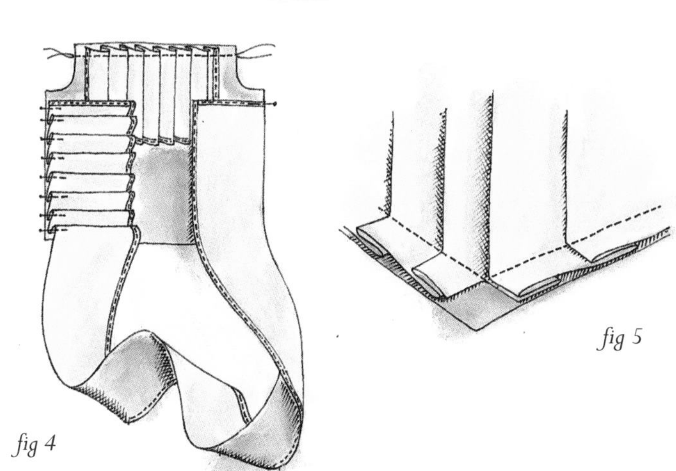

*fig 4*

*fig 5*

**4** Stitch together around the outside edge from 'b' (inner edge of tie) to 'b'. Keep the main fabric uppermost and sew over the existing seam. Double stitch the corners and ties. Clip the corners and turn right side out. Press under and slip stitch the top edge of the lining.

### *making up the chair back*

**5** With right sides facing, pin and stitch the two pieces together around the sides and top, 1.5cm from the edge. Turn right side out and press. Join the short ends of the frill with right sides together and press the seam open. With wrong sides together, fold in half lengthways and press.

**6** Match the join and notch on the frill to the side seams on the chair back cover and pin. Fold, pin and stitch the frill into pleats all around the opening (*fig 7*). Press the seam allowances inwards, and finish with a line of top stitching, 3mm above the seam.

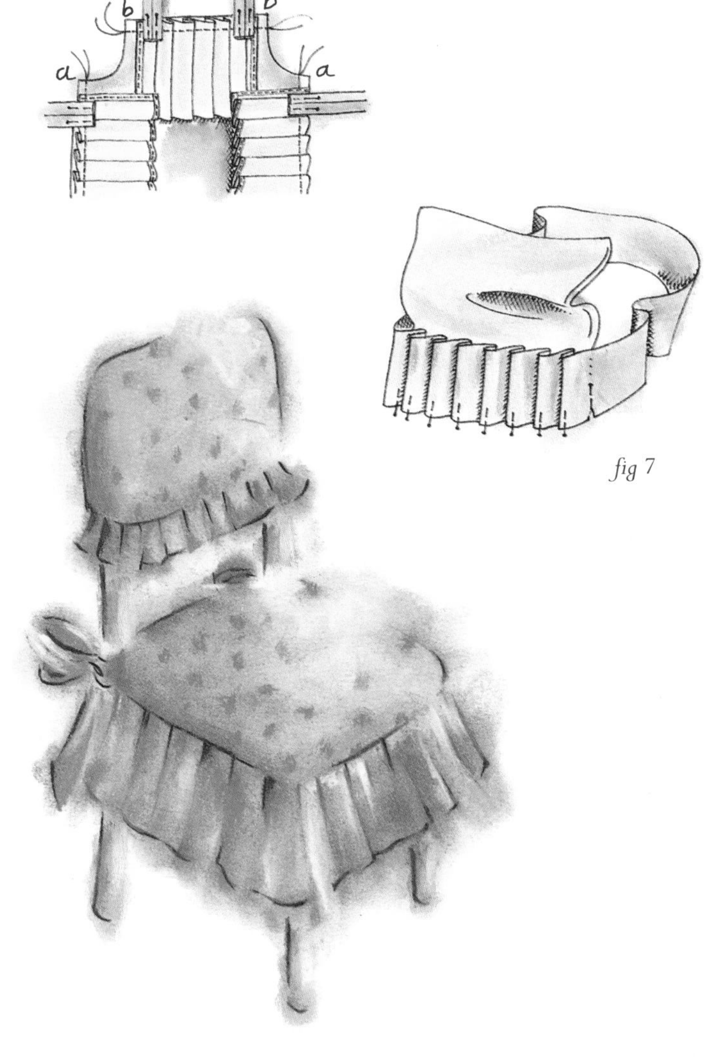


*fig 6*

*fig 7*

## box-pleated seat cover

This long-skirted variation is ideal for firmer fabrics such as woollen plaids which would be too stiff for pleats. A solid-backed chair does not require a back skirt.

### *materials*

Main fabric, lining fabric

### *measuring & cutting out*

Seat: cut two pieces, one from main fabric and one from lining. Notch the centre front and centre sides

Front skirt: cut one piece, length = 2e + f + 50cm, width = approx 20cm. Notch the centre top edge

Ties: cut four, length = 5cm, width = 30cm

### *making up*

Make a 1cm double hem along the side and bottom edges of the skirt. Fold a 2cm pleat either side of the notch and with right sides together, pin to the centre front of the seat. Do the same at the corners and centre of each side. Fold under the surplus fabric at each edge so that it lies 1.5cm in from the curve (*fig 8*). Stitch along the seam allowance, clipping at the corners (see *fig 5* left). Complete as for steps 3 and 4 above.

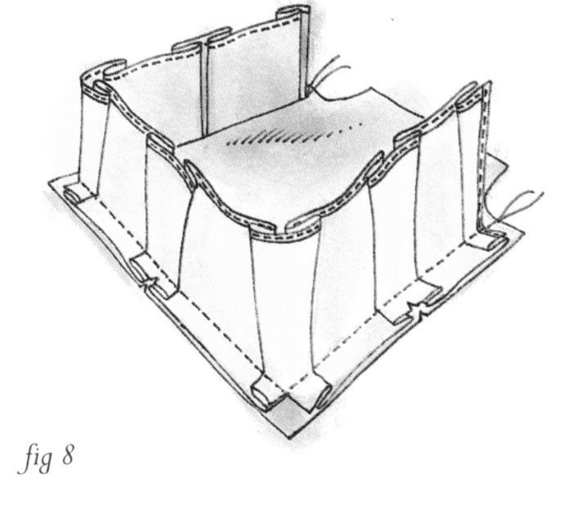

*fig 8*

## flounced cover

The feminine flounces of this cover, designed for a chair with a round seat, recall a lavish silk ballgown. It has a full, gathered skirt trimmed with braid, and the back is decorated with a sash and luxurious long-tailed bow.

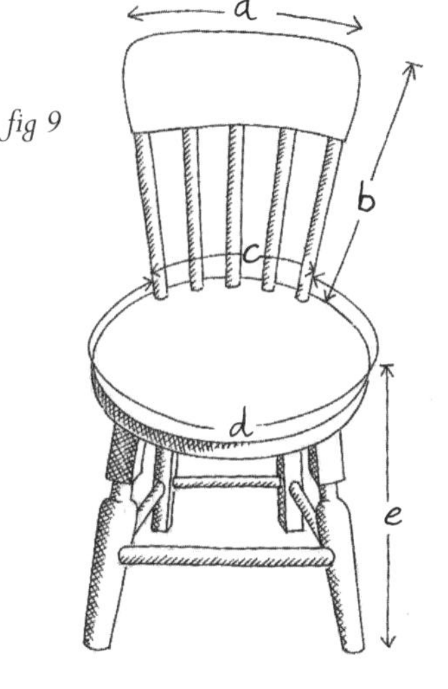

*fig 9*

### *materials*

Paper, pencil, masking tape, main fabric, sash and bow fabric, covered piping cord (length = a + 2b + d), 50cm zip, 1 large press stud (optional), braid (length = 2c + 2d), button hole thread for gathering

### *measuring & cutting out* *(figs 9 & 10)*

Measure your chair, noting the shape and thickness of the back. If the top edge is the same width or narrower than the bottom edge, the cover will slip easily over the chair and you can omit the zip. Make a toile of the back and seat; it may be necessary to cut the inside back slightly smaller than the outside to get the best fit. Add 1.5cm around each piece for the seam allowance. Make a template for the seat (see *fig 2* on p. 168).

Inside and outside back: cut two pieces, top width = a + 5cm (depending on thickness), bottom width = c, height = b
Seat: cut one piece, as template
Skirt: cut one piece, width = e (highest point of top edge of seat to floor), length = 2c + 2d
Sash: cut two pieces, length = ½c + 5cm, width = 25cm
Bow: Main part: cut one piece, width = 80cm, length = 40cm
Centre: cut one piece, width = 10cm, length = 20cm
Tails: cut two pieces, width = 90cm, length = 20cm

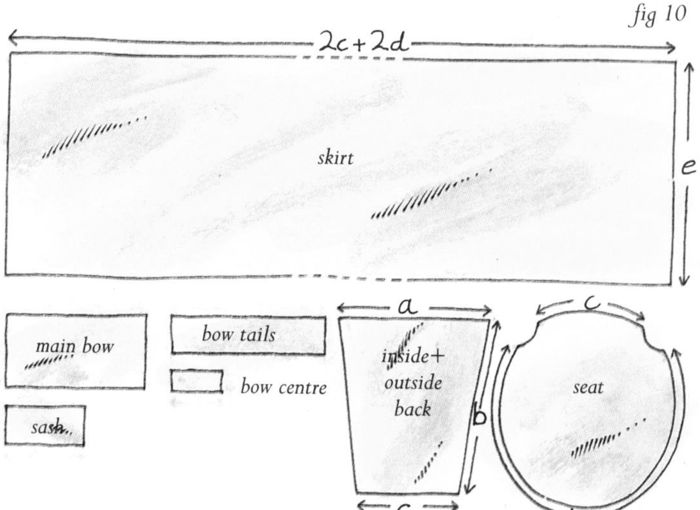

*fig 10*

### *making up*

**1** With right sides facing, pin and stitch the back of the seat to the bottom of the inside back, leaving a 1.5cm seam allowance. On the right side attach a round of piping to the outside edge (see p.141). Clip the seam allowance of the piping cover at regular intervals.

**2** Fold one of the sash pieces in half lengthways with right sides facing and join the long edges together. Turn right side out and press flat, so that the seam lies centrally. Fold the seam allowance at one end to the inside and sew a gathering thread to join the two neatened edges. Pull up and fasten securely *(fig 11)*. Make up the other part, gathering the opposite end to make a pair.

**3** With right sides together, pin and stitch the straight ends of the sash to either side of the inside back, so that the lower edges lie on the seam line *(fig 12)*.

**4** Pin the outside back to the inside back with right sides facing. Sew together around the sides and top, using a zipper foot to sew close to the piping. Leave 1.5cm unstitched at the lower edge. If you are going to put in a zip, leave 30cm unstitched on the right edge *(fig 13)*.

**5** Stitch the short edges of the skirt with right sides facing. Leave the top 23cm of the join open for the end of the zip. Make a zigzag gather (see p.142) 1.5cm down from the top edge, starting and finishing 1.5cm in from the edges. Draw up

*fig 11*
*fig 12*
*fig 13*

the cord to half its length.

**6** Slip the back and seat on to the chair, wrong side out. Pin the skirt to the outside back and seat edge, lining up the seam or opening with the right-hand edge of the back, and distribute the gathers evenly *(fig 14)*. Remove from the chair and stitch in place using a zipper foot, and sewing close to the piping on the seat. Insert the zip at this stage, following the instructions on p.144. Clip the curves, turn right side out and press lightly.

**7** Make up the bow as on p.144. Stitch the gathered end of the right-hand sash to the centre back seam and stitch the bow securely on top. Sew one half of the press stud to the end of the left-hand sash and the other half under the bow, close to the centre *(fig 15)*. If there is no zip, sew both ends of sash to the cover.

**8** Put the cover on the chair, then turn up the hem level with the floor and neaten. Sew braid around the hem.

*fig 14*

*fig 15*

## pleated cover

This elegant variation is assembled in exactly the same way, but without the sash. Its skirt is box-pleated instead of gathered, and the seams are not piped but concealed with gold braid, sewn on by hand once the cover is complete. Measure around the seat and the top edge of the back to find out how much braid is needed.

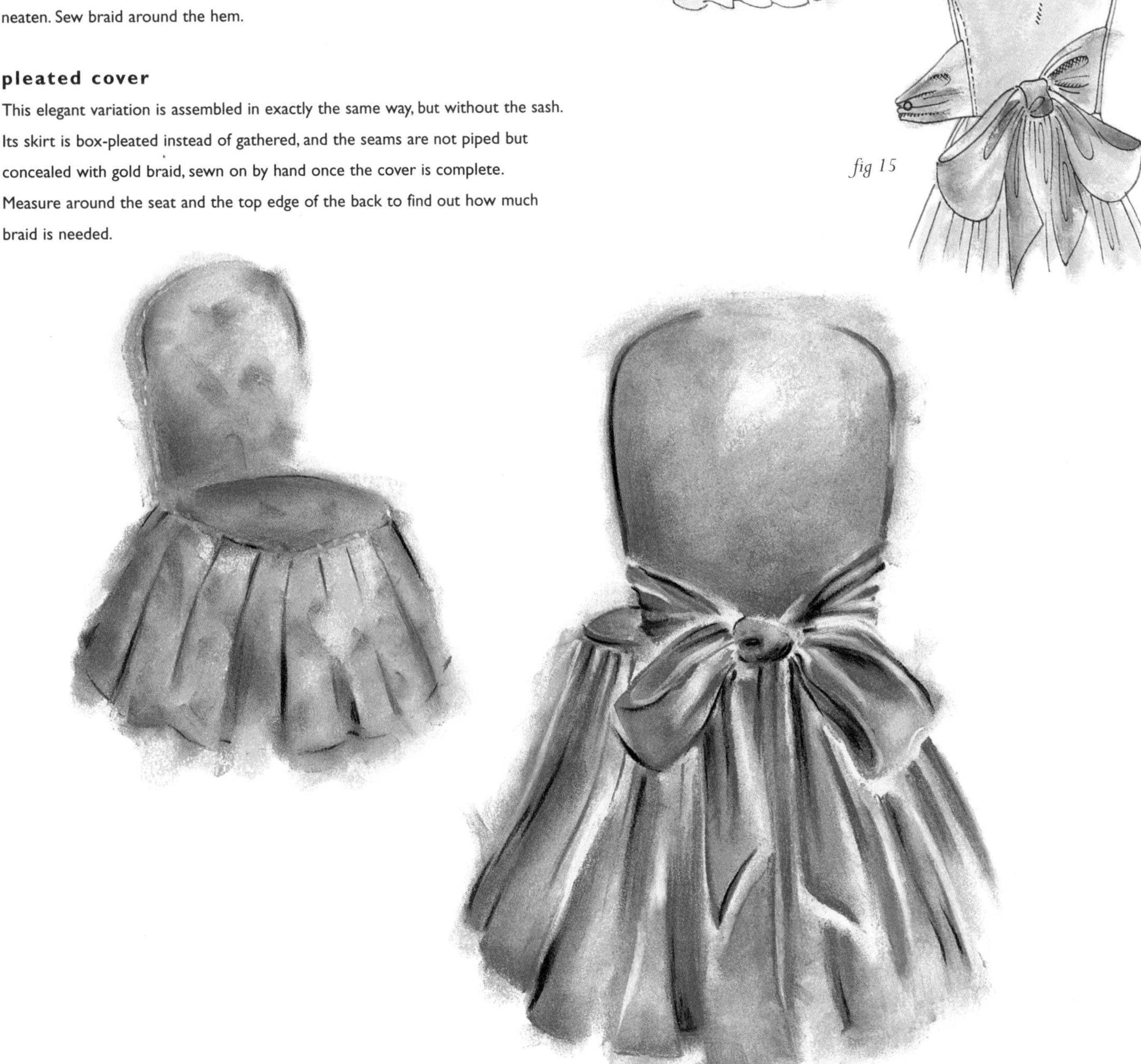

## tailored cover

The boxy lines of this cover are intended for an upright dining chair with a square seat. It looks particularly effective when made in checks, tartan or stripes. The optional side pockets are a useful place to store a book or magazine.

### *materials*

Main fabric

### *measuring & cutting out (figs 16 & 17)*

The shaded areas indicate a seat or back which is wider at the top or bottom edge and the broken lines represent fold lines. The 10cm pleats should allow the cover to fit most chairs, but if the legs are very splayed, work out the extra amount needed and add one eighth of this to each pleat. Add 1.5cm all round each piece. NB: z equals 5cm in the cutting instructions below.

Inside back: cut one piece, top width = a + z (depending on thickness), bottom width = d, depth = h. Notch the centre top edge

Seat: cut one piece, top width = d, bottom width = f, side depth = e

Front skirt: cut one piece, width = f + 4z, depth = i. Notch fold lines at top and hem

Side skirt: the back legs may be a different height to the front legs; measure 'i' and 'j' carefully, so that the skirt hangs straight.

Cut two pieces, width = e + 4z, height at one edge = i, the other j. Notch fold lines at top and hem

Pockets: make a rectangular template to fit on to the side skirt.

Cut two pieces, as template

Outside back: add 5cm or more to 'a', depending on thickness of back. If you are working with stripes or plaids, add extra fabric so that the box pleat folds along the pattern lines and alter the centre 20cm allowance accordingly.

Cut one piece, as pattern. Notch the centre top and the fold lines at top and hem

Ties: cut six, width = 5cm, length = 35cm including seam allowance

### *making up*

**1** Make the box pleat on the right side of the outside back by lining up the fold lines at top and bottom, and turning to the centre. Press well for a sharp crease. Pin in place along top edge, then stitch down, 1cm from the edge *(fig 18)*.

**2** Sew a 1cm double hem at the top of each pocket. Press under the seam allowance on the other sides. Pin one to each side skirt and top stitch down.

**3** With right sides facing, pin and stitch together the side and front skirts, matching the edges of pleats 'i'. Join the edge of pleats 'j' to the outside back *(fig 19)*. Make the corner pleats 'i' by matching the notches. Pin at the top and bottom edges and fold towards the middle. Press well. Stitch together along the top edge to hold in place. Do the same with the back pleats 'j' *(fig 20)*.

**4** Pin the inside back to the outside back with right sides facing. Sew together around the sides and top, 1.5cm from the edge, leaving the seam allowance on the lower edge unstitched. With right sides together, pin and stitch the top edge of the seat to the lower edge of the inside back.

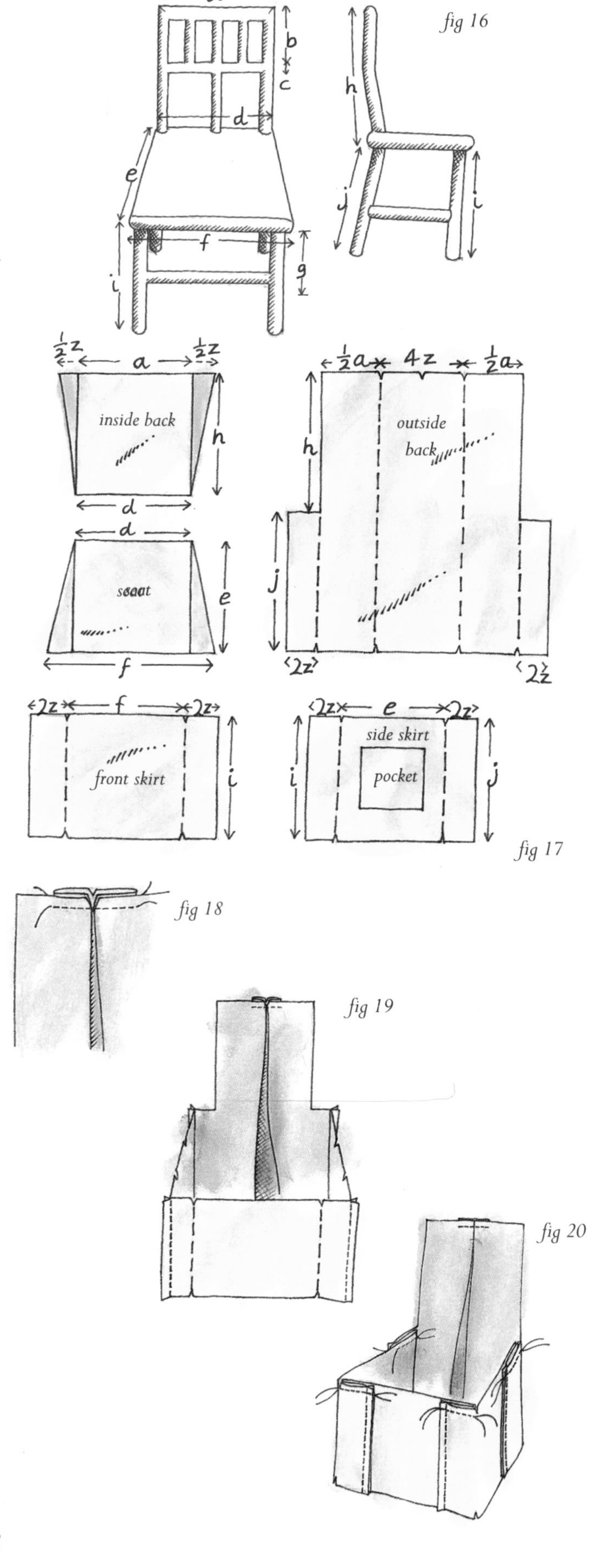


*fig 16*

*fig 17*

*fig 18*

*fig 19*

*fig 20*

**5** Pin the top edge of the skirt to the sides and lower edge of the seat, ensuring that the pleats are in position. Stitch along the seam allowance, reinforcing the corners.

**6** Turn right side out. Check that the lower edge is level, then neaten and turn up the hem. Make up the ties as on p.144 and sew in pairs to the inner edges of the box pleat at 15cm intervals.

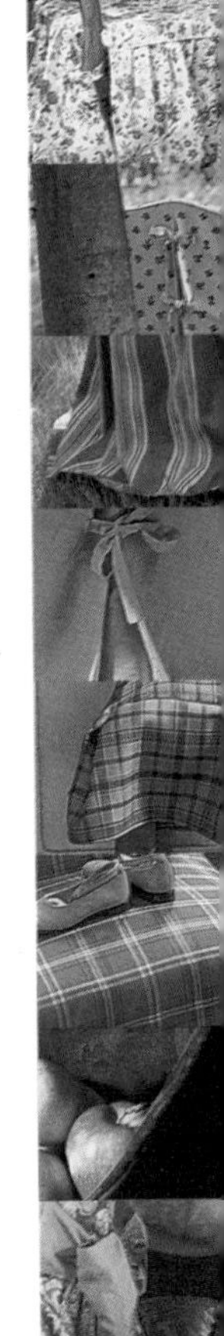

## basket chair cover

This deceptively sophisticated cover is designed to go over a traditional Lloyd Loom chair, but could easily be adapted for any tub-shaped armchair or cane garden seat. It is skilfully cut, in just five main pieces, with box pleats at the back.

### *materials*

Newspaper, marker pen, masking tape, main fabric

### *measuring & making the pattern* *(figs 1 & 2)*

The seat, sides and back can be cut out easily, but the inside back piece is more complicated and the shaping has to be accurate. Make a paper pattern first, and if you want to be extra sure, sew a toile before cutting the main fabric. Cut four paper rectangles as indicated in *fig 2*. Tape them to the chair and cut to the exact shape. The shaded areas represent areas that will be cut away and the broken lines are folds. NB: z equals 5cm in the cutting instructions below.

Side: width = h + z, depth = m + n. Cut away a rectangle (m x z) from the top right corner, to leave the fabric for the box pleat (n x z) at the bottom right edge. Shape the top edge to the outside curve of the arm (d).

Outside back: width = l + 6z, depth = m + n.

Cut away a rectangle (m x 3z) at each top corner. Shape the top edge to the outside curve of the back (c).

Seat: width = k, depth = i + f

Cut the upper part to fit the shape of the chair seat (a).

Inside back: width = a + 12z, depth = b + 3z (or more, depending on angle of back)

Fold in half widthways and tape to the centre back, so that the top of the fold lies on the outside edge (b). Cut the curve along the outside edge of the back and arm. Mark line 'j' (inside front arm). Cut the bottom edge of the pattern into a curve so that it fits around 'a', as far as 'j'. Remove from the chair, and draw a line which continues curve 'd' to the edge of the paper. Cut along this line. Retape to the chair, fitting the extended curve to the outside front arm. Fold the surplus paper to fit around the front arm, pinning along 'j' *(fig 3)*. Trim the bottom of the front arm so that it continues curve 'a'. Take the pattern off and cut along the pinned line.

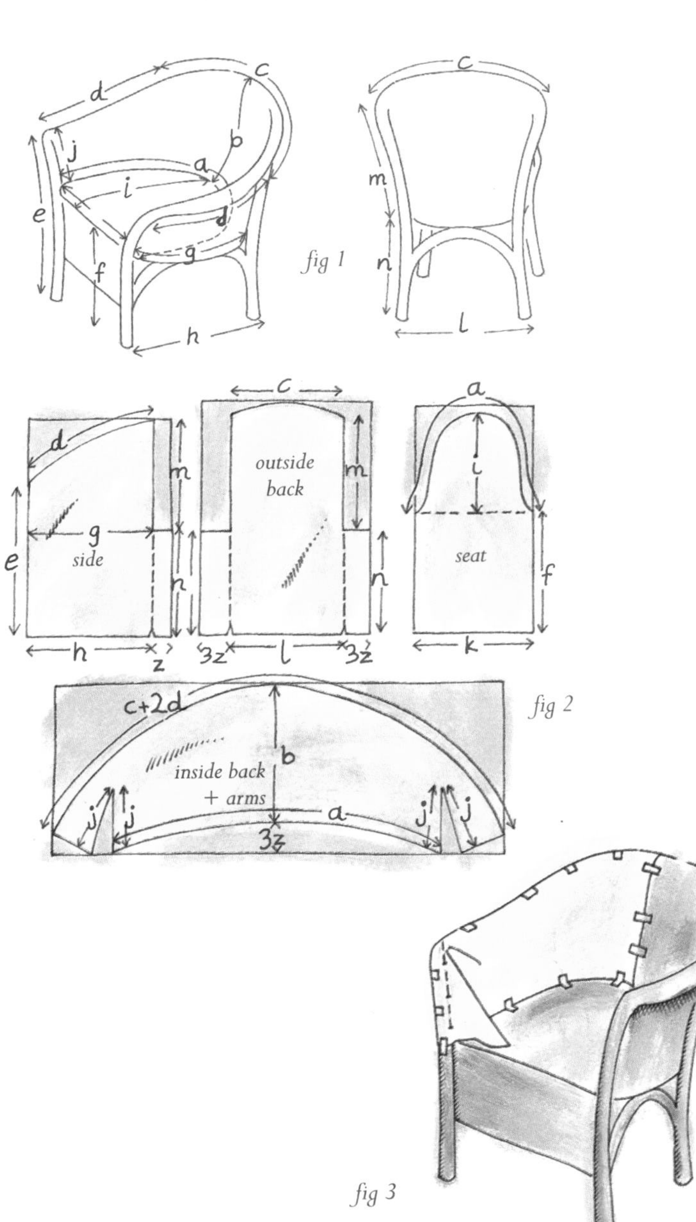


*fig 1*

*fig 2*

*fig 3*

*cutting out*

Add 1.5cm seam allowance around the edge of each pattern piece. Cut out from main fabric:

Sides: cut two pieces

Inside back: cut one piece. Notch the centre of top and bottom edges

Seat: cut one piece. Notch the centre of top curved edge

Outside back: cut one piece. Notch the centre of top edge, fold lines at the hem

Ties: cut four, 6 x 40cm

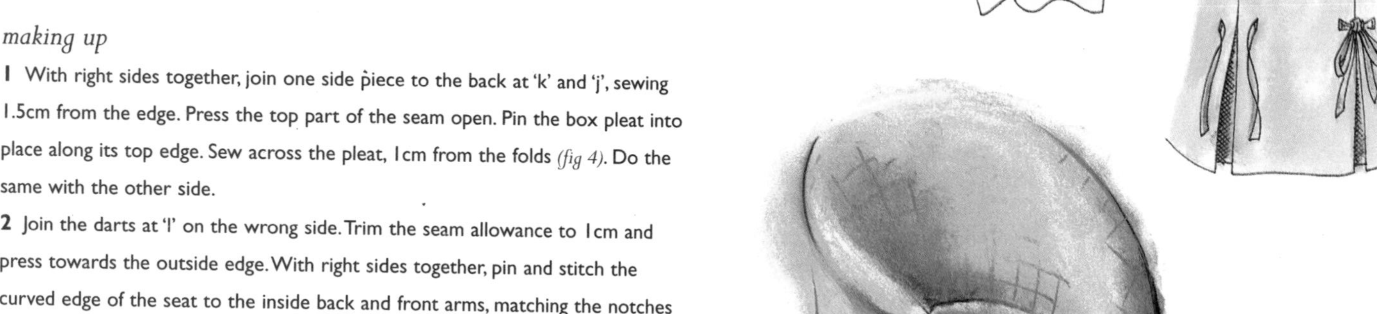


*making up*

**1** With right sides together, join one side piece to the back at 'k' and 'j', sewing 1.5cm from the edge. Press the top part of the seam open. Pin the box pleat into place along its top edge. Sew across the pleat, 1cm from the folds *(fig 4)*. Do the same with the other side.

**2** Join the darts at 'l' on the wrong side. Trim the seam allowance to 1cm and press towards the outside edge. With right sides together, pin and stitch the curved edge of the seat to the inside back and front arms, matching the notches *(fig 5)*. Trim the seam allowance to 1cm and zigzag to neaten and strengthen.

**3** With right sides together, and matching the notches at centre top, pin the back and sides to the seat and inside back. Clip the seam allowance on the inside back at the point where it meets the side corners, on the front arm. Stitch along the allowance, then trim back to 1cm and zigzag.

**4** Fold the pleats, lining up the notches and press well. Make up the ties as on p.144 so both ends are squared off. Stitch a pair 5cm from the top edge of each pleat and tie bows *(fig 6)*.

**5** Slip the cover on to the chair. Check that the lower edge is level. Neaten, and turn up and stitch the hem.

## director's chair cover

The folding director's chair is a classic, but this cover gives it a new twist. The skirt is made separately and stitched into box pleats, then sewn to the back, seat and arms. The opening is concealed down one side.

*materials*

Main fabric, marker pen, large press stud

*measuring & cutting out (figs 1 & 2)*

Cut the pieces to the measurements on *fig 2* from the main fabric, or calico if working with a toile, adding on 1.5cm all round. Add an extra 5cm (½z) to the back and the left arm, as shown by the dotted lines, where the opening will be. Add an extra 6cm to the lower edge of the skirt pieces for the hem. Notch all skirt pieces at top and hem to mark the folds, indicated by the broken lines. Cut the back and arms to shape as shown; the shaded areas represent the fabric to be cut away. NB: z equals 10cm in the cutting instructions opposite.

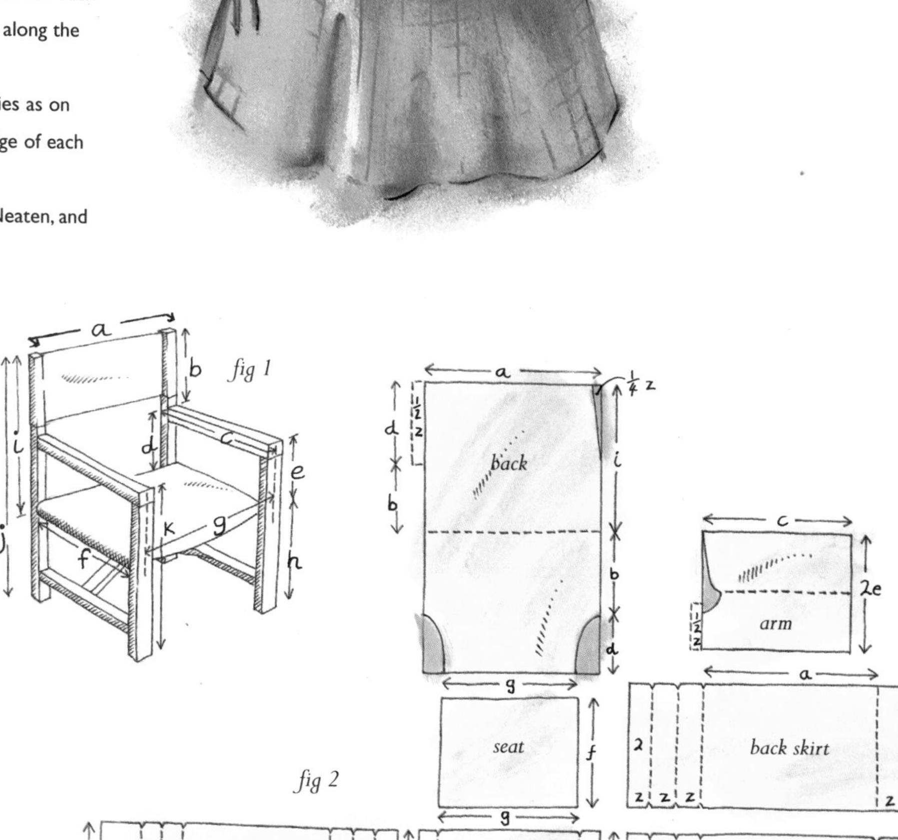

Back: cut one piece, width = a, length = i + b + d. Fold in half widthways and pin the edges together along the upper part (b). Pin a small box pleat at the fold to accommodate the width of the frame

Arm: cut two pieces, width = c (outside edge of back to centre front of arm), length = 2e (centre top of arm to top of seat). Fold in half widthways, place over one arm and pin the outside edge to the side of the seat. Pin the inside edges to both sides of the back, following the lines shown, so that the seam lies down the centre side of the back strut. Mark along the pinned line, then trim the seam allowance to 1.5cm

Seat: cut one piece, width = g, depth = f
Left skirt: cut one piece, width = c + 7z, length = h
Right skirt: cut one piece, width = c + 4z, length = h
Front skirt: cut one piece, width = g + 2z, length = h
Back skirt: cut one piece, width = a + 4z, length = h

## *making up*

**1** Fold the back in half widthways with right sides together. Pin and sew the top edges together to within 2cm of the fold, 1.5cm from the edge. Make a small box pleat from the unstitched fabric and stitch down, sewing from each side to the centre in turn *(fig 3)*. Do the same on the outside arm edges.

**2** With right sides facing, pin and stitch the back edge of the seat to the bottom edge of the inside back. Join the inside edge of the arms to the lower edges of the back (d), along the seam allowance. Clip the seams where necessary. Sew the outside edge of the right arm to the back. Neaten and hem the raw side edge of the left arm. Sew the seat to the bottom edge of the arms *(fig 4)*.

**3** Sew the side skirts to the front skirt with right sides facing at (1), then join the left side of the back skirt to the right side skirt at (2). Hem the two short edges. At the three joins, match the notches and seam lines to make 10cm box pleats. Make a single pleat at the right edge of the back skirt *(fig 5)*. Pin in place, and stitch down, 1.5cm from the top edge.

**4** Pin the top edge of the skirt to the main part with right sides together, so that the corners of the front seat and the right back line up to the centre of each pleat. Stitch along the seam allowance, reinforcing the corners. Turn right side out and press the pleats, using the notches on the hem as a guide.

**5** Put the cover on to the chair and check that the skirt is hanging level. Neaten and turn up a 6cm hem. Turn the surplus fabric at the left-hand edge of the back skirt to the wrong side and press. Sew the press stud to either side of the opening as shown *(fig 6)*.

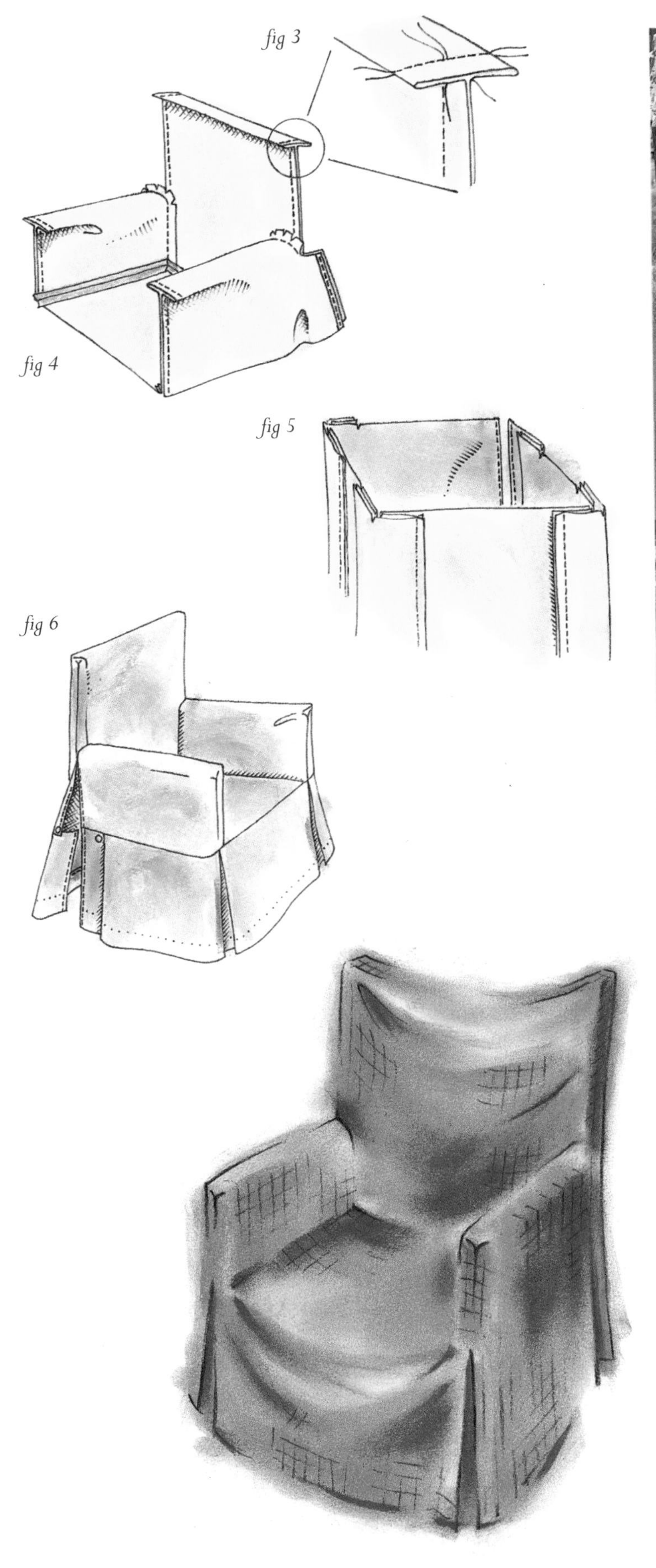

## director's chair with hood

This variation is much simpler in structure – it does not have a separate skirt – but in a flight of fancy, the back extends to form a long tassel-trimmed hood.

*materials*

Main fabric, covered piping cord (length = 2k + 2c + distance around edge of hood), large tassel

*measuring & cutting out* *(see figs 1 on page 174 & fig 7)*

Cut the pieces as shown in the diagram. The small curves on the side edges of the outside and inside back pieces allow the cover to fit over the thickness of the arms. Take the measurements for the inside back and inside arm to the outside edges of the arms. Add a 1.5cm seam allowance all round.

*making up*

**1** With right sides facing, sew the top edge of the seat to the lower edge of the inside back. Sew sides 'd' and 'f' of the inside arms to the inside back and seat *(fig 8)*.

**2** Stitch the outside arms to either side of the outside back, so that the curves line up. With right sides together, fold the top edge of the back in half. Pin and stitch to form the hood *(fig 9)*. Do the same with the inner back.

**3** Stitch a line of piping (see p.141) around the outside edge of the arms and back. With right sides facing, pin the inner part of the cover to the outside, and sew together around the arms and back, using a zipper foot. Turn right side out and press. Hem the bottom edge, and sew the tassel to the point of the hood.

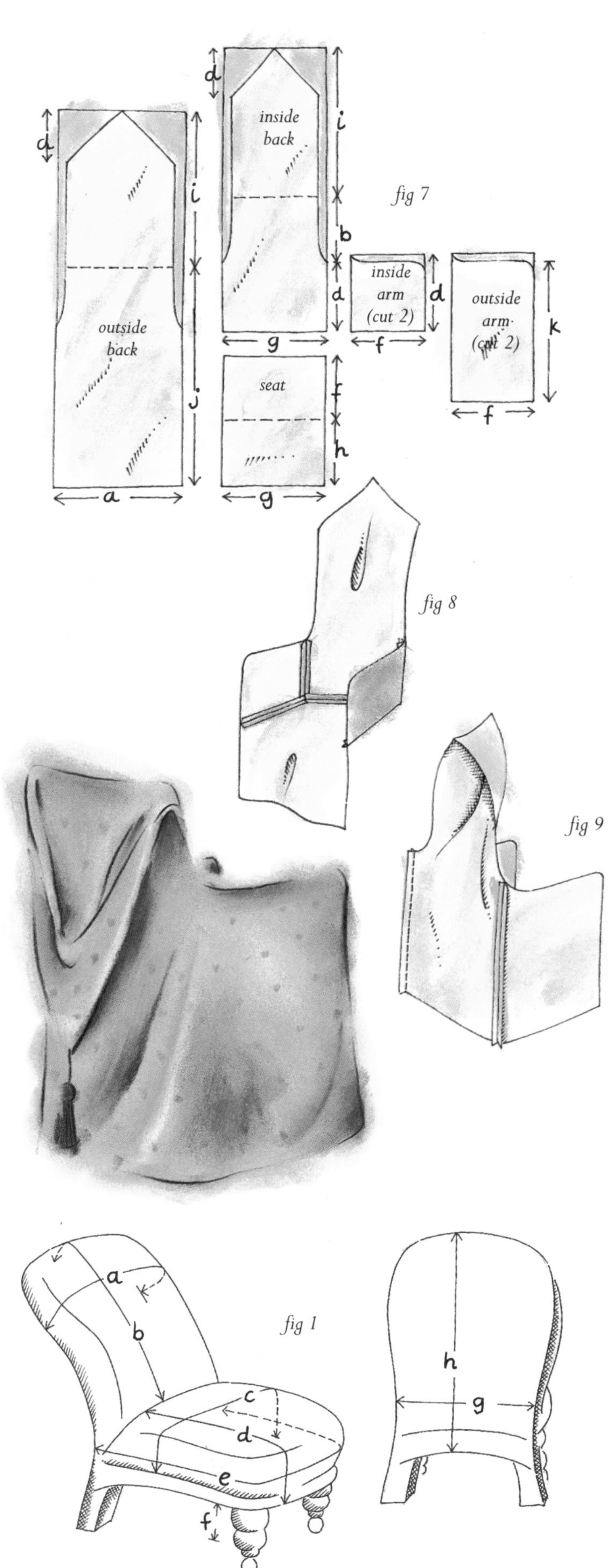


fig 7

fig 8

fig 9

fig 1

## bedroom chair cover

This low armless chair provides a good introduction to the techniques involved in making loose covers for upholstered furniture, which have to accommodate the thickness of the padding. Extra fabric (tuck-in) also has to be added where the seat and back meet to prevent the cover from straining at the seams during use.

*materials*

Calico, tailor's chalk, waterproof marker pen, main fabric, covered piping cord (length = a + 2h + f + 15cm), 30cm zip

*measuring & cutting out* *(figs 1 & 2)*

Cut three calico rectangles for the main pieces, adding 5cm all round and a 15cm tuck-in at the bottom of the inside back and the top of the seat. Label each piece.

Inside back: cut one piece, width = a, depth = b + tuck-in

Seat: cut one piece, width = c, depth = d + tuck-in

Outside back: cut one piece, width = g, depth = h

Frill: cut one piece, length = 2e + 2g, depth = f

*cutting a toile*

The calico pieces can be moulded to shape on the chair itself, using the seams on the existing upholstery as a guide to pinning them together. They can then be used as a pattern to cut out the main fabric. The shaded areas on *fig 2* show the areas that will be cut away to give the final shape.

**1** Chalk a vertical line on the chair to mark the centre seat and back. Each piece is folded in half lengthways, and pinned to this guide line at top and bottom to ensure that the cover is symmetrical. Smooth the fabric as you work and keep the grain straight. Insert the pins at 10cm intervals at right angles to the seam lines. Pin each piece through the padding to the outside edges of its respective section and to the adjacent pieces in the following order:

**a** inside back: pin to the outside edge of the chair back, making two pleats at each top corner.

**b** outside back: pin to the chair back. Inserting the pins in a straight line, pin the two pieces together across the top, then down each side. Trim back the seam allowance to 2cm *(fig 3)*. Notch the centre sides and back, and mark where the pleats lie.

**c** seat: pin over the side and front edges, making an inverted box pleat to fit the surplus fabric around the front seat corners. Pin the top edge to the outside back and outer edge of the inside back where they meet, along the existing seam lines.

**d** Fold back the tuck-in on the lower inside back and pin to the tuck-in on the seat. Slip inside the join and adjust as necessary for a neat fit. Trim back the surplus fabric to 2cm *(fig 4)*. Notch the centre front and sides and mark the front corner pleats. Draw over the pinned lines with a marker pen before separating the sections. Neaten the edges, press, and cut out the main fabric.

*making up the cover*

**2** Stitch down the pleats at the front corners of the seat and top of the inside back. With right sides facing, pin and stitch the top of the seat to the lower edge of the inside back.

**3** Sew a line of piping (see p.141) to the sides and top of the outside back. With right sides facing, pin and stitch the inside back and top edges of the seat to the outside back using a zipper foot. Leave 30cm unstitched at one lower edge and insert the zip in this gap (see p.144). Sew the rest of the piping around the lower edge of the cover.

**4** Neaten the lower edge and sides of the frill. Pin around the lower edge of the cover in a series of regular box pleats 5cm apart, and sew in place with a zipper foot. Clip any tight curves and turn right side out. Press.

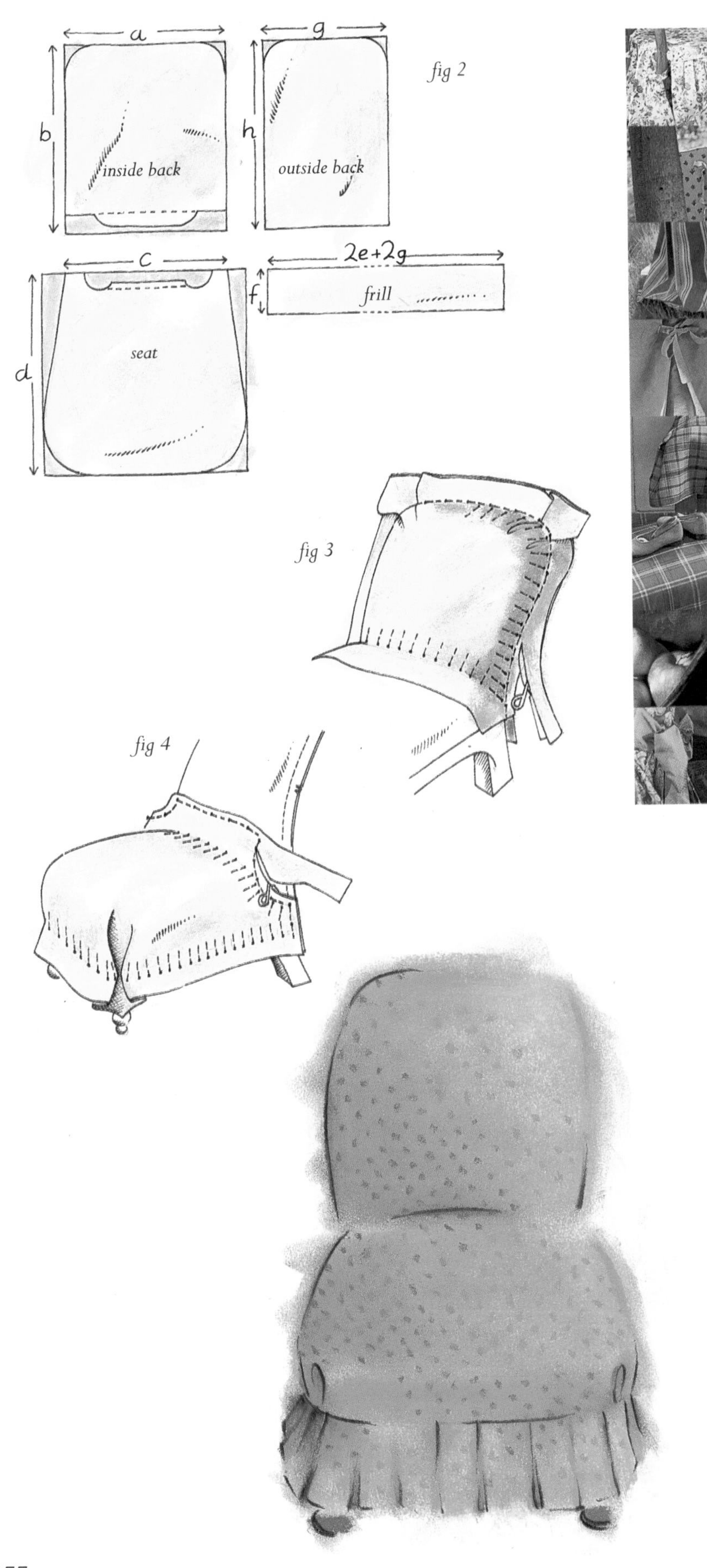


*fig 2*

*fig 3*

*fig 4*

## tie-backed armchair

All armchairs look different but the basic structure is the same. Although this cover may appear complicated, it consists of just ten pieces which are assembled in a set order. The instructions given are for a tie-back cover with a scalloped edge, but it can easily be adapted for a zipped opening and a separate valance.

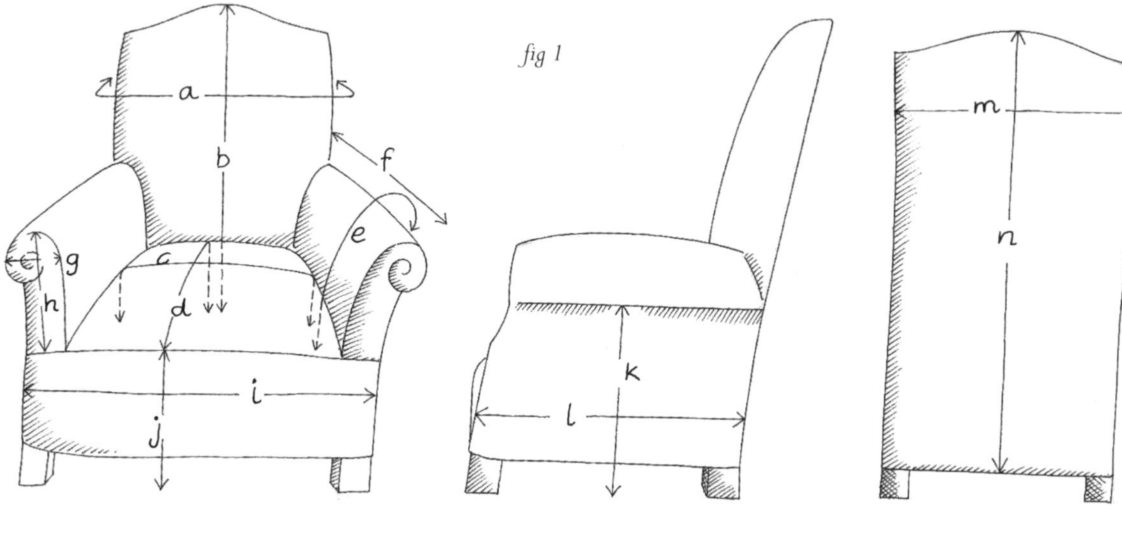


*fig 1*

### *materials*

Calico, tailor's chalk, waterproof marker pen, main fabric, covered piping cord (length = 2g + 4h + i + 2l+ 2n + m)

### *measuring the toile (figs 1 & 2)*

Cut seven rectangles from calico – one for each piece, using *fig 2* as a guide. Take each measurement at the widest point of the section and add 5cm all round. Include 15cm extra tuck-in at the bottom edge of the inside back, inside arms, and the side and back edges of the seat.

### *cutting the toile*

Following the pinning and cutting method for the bedroom chair (p.177), cut each piece to shape. It is only necessary to make up the arm cover for one side.

**1** Outside back: pin flat to all four side edges of the back, following the shape of the chair. For a back cover with ties, cut the back in two vertically when you eventually unpin the pieces and add an extra 5cm to each inside edge; for a zipped opening leave it in one piece.

**2** Inside back: pin to the side and top edges of the chair back. Make a dart around the thickness of the back if the corners are square, or pleat a rounded corner. Cut a rough curve at each bottom edge so that the calico will fit around the back and along the line where the arm joins the back, avoiding the tuck-in allowance. Pin the calico to the inside back of the chair around these curves and the bottom edge. Neaten and clip the fabric. Pin the two back pieces together around the top and sides as for the bedroom chair.

*fig 2*

**3** Seat: fold over the tuck-in at the inside edge and sides temporarily, and pin the calico to the four sides of the seat *(fig 3)*.

**4** Inside arm: pin one inside arm piece to the right arm of the chair, so that the seam allowance on the top edge overlaps the widest point of the arm and the front arm. Pin and cut to match the curve on the lower inside back, then pin the tuck-in to the side of the seat tuck-in. Cut away a triangle at the front corner of the tuck-in *(fig 4)*.

**5** Outside arm: pin the top edge to the top edge of the inside arm, keeping the lower edge parallel to the floor. Pin the back edge to the edge of the chair, and then to the lower edge of the outside back.

**6** Seat: the shaping of the seat can now be completed. Pin the top edge to the lower edge of the back. Fold the corners inwards, and pin the surplus fabric into two darts, forming an inverted box shape. Trim the seam allowance to 2cm. This box should now tuck neatly down around the edges of the seat.

**7** Front arm: pin to the front arm, keeping the grain straight, then pin to the inside and outside arms *(fig 5)*. Ease in any fullness; for a very curved arm you may need to make a few small darts in the main arm pieces.

**8** Front seat: fold in half, then pin in place along the bottom edge of the seat and front arm, and the lower edge of the outside arm. Trim the hem around the cover so that it is level with the floor.

## *cutting out the main fabric*

**1** Trim the seam allowance back to 2cm and notch two or three sets of balance marks on each edge so that the pieces will match up exactly. Unpin and press.

**2** Plan the layout before you cut out the pieces. If you are using a patterned fabric, centre any large motifs on the seat and back. A directional design should always be upright – this is why the arms are cut in two pieces – and must line up across the whole chair so that one side is a mirror image of the other.

**3** Cut out the ten main pieces, using the calico pattern, and transfer the notches. Also cut out eight 8 x 50cm ties and a strip of fabric 15cm x the length around the lower edge of the chair cover to face the scalloped edge. As a final check, pin each piece, right side up, on to the chair, then pin the seams in the order in which they will be stitched. Adjust as necessary.

## *making up the cover*

Unpinning each piece as it is required, pin and sew the cover with right sides together, leaving a 2cm allowance. Pipe the seams (see p.141) where indicated.

**1** Join the top corners of the inside back, then sew the lower edges to the inside arms, double-stitching to reinforce the curves.

**2** Sew a line of piping to the top of the outside arms, then stitch to the top of the inside arms, using a zipper foot. Cut away 2cm of piping cord from inside its casing at each end of the seam, so that the next seam will lie flat against it. Join

*fig 3*

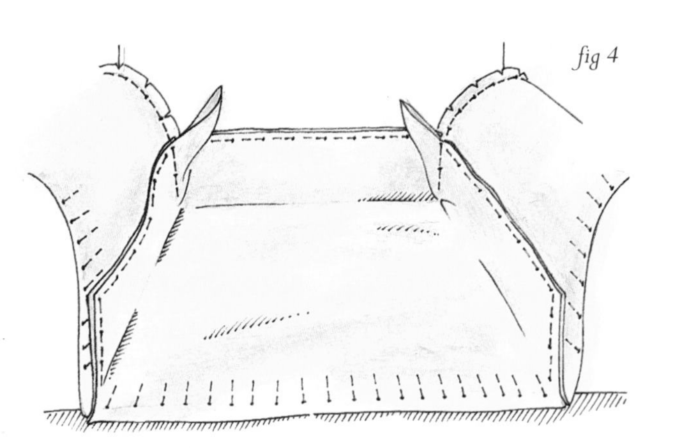

*fig 4*

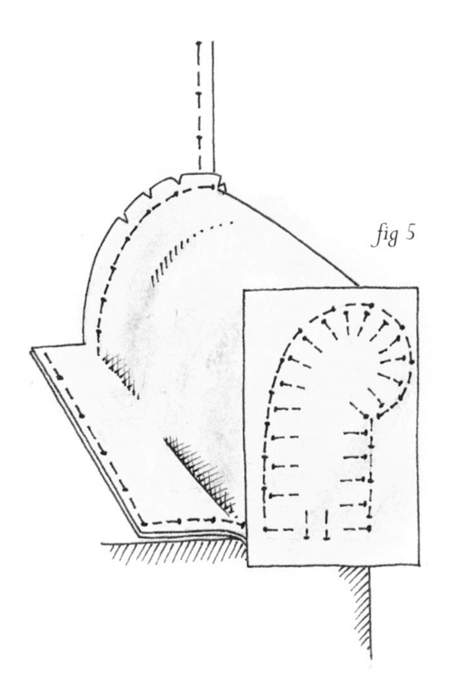

*fig 5*

the corners of the tuck-in on the seat, then sew the seat to the lower back and inside arms *(fig 6)*.

**3** Pipe around the top and sides of the arm fronts, again removing the end of the cords, then sew in place. Pipe the top edge of the front seat and sew to the bottom edge of the seat and the sides of the outside arms.

**4** Make a 1cm double hem on the inside edges of the back pieces. Overstitch the top 3cm together by hand and sew a line of piping across the top and down the sides. Pin and stitch to the front of the cover using a zipper foot. Turn right side out and press. Make the ties (see p.144) and sew in pairs, one on either side of each open edge, 25cm apart. If the chair has a plain back, leave three-quarters of one side seam unstitched and insert a zip.

**5** Zigzag the top edge of the facing and pin to the bottom edge of the cover with right sides facing. Chalk a series of shallow scallops on to the facing, reaching to within 1cm of the edge. Stitch along this line, and trim the surplus fabric, leaving a 1cm seam allowance *(fig 7)*. Clip the curves, turn the facing to the wrong side and press.

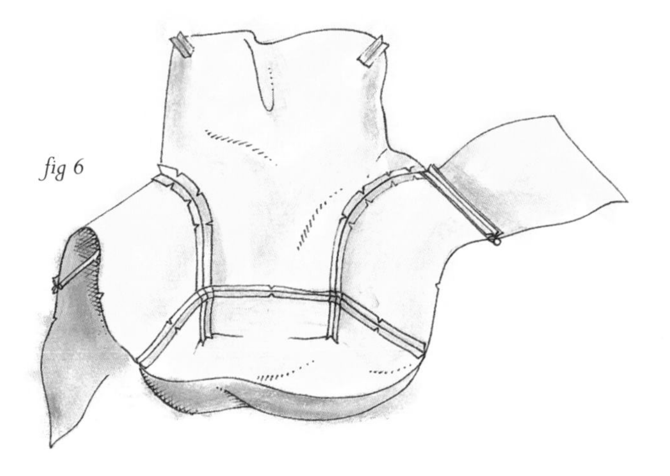

*fig 6*

*fig 7*

## variations

If the seat projects in front of the arms, make allowance for this by extending the seat cover. A chair with a separate seat cushion will require a shallower tuck-in, and a fitted box cover for the cushion.

A sofa is, in effect, a very wide chair and a loose cover can therefore be made in a similar way. A separate valance, which can have a plain or scalloped edge, can be cut in one or four pieces. The main cover will need to be cut to finish at the top of the chair legs and then a line of piping can be sewn around the lower edge before attaching the valance *(fig 8)*.

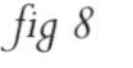

*fig 8*

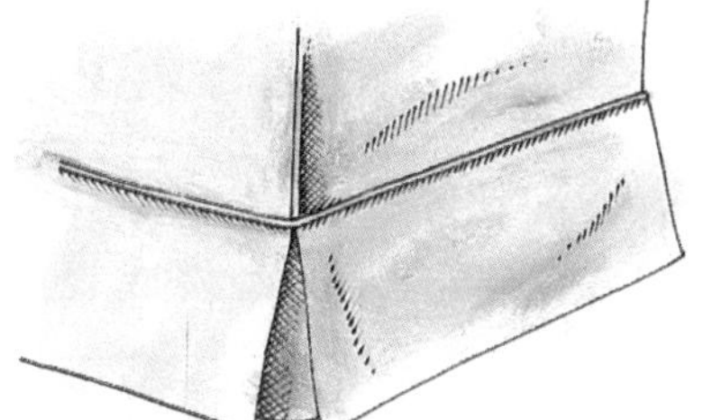

# footstools

*A matching footstool is a fanciful, although not necessarily essential, accessory for a covered chair. It is, however, a practical way to use up any left over fabric. Here are two versions, one made from a simple rectangle, the other with an extravagantly gathered and ruched skirt.*

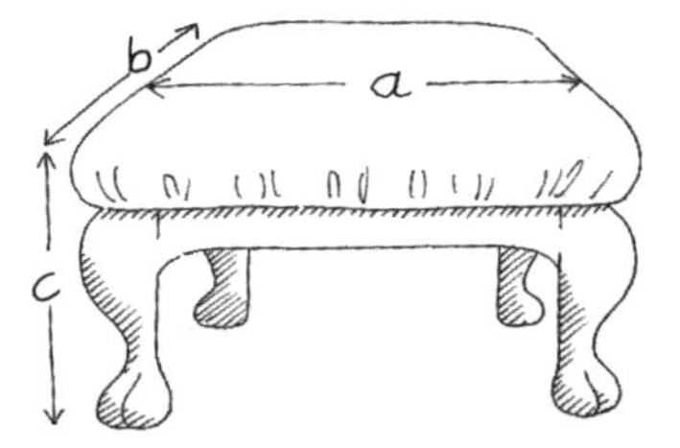


*fig 1*

## loose cover with bows

*materials*

Main fabric, tailor's chalk, saucer, 5cm-wide ribbon (length = 30cm)

*measuring & cutting out (fig 1)*

Cut a rectangle, width = a + 2c, depth = b + 2c

Draw a curve at each corner, using the saucer as a guide, and cut to this line

*making up*

**1** Neaten the outside edge, then turn up a 1cm hem all round. Place the cover centrally over the stool and pin to the top at the corners. Make a pleat on each side of each corner so the fabric fits tightly over the padded top, and secure with a few stitches *(fig 2)*.

**2** Cut the ribbon into four equal lengths and trim each end into a swallow tail. Tie into bows and sew one bow firmly to each corner.

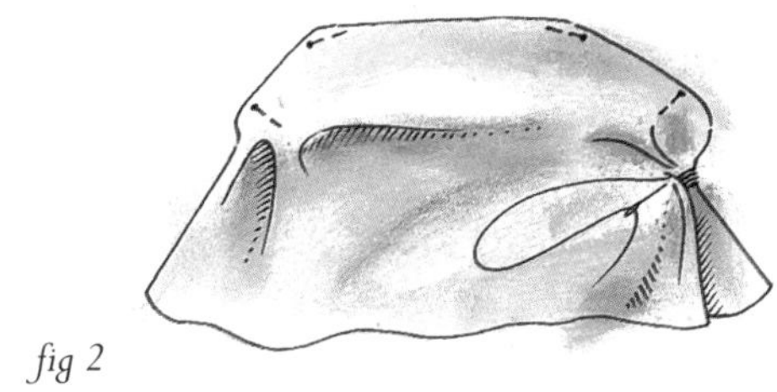

*fig 2*

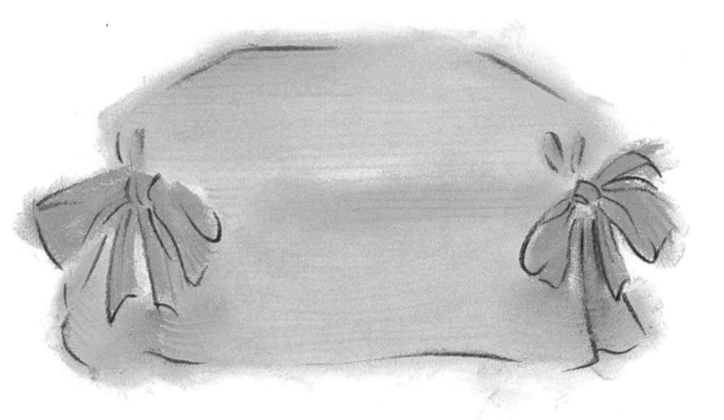

## ruched cover

*materials*

Main fabric, 5cm-wide fringing (length = 3a + 3b), buttonhole thread

*measuring & cutting out (fig 1)*

Top: cut one piece, width = a, depth = b, + 1.5cm all round

Skirt: cut one piece, length = 3a + 3b, width = 2c, + 1.5cm all round

*making up*

**1** Join the two short ends of the skirt with right sides facing and press the seam open. Make a 1cm double hem around the lower edge. Sew on the braid so that the cut edge is level with the fold and neaten the join. Make a zigzag gather (see p.142) 1.5cm from the top and pull up the thread to two-thirds of its length.

**2** With right sides together, pin the frill to the top, distributing the gathers evenly (see p.142). Stitch down 1.5cm from the edge and clip into the seam allowance for a neat corner.

**3** For a ruched look, make two pleats 5cm apart at each corner of the skirt, and catch together with a few invisible stitches *(fig 3)*. If the footstool has decorative feet, make the skirt short enough to show them.

*fig 3*

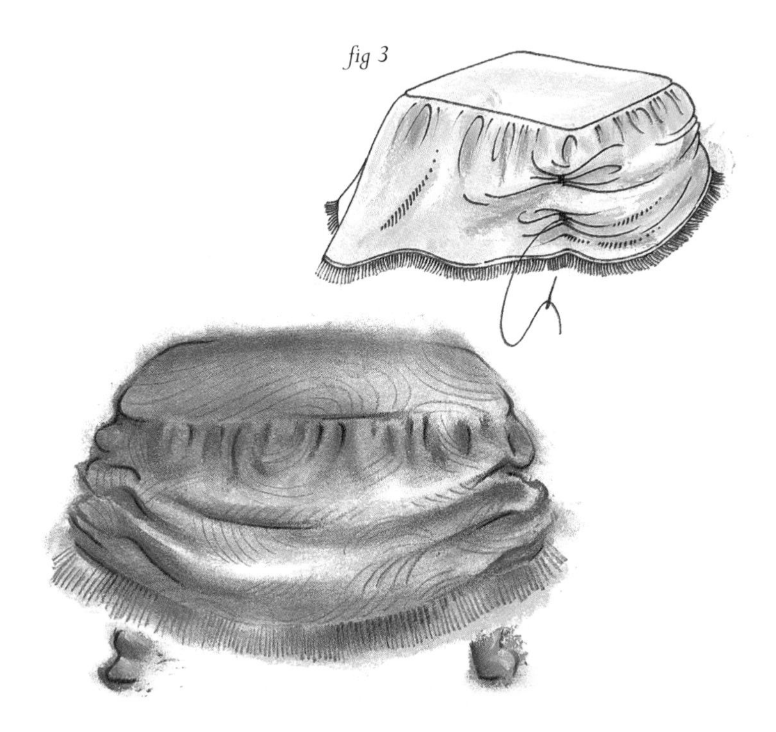

# bed dressings

*Bed coverings are straightforward and relatively quick to make. Only the most basic sewing techniques – straight seams, hems and gathers – are involved, although the scale is larger than you may be used to. A new duvet cover in a cotton print or a throw-over bedspread in heavier furnishing fabric will instantly transform your bedroom, and a co-ordinating valance will complete the effect. See pages 155–60 for how to make pillowcases and cushion covers to match.*

## throws

Throws are very versatile – they can be made to any size, and in almost any fabric, from brocade to fake fur. Small rectangular throws may be draped over the back of a chair or sofa, whilst larger versions serve as picnic rugs or bedspreads. A reversible throw is put together using the bagging method described on p.143 and can be given a backing of quilted fabric for extra warmth. A single-sided version is made in the same way as the rectangular tablecloth on p.184. Fringing, braid, binding or a narrow ruffle can be added to trim the edge.

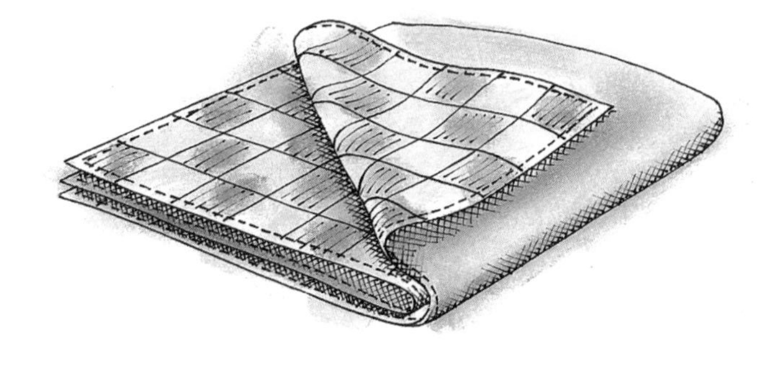

## tie-on duvet cover

The basic construction for this cover is the same as for the Decorative Housewife pillowcase on p.155. Choose sheeting or extra-wide cotton to avoid any seams.

fig 1

fig 2

fig 3

*materials*

Main fabric, contrasting fabric for flap and ties

*measuring & cutting out (fig 1)*

Front: cut one piece, width = a + 3cm, length = b - 5cm

Back: cut one piece, width = a, length = b, + 2cm all round

Flap: cut one piece, width = a + 3cm, length = ¼b + 10cm

Ties: cut six, width = 8cm, length = 53cm

*making up*

**1** Sew a 4cm double hem along one long edge of the flap. With right sides together, pin the opposite edge to one short edge of the back, and stitch together along the seam allowance. Double hem one short edge of the front. Sew the other short edge to the end of the back, with right sides facing.

**2** Pin the front to the back along the sides, with the flap lying between them *(fig 2)*. Sew together, double stitching to reinforce the corners. Trim the seam allowance to 1cm and zigzag to neaten. Turn right side out and press.

**3** Measure the flap and divide into four. Place three pins along the unstitched long edge to mark the quarters. Make up the ties as on p.144. Stitch three to these points along the seam line and three to the corresponding positions on the top *(fig 3)*.

## valances

A valance fits under the mattress to disguise the base of a divan. When working with expensive fabric it is more economic to cut the centre of the panel from lining, and sew on a border of the main fabric. A line of piping can be added, between the frill and the panel, to either of the valances shown.

*fig 4*

*fig 5*

## gathered valance

*materials*

Main fabric for frill (and panel border if required), lining fabric for panel

*measuring & cutting out (fig 4)*

Plain panel: cut one piece, width = a + 3cm, length = b + 4.5cm, + 1.5cm all round.
Curve the bottom corners to fit the shape of the bed if necessary
Bordered panel: from lining, cut panel centre, width = a - 30cm,
length = b - 15cm; from main fabric, cut one bottom strip,
width = 15cm, length = a - 30cm, and two side strips,
width = 15cm, length = b, + 1.5cm all round each piece
Frill: cut one piece, width = 2c, length = 2a + 4b, plus 1.5cm all round

*making up*

**1** To make a bordered panel, stitch the bottom strip to one short edge of the centre panel with right sides together. Press the seam open. Sew the side strips to the long edges and press open. Curve the corners to fit the bed base if necessary. Make a 1cm double hem along the top edge.

**2** Fold the frill in half lengthways and join the side seams. Clip the corners, turn right side out and press. Attach to the three unhemmed edges, following the method on p.142 *(fig 5)*.

## box-pleated valance

*materials*

Main fabric for frill and panel, lining fabric for panel, contrast fabric for inserts

*measuring & cutting out*

Panel: as for the Gathered Valance
Side frills: cut two pieces, width = c, length = 1⅓ x b, + 1.5cm all round
Bottom frill: cut one piece, width = c, length = 1⅓ x a, + 1.5cm all round
Corner inserts: cut two pieces, width = 20cm, length = c, + 1.5cm all round

*making up*

**1** Make up the panel as for the Gathered Valance. With right sides facing, join one corner insert to each end of the bottom frill, then join the side frills to the corner inserts. Make a 7mm double hem along the lower edge and the two ends of the frill.

**2** Clip into the seam allowance at the centre top edge of both corner inserts. Fold the sides of the frill pieces to the centre to make box pleats and pin. With right sides together, pin the ends of the frill to the top corners of the panel and the centre of the pleats to the bottom corners. Pin down the rest of the frill in a series of 10cm box pleats, 15cm apart *(fig 6)*, then stitch in place 1.5cm from the top edge.

*fig 6*

# table linen

*A tablecloth, or even a set of co-ordinating table linen, is a simple project for a beginner, but one which has immediate visual impact. A contrasting square can be draped over a full-length round cloth in a bedroom, whilst a floral cover for a buffet table, with a plain rectangular cloth underneath, could be the focus of a celebration meal. See p.143 for how to join lengths of fabric to make a large cloth.*

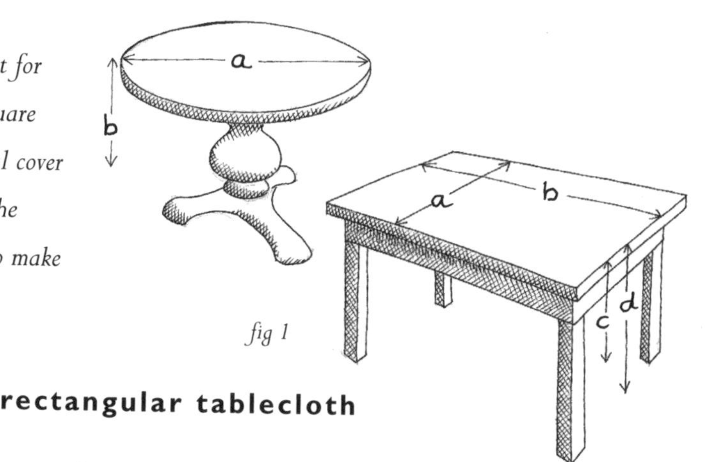


*fig 1*

## tablecloths

Consider how the cloth will be used when deciding the length of the overhang. A decorative cover may skim the floor, but a kitchen tablecloth should not be longer than the seats of the surrounding chairs. Decorative fringing or binding can be added to the hem of a cloth of any shape.

*fig 2*

½a
½a

## round tablecloth

*materials*

Main fabric, paper, pencil, string, drawing pin

*making the template (figs 1 & 2)*

Cut a square of paper with sides equal to the radius of the cloth – ½(a + b) – plus 1.5cm. Tie one end of the string near the point of the pencil. Pin the other to a corner of the paper, so that the string is the same length as the side of the square. Keeping the string taut and the pencil upright, draw a quarter-circle curve. Cut out.

*measuring & cutting out*

Cut a square of fabric, with sides equal to a + 2b. Fold into quarters and pin the pattern through all four layers, matching the corner of the pattern to the folded corner of the fabric. Cut along the curve.

*making up*

Sew a line of stay-stitch 1.5cm from the edge. Press the seam allowance to the wrong side, so that the stitching lies just inside the fold. Turn under and tack down half the remaining allowance. Hem by hand or machine.

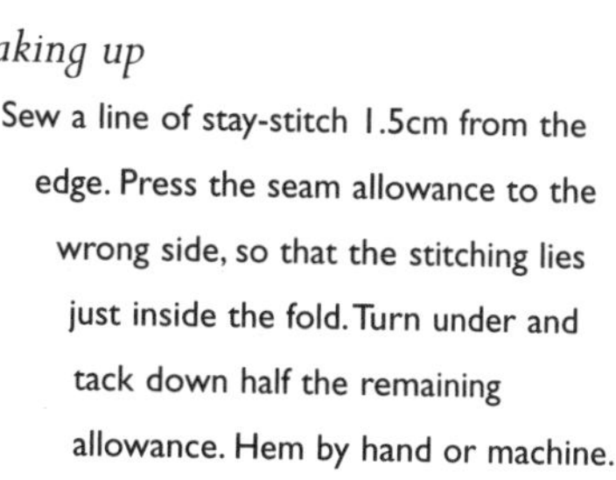

## rectangular tablecloth

*materials*

Main fabric

*measuring & cutting out (fig 1)*

Cut a rectangle, width = a + 2c, length = b + 2c or 2d, plus 5cm all round

*making up*

Press under 2cm along each side, then a further 3cm. Unfold and mitre the corners (see p.140). Tack and stitch down the hem.

## fitted buffet tablecloth

*materials*

Main fabric

*measuring & cutting out (fig 1)*

Top: width = a, length = b, + 1.5cm all round

Skirt: width = d + 6cm, length = 3a + 3b + 3cm

Bow: (make four)

Main part: width = 25cm, length = 35cm

Centre: width = 15cm, length = 20cm

Tails: width = 24cm, length = c + 1cm all round

*making up*

Join the two short edges of the skirt with right sides facing and turn up a 2cm double hem along the lower edge. Attach to the top following the method on p.142 to ensure the gathers are even. Make up the bows as on p.144 and sew one firmly to each corner.

## napkin

A simple square napkin is made from a 50cm or larger square of fabric. Finish the edges with a double 1.5cm hem, mitring the corners if preferred.

## quilted table mat

Mats provide protection for a polished tabletop, as well as completing a table setting. They are a good way of using up any fabric left over from a tablecloth.

*materials*

Main fabric, polyester wadding, backing fabric, ruler, chalk pencil

*measuring & cutting out*

Front: cut one piece from main fabric, width = 40cm, length = 30cm

Back: cut one piece from backing fabric, as front

Wadding: cut one piece, as front

Binding: cut a 5cm bias strip, 140cm long

*making up*

**1** Mark two lines on the right side of the front piece, from corner to corner, with a chalk pencil. Rule a series of lines, 5cm apart, which are parallel to these, so that the whole top is covered with a grid *(fig 3)*.

**2** Sandwich the three pieces together, with the marked front and the back facing outwards and the wadding in the middle. Tack from corner to corner, then around the outside edge, keeping the layers smooth. Work several more rows of tacking parallel to the long sides, roughly 10cm apart.

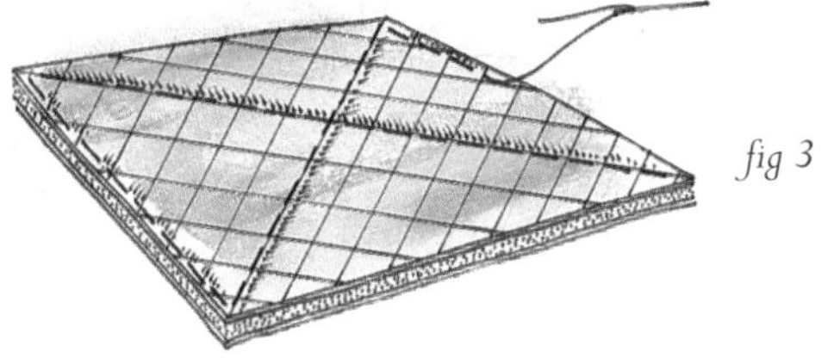

*fig 3*

**3** Stitch over the marked lines, then remove the tacking and round off the corners of the mat. Bind the edges as on p.140.

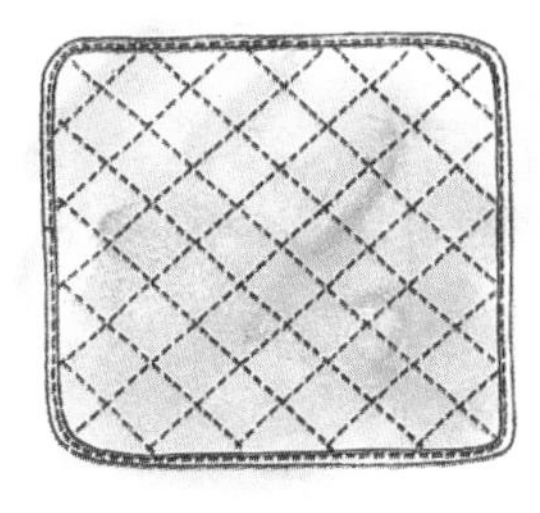

## cutlery roll

This rolled-up mat is an ideal accessory for a picnic.

*materials*

Main fabric, contrast fabric, 7cm-wide ribbon (length = 90cm)

*measuring & cutting out*

Outside: cut one piece from main fabric, width = 50cm, length = 36cm

Inside: cut one piece from contrast fabric, as front

Pocket: cut one piece from main fabric, width = 30cm, length = 20cm

*fig 4*

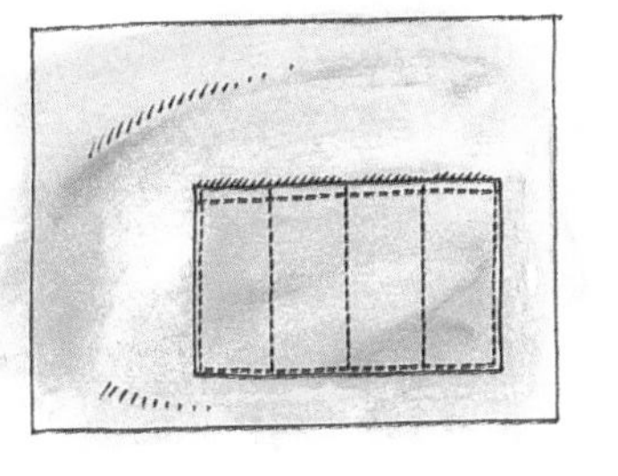

*making up*

**1** With right sides facing, pin the two main pieces together. Stitch, 1cm in from the edges, leaving a 10cm gap along one side. Turn right side out and close the gap with slip stitch. Press.

**2** Turn under a 1cm double hem along the top of the pocket, and press under 1cm along the other three sides. Pin to the lower right-hand corner of the inside, 5cm in from the edges. Sew down along the sides and bottom, 3mm from the folded edges. Divide the pocket into four equal sections with vertical lines of stitching *(fig 4)*.

**3** Trim the ends of the ribbon on a slant and fold in half. Sew to the outside, two-thirds of the way down and 10cm in from the right-hand edge.

# suppliers

*I would like to say a big thank you to all the companies who so generously supplied me with the most beautiful fabrics, lent me their exquisite furniture and accessories and made the soft furnishings to such a high standard. Needless to say, without their help and trust, I could not have produced the projects and photographs, and finally the book. Here are the names and addresses of the suppliers.*

## *spring* **awakening**

Antiques & Things, 91 Eccles Road, London SW11 1LX, tel: 0171 350 0597.
French antique furniture and accessories, *(pages 10, 24, 26, 34, 35, 36).*

Celia Birtwell, 71 Westbourne Park Road, London W2 5QH, tel: 0171 221 0877.
Unusual printed furnishing fabrics in silk, linen, cotton and voile, *(page 10).*

Christopher Moore Textiles
Available from Lee Jofa, tel: 0171 351 7760.
Toile de Jouy fabrics and wallpapers taken from original designs, *(pages 24, 35, 36).*

Ciel Decor, 187 New Kings Road, London NW6 4SU, tel: 0171 731 0444.
Provençal cotton prints, *(pages 19, 20, 21, 22).*

Colefax and Fowler, 110 Fulham Road, London SW3 6RL, tel: 0171 244 7427. For stockists, tel: 0181 874 6484, *(pages 19, 21, 22, 23).*

Design Archives, The Decorative Fabrics Gallery, 278-280 Brompton Road, London SW3 2AS, tel: 0171 589 4778. For stockists call 01202 753248, *(pages 30, 32).*

FR Street
For mail order details, tel: 01268 766677.
Natural fabrics, ticking, calico, muslin, *(page 33).*

Hodsoll McKenzie, 52 Pimlico Road, London SW1W 8LP, tel: 0171 730 2877.
Wide range of weaves and prints, *(page 18).*

J & M Davidson, 62 Ledbury Road, London W11 2AJ, tel: 0171 243 2089.
French inspired bedlinen and fabrics, *(pages 10, 35).*

Jane Churchill, 151 Sloane Street, London SW10 9B2, tel: 0171 730 9847. For stockists, tel: 0181 874 6484. *Trimmings throughout.*

Judy Greenwood Antiques, 657 Fulham Road, London SW6 5PY, tel: 0171 736 6037.
French painted antique furniture, accessories, quilts and linen, *(pages 24, 34).*

Lewis & Wood
For stockists, tel: 0181 748 6681.
Simple cotton stripes and florals, *(page 24).*

Liberty Furnishings at Osborne & Little
For stockists, tel: 0181 675 2255, *(pages 24, 30, 32).*

LM Jakobsson, 35 Walcot Street, Bath BA1 5BN, tel: 01225 480660.
Soft furnishing service, antique Swedish furniture and accessories, fabrics, *(pages 19, 20, 21, 22, 24, 30, 32).*

Marvic Textiles
For stockists, tel: 0181 993 0191.
New toile fabrics taken from old documents, *(pages 26, 27, 35, 40, 41).*

Marylin Garrow, 6 The Broadway, White Hart Lane, Barnes, London SW13 ONY, tel: 0181 392 1655.
Antique fabrics and accessories, *(pages 24, 34).*

McKinney & Co, 1 Wandon Road, London SW6 2JF, tel: 0171 384 1377.
Decorative curtain poles and finials, *(pages 26, 30).*

Nina Campbell at Osborne & Little, tel: 0181 675 2255. *Trimmings throughout.*

Nobilis–Fontan
For stockists, tel: 0171 351 7878.
Beautiful French woven and printed fabrics, *(pages 18, 24).*

Osborne & Little
For stockists, tel: 0181 675 2255, *(page 18). Trimmings throughout.*

Percheron
For stockists, tel: 0171 580 5156, *(pages 24, 32).*

Pierre Frey
For stockists, tel: 0171 376 5599.
French woven, printed and plain fabrics in cotton, linen, voile, silk and velvet, *(pages 24, 33, 40).*

Shelfstore (shelf unit for tent)
For stockists, tel: 0171 794 0313, *(pages 26, 27).*

Sue Holley at Susannah, 142–144 Walcot Street, Bath BA1 5BL, tel: 01225 445069.
Decorative old floral quilts, fabrics and accessories, *(pages 30, 32).*

Sue Ralston Designs
For soft furnishing commissions, tel: 0181 940 7756, *(pages 34, 35, 36, 37, 40, 41).*

The Blue Door, 77 Church Road, London SW13 9HH, tel: 0181 748 9785.
Antique French and Swedish furniture and accessories, Swedish reproduction furniture, fabrics and accessories, *(pages 24, 33).*

The Natural Fabric Company, Wessex Place,
127 High Street, Hungerford, Berkshire
RG17 0DL, tel: 01488 684002.
Classic natural fabrics, checks, toiles and stripes,
*(pages 23, 31, 35, 37).*

Titley & Marr
For stockists, tel: 01730 894351.
Prints, weaves, florals and toiles,
*(pages 19, 21, 24, 25, 30, 31, 34, 35, 37, 41).*

Turnell and Gigon
For stockists, tel: 0171 351 5142.
Wide range of beautiful classic fabrics,
*(pages 18, 19, 24, 25).*

Valerie Howard, 2 Campden Street,
London W8 7EP, tel: 0171 792 9702.
Antique Mason's and other ironstone china,
faience of Quimper and Rouen, French antique
accessories, *(pages 11, 12, 13, 34, 35, 40, 41).*

VV Rouleaux, 10 Symons Street, London
SW3 2TJ, tel: 0171 730 3125. *Trimmings throughout.*

Wemys Houles
For stockists, tel: 0171 255 3305. *Trimmings throughout.*

Wendy Cushing, Unit G7, Chelsea Harbour Design
Centre, London SW10 0XE, tel: 0171 351 5796.
*Trimmings throughout.*

## *summer* **lightness**

Antiques & Things, as before, *(pages 42, 76).*

Bennison Fabrics, 16 Holbein Place, London
SW1 W8NL, tel: 0171 730 8076.
Printed linen and cotton inspired by old documents,
*(pages 52, 53).*

Chelsea Textiles, 7 Walton Street,
London SW3 2JQ, tel: 0171 584 0111.
Embroidered cotton, voile, linen and wool fabrics,
*(page 76).*

Colefax & Fowler, as before, *(pages 58, 59)*

Design Archives, as before, *(page 61).*

Cover Up Designs of Kingsclere, tel: 01635 297981
Soft furnishings, *(page 52).*

Designers Guild, 267–271 & 275–277 Kings Road,
London SW3 5EN, tel: 0171 243 7300.
Contemporary fabrics and accessories,
*(pages 64, 65, 66, 67, 68, 69, 76, 78).*

De Le Cuona Designs, 1 Trinity Place,
Windsor, Berkshire, SL4 3AP, tel: 01753 830301.
Hand-loomed linen cloth, flax, silk, woven paisleys,
accessories, *(pages 42, 43).*

Ian Mankin, 109 Regents Park Road,
London NW1 9UR, tel: 0171 722 0997
and 271 Wandsworth Bridge Road,
London W6 2TX, tel: 0171 371 8825.
Natural fabrics, stripes and checks, *(pages 64, 67).*

Liberty, 210-220 Regent Street,
London W1R 6AH, tel: 0171 734 1234, *(pages 72, 73).*

Liberty Furnishings at Osborne & Little,
as before, *(pages 52, 60, 62, 63, 72, 73).*

Malabar Cotton Company
For stockists, tel: 0171 5014 200.
Indian woven silks and cottons in natural and bright
colours, *(page 42).*

Mulberry, 41–2 New Bond Street, London W1Y 9HB
For stockists, tel: 01749 340594, *(pages 50, 51).*

Old Town
For mail order details, tel: 01603 628100.
Gingham bedlinen, *(pages 76, 78).*

Ralph Lauren (Fabrics)
For stockists, tel: 0171 229 1000, *(pages 64, 65).*

Sanderson
For stockists, tel: 0171 584 3344, *(pages 54, 62).*

Sue Holley at Susannah, as before,
*(pages 48, 50, 51, 60, 61).*

The Conran Shop, Michelin House, 81 Fulham Road,
London SW3 6RD, tel: 0171 589 7401.
Best of contemporary design for interiors and
gardens, *(pages 42 63, 74, 75).*

The Iron Bed Company
For branches, tel: 01243 574049, *(pages 72, 76).*

The Sofa Workshop
For stockists, tel: 01798 343400.
Sofas of all shapes and sizes, *(page 75).*

The White Company
For mail-order details, tel: 0171 385 7988.
Bedlinen, duvets, pillows, towels available by
mail order, *(page 72).*

VV Rouleaux, as before. *Trimmings throughout.*

## *autumn* **warmth**

Anta Fearn, Tain, Ross-shire IV20 1TL Scotland,
tel: 01862 832477 and the High Street, The Royal
Mile, Edinburgh EH1 1TB, tel: 0131 577 8300,
*(pages 79, 80,84, 85, 86,87, 88, 89, 92, 93, 94, 95, 98, 102, 103).*

Brora, 344 Kings Road,
London SW3 5UR, tel: 0171 352 3697.
Fine woollens, tartans, tweeds. Accessories
and fabrics, *(pages 96, 97, 99).*

Christine Anderson, Unit 6&7, The Estate Yard,
Pandy Road, Llanbrynmair, Powys SY19 7DU,
tel: 01650 521596.
Soft furnishings, *(pages 91,102, 103).*

Mulberry, as before, *(page 97).*

Nina Campbell at Osborne & Little, as before,
*(pages 84, 90, 98, 99).*

Tate & Style, Bray Studio, Back Road, Stromness,
Orkney KW16 3AW Scotland, tel: 01856 851186.
Unusual soft furnishings made out of felt and wool,
mohair and appliqué, *(pages 84, 94).*

Designers Guild, as before, *(pages 97, 99).*

The Isle Mill, 12 West Moulin Road, Pitlochry PH16
5AF, Scotland, tel: 01796 472390, *(page 100).*

The Loose Cover Company, 8 Abercromby Avenue,
High Wycombe, Buckinghamshire HP12 3AX,
tel: 01494 471226, *(pages 96, 100).*

Thomas Dare, 341 Kings Road, London SW3 5ES,
tel: 0171 3517991, *(page 101).*

Titley & Marr, as before, *(pages 78, 90, 91, 100).*

VV Rouleaux, as before. *Trimmings throughout.*

## *winter* **glow**

Antiques & Things, as before, *(pages 120, 121, 122).*

Bonpoint, 35b Sloane Street, London SW1X 9LP,
tel: 0171 235 1441.
Exquisite French children's clothes, *(page 127).*

Calver & Wilson, tel: 0171 724 6771.
Velvet and silk fabrics, scarves, accessories,
*(pages 126, 127).*

Christopher Moore, as before, *(pages 118, 120, 132).*

Cover Up Designs, as before, *(pages 136, 137).*

De Le Cuona Designs, as before
Silk and wool paisley fabrics, natural linen, silk
and cotton, *(page 125).*

Design Archives, as before, *(pages 113, 120, 122, 125).*

Designers Guild, as before,
*(pages 107, 113, 114, 136, 137).*

Gainsborough Silks
For stockists, tel: 01787 372081,
*(pages 113, 122, 123, 125).*

G P & J Baker
For stockists, tel: 01494 467467.
Also at The Decorative Fabrics Gallery, 278–280
Brompton Road, London SW3 2AS,
tel: 0171 589 4778, *(pages 113, 122, 123, 124).*

JAB, as before, *(pages 123).*

J & M Davidson, as before, *(pages 121, 132).*

Joss Graham Oriental Textiles, 10 Eccleston Street,
London SW1W 9LT, tel: 0171 730 4370.
Shop specializing in decorative textiles, ceramics,
jewellery and clothing, *(page 112).*

Judy Greenwood, as before, *(pages 122, 123).*

Liberty, as before, *(page 118).*

Malabar, as before, *(pages 106, 113, 120, 121, 122).*

Mulberry, as before,
*(pages 122, 124, 125, 130, 131, 134, 135).*

Neisha Crosland
For stockists, tel: 0171 978 4389.
Contemporary velvet accessories and furniture,
*(pages 136, 137).*

Nina Campbell at Osborne & Little, as before,
*(page 120).*

Nobilis-Fontan, as before,
*(pages 107, 113, 122,126,127, 136,137).*

Osborne & Little, as before, *(pages 112, 113, 115, 119).*

Pierre Frey, as before, *(page 132).*

Shades of Choice, tel: 01275 373 025.
Lampshades made to order, *(page 125).*

Stroheim & Romann at JAB Anstoetz,
tel: 0171 349 9323, *(page 120).*

Valerie Howard, as before, *(pages 112, 113, 118,119).*

VV Rouleaux, as before. *Trimmings throughout.*

Warner Fabrics, tel: 0171 376 7578.
Classic damasks, weaves and prints, *(page 118).*

Warris Vianni, 85 Golborne Road, London
W10 5NL, tel: 0181 964 0069.
Beautiful Indian textiles, *(page 112).*

Wemyss Houles, as before. *Trimmings throughout.*

Wendy Cushing, as before. *Trimmings throughout.*

# index

# acknowledgments

*I would like to thank everyone who has helped me to produce Country Living's Seasonal Guide to Soft Furnishings – spiritually, mentally and physically!*

*Pippa Rimmer, Carl Braganza and Clara Thomas, my loyal, good-humoured and ever-supportive assistants at Country Living. Anna Lallerstedt, Valerie Howard, Elizabeth Brower, Kerry Woodbridge, Lauren Henry and Sue Rowlands who were generous enough to let us disrupt their lives by allowing us to photograph their beautiful homes.*

*Soft furnishing companies and crafts people who have all contributed with their work: Melanie Williams, Lillimore Jacobson, Sue Ralston, Cover Up Designs and The Loose Cover Company. A very special thank you to all the fabric manufacturers for their generosity in supplying the fabric.*

*I greatly enjoyed being associated with such professionals as Jane O'Shea and Mary Evans at Quadrille, who made this book possible. Francoise Dietrich for her elegant and brilliant page design. Lucy Naylor for her much needed additional prose. Lucinda Ganderton for deciphering all the projects and writing the instructions, and the illustrator, Alison Barratt, for her exquisite artwork. Alexa Stace, my editor, for staying calm over ever-changing pages. Francine Lawrence, the former editor of Country Living, for believing in me and suggesting my name to the publishers. Last, but not least, my dear friend and photographer Pia Tryde, whose individual style and personality shine through every photograph. And, of course, a big hug for my lovely husband Pierre for putting up with me in moments of stress and always being at hand when needed – especially loading and unloading the car before and after photographic shoots.*

## photographic acknowledgments

*The publisher thanks the following photographers and organizations for their permission to reproduce the photographs in this book.*

2-3 William Shaw; 5 top centre Simon McBride; 5 bottom Clay Perry; 6 Jan Baldwin; 8 top Jan Baldwin; 8 bottom Simon McBride; 19 top left William Shaw; 20 left Henry Bourne; 23 top centre Jan Baldwin; 42 -43 Frank Herholdt; 43 top right Pia Tryde; 43 bottom centre Pia Tryde; 44-45 Simon McBride; 44 left Elizabeth Zeschin; 48 bottom right (inset) David George; 49 top left (inset) Frank Herholdt; 49 top centre (inset) Pia Tryde; 58 Jan Baldwin; 59 top Jan Baldwin; 59 bottom right Elizabeth Zeschin; 61 top left Jan Baldwin; 62-63 David George; 72 left Pia Tryde; 72-73 David George; 73 top right Andreas von Einsiedel; 73 bottom right David George; 74 top left Christopher Drake; 74 top right Jan Baldwin; 75 Jem Grischotti/The Sofa Workshop; 76 top left Tom Leighton; 76 top right Andreas von Einsiedel; 76 centre left Frank Herholdt; 76 bottom left Frank Herholdt; 77 Frank Herholdt; 79 bottom centre Charlie Colmer; 84 top right (inset) Jacqui Hurst; 85 bottom right (inset) Leonard Smith; 85 bottom left (inset) Jacqui Hurst; 101 top right Mike England; 101 bottom Thomas Dare 'Multi' collection, 341 Kings Road, London SW3 5ES Tel: 0171 351 7991; 108-109 Clay Perry; 114 top left Jan Baldwin; 114 bottom right Pia Tryde; 117 top left Pia Tryde; 117 bottom right David George; 118 David George; 119 top left David George; 119 bottom left and right Fran Brennan; 122-123 Pia Tryde; 123 bottom centre Pia Tryde; 132 Christopher Drake; 133 top left Pia Tryde.

Special photography of all other images by Pia Tryde.